Healthy American Families

HEALTHY AMERICAN FAMILIES

A Progressive Alternative to the Religious Right

John H. Scanzoni

PRAEGER

AN IMPRINT OF ABC-CLIO, LLC
Santa Barbara, California • Denver, Colorado • Oxford, England

6-8-11
GB
$44.95

Library of Congress Cataloging-in-Publication Data

Scanzoni, John H., 1935–
   Healthy American families : a progressive alternative to the religious right / John H. Scanzoni.
      p. cm.
   Includes bibliographical references and index.
   ISBN 978-0-313-38401-1 (alk. paper) — ISBN 978-0-313-38402-8 (ebook)
1. Families—United States.   2. Families—Religious aspects—Christianity.
3. Parenting—United States.   4. Parenting—Religious aspects—Christianity.   I. Title.
   HQ536.S3364   2010
   306.6'6183585—dc22   2009051220

ISBN: 978-0-313-38401-1
EISBN: 978-0-313-38402-8

14   13   12   11   10   1   2   3   4   5

This book is also available on the World Wide Web as an eBook.
Visit www.abc-clio.com for details.

Praeger
An Imprint of ABC-CLIO, LLC

ABC-CLIO, LLC
130 Cremona Drive, P.O. Box 1911
Santa Barbara, California 93116-1911

This book is printed on acid-free paper ∞

Manufactured in the United States of America

For my grandchildren—Alex, Brett, Bryan, Chris,
Jason, Ken, Morgan, and Sarah.
And also for all grandchildren and children everywhere as they pursue
the never-ending task of reinventing the futures of families. Lest they
forget, the Prophet reminds them that what they're creating is by
no means the Last Word. Their offspring are likely to take as dim
a view of their efforts as they have of ours.

Your children are not your children . . .
You may give them your love but not your thoughts,
for they have their own thoughts.
You may house their bodies but not their souls,
for their souls dwell in the house of tomorrow, which
you cannot visit, not even in your dreams.
You may strive to be like them, but seek not to make them like you.
For life goes not backward nor tarries with yesterday.

—*Kahil Gibran*, The Prophet (1980)

Contents

Preface: A Recovering Evangelical Weighs In

I have sworn upon the altar of God eternal hostility against every form of tyranny over the mind of man.[1]

— *Thomas Jefferson*

Ever since the Puritans landed in the early 1600s, America's families have refused to stand still. Now, in the 21st century, our families remain very much a work in progress. As I see it, many of the changes happening right now are good. Not everyone agrees with me, of course. The religious right, for instance, claims that most of the changes in today's families are bad. Its way of coping with the changes is to force us back to the days before (as they see it) everything went topsy-turvy.

But my suggestions for managing change are quite different. Why not try to figure out which of today's changes are positive, which are negative, and which are simply neutral? And once we figure that out, why not do all we can to help make desirable changes? And on the flip side, why not help lessen the chances for undesirable changes? Answering those three questions is precisely what this book is all about.

I'm writing this book from two vantage points—the first is *professional*.

I'm a social scientist and, more specifically, a sociologist.[2] My career began in the mid-1960s around the time that what's now called the religious right was being spawned. I've been a professor at several universities, teaching numerous types of courses about families. Alongside my teaching, I've done a great deal of research and writing about families. The question of why and how families have never stood still has fascinated me for many years. I am, in short, a professional insider who's made a career of trying to understand the evolution of families.

I'm also an insider when it comes to my second vantage point, which is *personal*. More accurately, I'm an *ex*-insider, renegade, or backslider, as some might say. As an infant I was baptized Roman Catholic, but grew up a Protestant fundamentalist. At college I morphed into being evangelical, and from there evolved into being simply a person of faith, which is what I am right now.[3] Persons like me who have developed beyond evangelicalism are often referred to as a *recovering* evangelical.[4] We're like the recovering alcoholic or addict who, though clean, never entirely escapes the negative effects of his or her former circumstances. In any case, I do not write this book as an outsider peering through stained glass windows into unfamiliar territory. I write instead as a former insider.

A person of faith is by no means the same thing as a Religious-Right person or a "christianist," which is Andrew Sullivan's convenient label for the religious right.[5] A big difference between christianism and simple faith was expressed (in the chapter epigraph) by Thomas Jefferson. His lifelong quarrel was never with religion, or faith, or God, but with christianism—the attempt to employ political and legal means to impose a particular set of ideas, values, and behaviors on society: tyranny, he called it. In this book, the christianist is someone using politics and/or the law to inflict his values about families on the rest of us.

Though evangelicalism (in contrast to the religious right) tends to refrain from imposing its way of life on the unbelieving world, it is nonetheless relentless and uncompromising in its determination to enforce uniformity of thought and action on its insiders. Evangelicals are compelled to conform to the Bible's commands as to how they must think and behave—especially when it comes to families. Evangelicalism is but one example of that singular type of group—whether religious or political—that the people's philosopher Eric Hoffer once called "True Believers."[6] Every set of true believers is marked by at least two characteristics: one is the arrogance of absolute certainty; another is the intolerance of a crusader. One noxious effect of these twin characteristics is to cripple the insider's capacity to think creatively about faith, life, and the society and culture in which she lives.

I was recently reminded of the boxed-in feelings I'd experienced as an evangelical while reading a 2008 story in the national press about Kent Gramm.[7] He was a professor at the evangelical Wheaton College (my alma mater) who was forced to resign his position because he refused to explain to college officials why, after 34 years of marriage, he'd gotten divorced. College policy is to fire professors who divorce for reasons other than on the grounds it says are permitted by the Bible (adultery or abandonment). But Gramm felt that the reasons for his divorce were between him and God. Needless to say, college officials felt they were speaking for God and so he had to 'fess up or leave. Gramm was profoundly hurt. After serving the college for 20 years, why, he wanted to know, couldn't officials trust him to do the right thing?

Studying the social sciences has, over the years, had an enormously liberating effect on my mind and life. I've gradually begun to feel free to think and act outside what I felt was the stifling box of evangelicalism, and to escape the party lines to which evangelicals hew unwaveringly. My studies began to release me from the tyranny of absolute certainty and the intolerance of a crusader. In particular, I slowly gained permission to think outside the box about families. Eventually, it became apparent to me that I could not be a free, whole person and still remain evangelical: And so I choose wholeness and freedom.[8]

As anyone who's been through this sort of gut-wrenching transition can testify, the process is both lengthy and agonizing. I was overwhelmed with self-doubt, anxiety, and downright fear. I kept on asking myself whether or not I was doing the right thing. I felt I was finally okay when I could look in the mirror and affirm, "You are no longer evangelical." But what was I? Where did I belong? A number of similarly disillusioned evangelicals I've met over the years chose to become agnostic. That was the experience of one-time evangelical Bart Ehrman (also a Wheaton graduate). Ehrman wrote a book that "picks apart the Gospels that made a disbeliever out of him."[9] But I knew I was not agnostic—I became instead simply a person of faith. Not too long ago, my seven-year-old granddaughter (Morgan) jumped onto my lap to ask, "Do you believe in God?" "Yes," I said, and she wanted to know why, given that her father is agnostic. As best I could, I tried to explain to her the pilgrimage of faith I've been on for many years.

The basis for my personal faith draws deeply from the tortured experiences of the profoundly anguished 19th-century Danish philosopher/theologian Soren Kierkegaard.[10] I first encountered him in a college philosophy class where the professor informed us that Kierkegaard's personal torment was the inevitable result of someone forsaking his allegiance to the Bible. Kierkegaard helped set the stage for what later came to be known as 20th-century existentialism. At its core, it sought to fathom how the individual, surrounded by the impersonal, capricious, and menacing forces of nature and society, somehow manages to make sense of life. Although I remember being struck by his ideas, I thought little about Kierkegaard until some time later when I too like him was agonizing over my own crises of faith. Several years ago, I recall being profoundly moved as I stood before the imposing monument to his life and work set in the center of Copenhagen, testifying to the respect and admiration that the Danes continue to feel for him.

Kierkegaard's way out of his deep spiritual crises was to assert that in order to survive, "I must," he said, "believe in God." But because no one and nothing can prove that God does or does not exist, "I am," said Kierkegaard, compelled to take a "leap of faith into the darkness" in order to discover God and thus to live. "I believe in God in order to survive," he said, and it is the same for me. I too am obliged every moment of my life to take that same leap of faith into the darkness to discover God and to practice the relationship with Her (or Him) begun while still a child.

During my pilgrimage, I've met numerous people of goodwill—persons of faith from many other religious traditions (Jews, Muslims, Hindus, Buddhists, religions of native peoples here and around the world, as well as Christians of every stripe) pursuing the same quest as I. My fellow pilgrims also include many persons of goodwill who do not believe in any sort of reality apart from what they can observe in the world around them. They may consider themselves agnostic ("I don't know"), or atheist, or simply nothing. Several of my agnostic friends attend church regularly, and think it amusing that I do not. I'm also a source of curiosity to friends, acquaintances, students, and colleagues wanting to know how a social scientist who managed to escape the constraints of evangelicalism can still remain a person of faith.

Many persons of goodwill believe (as did some of America's founders) that we can learn a great deal from the Bible. But we, like almost all our founders, believe that God—however God is defined—can also be experienced through any number of sacred texts, religious traditions, and various forms of faith. We believe that humans may encounter God almost anywhere, and especially through nature and in art—music, painting, sculpture, drama, and literature. Many of us follow the tradition of our nation's founders who, it is said, "worshipped in the cathedral of creation."[11] It is worth noting that Francis Collins, an evolutionary biologist (yet still evangelical) and head of the Human Genome Project takes a comparable tack by arguing that "advances in science present 'an opportunity for worship,' rather than a catalyst for doubt."[12]

Persons of goodwill cherish the liberty to differ from one another on any number of things—including families—and yet be seen as an honorable person. We are united by a common objective inherited from America's founders— an objective that can in fact be traced back to the pre-Christian Greek thinkers, Plato in particular. Our shared objective is to participate in creating a society in which people are free to enjoy personal freedoms (their private household) yet feel a keen sense of responsibility for others (the public household). And that is what this book is all about: *When it comes to families, how can persons of goodwill embrace freedom and responsibility at the same time?*

On a most encouraging note, it seems to me that people of goodwill make up the vast majority of Americans. A 2006 *Pew* survey reported that "96% of the public says they believe in God or some form of Supreme Being, roughly the same number as in a 1965 [*Time* magazine] survey."[13] America is thus a religious, though by no means a Christian nation. Neither is it evangelical nor christianist. And that blissful outcome is precisely what our founders intended.[14] Furthermore, another 2008 *Pew* survey vindicates our founders' hope that America should be a nation of rich religious diversity:

> [M]ost Americans have a non-dogmatic approach to faith. A majority of those who are affiliated with a religion, for instance, do not believe their religion is the only way to salvation. And almost the same number believes that there is more than one true way to interpret the teachings of their religion. This openness to a range of religious viewpoints is in line with the great diversity of religious affiliation, belief and practice that exists in the United States, as documented in a survey of more than 35,000 Americans that comprehensively examines the country's religious landscape.[15]

NOTES

1. An oath taken by Jefferson and carved on the inside of his Washington, D.C., monument.

2. Scanzoni 2002.

3. I was "saved" and thus "born again" at the tender age of 7. After finishing high school, I was graduated from Chicago's Moody Bible Institute. I then enrolled in Wheaton College (Illinois) and earned a bachelor's degree in sociology. Technically speaking, there are only minimal differences between fundamentalism and evangelicalism. Both groups subscribe strongly to the twin tenets of traditional Christianity: an error-free Bible and the necessity of a born-again experience in order to escape eternal punishment in hell (Barr 1977; Marsden 1991). Hannah Rosin recently studied the staunchly evangelical Patrick Henry College. She reports (2007:8) that her husband asked a student, "So, are we going to hell?" The student's response was unequivocal: "All who die outside of Christ shall be confined in conscious torture for eternity."

The two groups differ, however, on how to reform society—how to make life better for people in the here and now.

Fundamentalists believe that getting people saved and making a better society are inseparable tasks—an indivisible package, but *only* in that sequence. That logical progression was preached by the 18th-century evangelists Jonathan Edwards and George

Whitfield. It was also advocated by the 19th-century evangelists Charles Finney and Dwight L. Moody. The 20th-century evangelist Billy Graham likewise preached that same message. Fundamentalists reason that if enough people are born again, evils such as pornography, adultery, divorce, homosexuality, murder, and fornication will slowly wither on the vine. That being the case, they argue that born-again folk should invest most of their time and energy getting sinners saved. Too much time spent on social or political action to change laws regarding abortion or gay marriage (or anything else) may, from their point of view, be pointless. They are critical of the religious right precisely because it expends so much energy trying to rid society of evils. Fundamentalists ask, "What good does it do to make society better if those better-off citizens are still bound for hell?"

Today's younger evangelicals seem to be caught in the middle between fundamentalists and the Religious Right. Unlike the former, they tend to embrace the idea that it's okay to try to make the world a better place quite apart from getting people saved. They aim to penetrate all parts of society acting as salt, light, and leaven. By example and reason, they hope to persuade unbelievers of the soundness of evangelical ideas for social betterment. If the goal, for instance, is reduce the spread of HIV/AIDS in Africa, or to slow global climate change, evangelicals reckon they can work with unbelievers in order to accomplish that goal. But unlike the christianist, they do not typically seek to impose their religious views on outsiders by legal or political means (see Lindsay 2007).

4. See Michael Spencer for a discussion of what he calls the "post-evangelical wilderness" at http://www.internetmonk.com.

5. Sullivan 2006.

6. Hoffer 1951. See Sullivan 2006 for the same point.

7. Einhorn 2008.

8. See *The Other Side of Sunday* (a 1996 Danish film) for a contemporary portrayal of this same quest for freedom.

9. Neely Tucker, "The Book of Bart." *Washington Post*, p. D01, 5 March 2006. His book is Ehrman 2005. See also Lobdell 2009; Reece 2009; Schaeffer 2008.

10. Ferreira 2009.

11. Kowalski 2008:7.

12. Masci 2008b; Collins 2006.

13. Masci and Smith 2006.

14. Meacham 2006, 2007.

15. "Religion in America: Non-Dogmatic, Diverse, and Politically Relevant." June 23, 2008; pewresearch.org.

Acknowledgments

I'm obviously much obliged to many people for their efforts in support of this project. Among these are the numerous college students whose stories and comments appear in the following pages. Indeed, apart from their willingness to share their personal experiences, it's quite likely that this book would never have seen the light of day. In addition, colleagues in the sociology department at the University of Florida and elsewhere encouraged me to write the book and help me to work through its various stages. Department staff was, as always, superb in providing necessary assistance.

Over the course of several years spent discussing the project, my sons Steve and Dave continued their long tradition of being unconvinced about anything I might have to say. But as in the past, their doubts and questions eventually stimulated me to produce, I believe, a more compelling book. Similarly, during our daily walks in the local park, my wife and partner, Professor Jo Hasell, never ceased offering perceptive comments on how to express more effectively the things I wanted to say. I am profoundly grateful for her many contributions to the book during the several years of its gestation.

Patience also characterized my agent, Stan Wakefield, while guiding me through earlier versions of the manuscript en route to something that might entice both editors and readers. Once we had a reasonable manuscript, he wasted no time in identifying Praeger as the best publisher for this book. Michael Wilt, my editor at Praeger, has been extremely helpful in offering suggestions that might improve the book, as well as in guiding it along the path toward eventual publication. I'm compelled to express my heartfelt thanks to both Stan and Michael for their faith in the project and their efforts in bringing it to completion.

Finally, I feel obliged to acknowledge my long-term debt to certain professors I had while a student at Wheaton College. Over the years I've spoken with a number of fellow alumni who like me are now what the preface to this volume calls a recovering evangelical. All of us agreed that certain key professors felt called to the vocation of coaching sheltered evangelical youth on how to think—most of us for the first time in our life. They wanted us to taste the pleasures of what one professor called "the wine of the mind." All of us agreed that we are profoundly indebted to those brave professors for their priceless gift—"brave" because they risked operating beneath the radar of college officials whose passion was to enforce conformity rather than stimulate creative thinking. Our conversations, however, quickly turned bittersweet when we reflected on the fact that our professors didn't warn us that thinking can become addictive. Our inability to put the lid on the bottle is after all what eventually led us into the ranks of *recovering* evangelicals. As I look back on it now, I'm convinced our professors were well aware of the risks of addiction but felt compelled to entice us anyhow. For that, my fellow alumni and I are forever grateful.

Introduction
The Religious Right:
A Not-So-Classy Act

For more than 60 years, the fact that people in the West (North America, Europe) have been changing the ways we actually *do* families is obvious to just about everyone. Yet our values or image of what families *should* be are not in step with what we do—they've not kept pace. Social scientists describe that kind of gap as a cultural lag. The downside of any cultural lag is that we find ourselves trying to solve today's new problems using the answers for yesterday's old problems. It's like students who've memorized the answers to last year's test without realizing that the teacher has made up a new test.

And that is surely the case when it comes to contemporary families. Furthermore, as we continue on into the 21st-century information age we can expect that the problems facing families will get even more complex and tougher to solve. It follows that if yesterday's answers don't have the juice to solve today's problems, they'll be even more impotent tomorrow. An added and painful reality is that the strategy of relying on yesterday's answers to solve today's problems hits families who are less well off much harder than it hits families who are better off.

In this book, *families* is a shorthand term that covers just about everything that naturally belongs here. Families include our immediate (nuclear) family and our kin. Families also cover love, marriage (straight and gay), cohabitation, divorce, singleness, gender and work, parenting (dual and solo), children and youth, sexuality (adolescent and adult), and abortion. Moreover, social class and race/ethnicity are central to our understanding of families.

We do not, of course, make our choices regarding families in a social vacuum. Outside forces work both ways: they sometimes limit us, but they also provide opportunities to get creative about our choices. Some 200 years ago, the industrial revolution swept away the agricultural age—and with it a way of life that had existed for millennia. The traditional ways of doing families were gradually displaced by newer ways of doing families. Today, it's déjà vu all over again: the industrial age is steadily giving way to the *post*-industrial era, or what some call the information age. And that evolution—like the earlier revolution—both limits our choices *and* offers us chances to get creative about doing families.

That is the tide of history—ordinary persons responding as best they can to relentless social, political, and economic forces. But like children on the beach, there are always a few people hoping to preserve their sandcastles by turning back the tide. Though doomed to fail in the long run, their resistance hurts a lot of people in the meantime. Today, the most politically powerful social force aiming to reverse the tide of history goes by the label *religious right* (RR). "Christianist" is *Atlantic* editor Andrew Sullivan's label for the RR—persons who use politics and/or the law to impose their views about families on the rest of us.[1] In 2000, for instance, R. A. Mohler (a leader of the Southern Baptist Convention, which is strongly christianist) declared that the SBC stands like a rock against the "immoral tide" of change sweeping over American families.[2] His very first example of the "immoral tide" is the fact that many Americans have forsaken "traditional roles for women." SBC believes that the wife should submit to the God-given authority of her husband, and that women should *not* be ordained as clergy. Mohler added:

> Southern Baptists know they are in a race against time and the direction of the culture. As issues like homosexual marriage, abortion, euthanasia, and attacks upon the natural family have exploded, Baptists have held themselves captive to God's word.

To make his case, Mohler uses the strongest tool in the christianist arsenal—the notion that its vision of the family is supremely moral or right. Their flip side is that all other visions of families have little or no virtue—they are *im*moral and *not* right. Many Americans, however, believe that the RR's vision is badly flawed. Recent surveys reveal a generation gap between younger and older Americans when it comes to the christianist agenda.[3] Younger citizens (evangelicals and Roman Catholics among them) are less likely than their elders to roll over and accept without question the RR's spin on families. Accordingly, a major objective of this book is to come up with a vision of families that is morally superior to christianists' defective vision. And part of doing that is to point out that the RR is not an equal-opportunity mischief-maker. The pain and suffering it inflicts on society via its political clout is felt most keenly by the less advantaged citizens among us—persons whom Jesus called the "least of my brothers [and sisters]" (Mat. 25:40 KJV). Persons who are better off in socioeconomic terms are much more insulated against christianist slings and arrows.

To be sure, some citizens wonder aloud if christianists are a spent political force. They suggest that because the RR was unable to elect its 2008 presidential ticket (as it had in 2000 and 2004) it is therefore no longer a serious threat to Americans' freedoms to get creative about 21st-century families. For instance, the evangelical spokesperson Jim Wallis asserted that we've now entered a "post-religious right America."[4] Also, *Washington Post* essayist E. J. Dionne, Jr., wrote about the future of American faith and politics "after the religious right."[5] However, such undue optimism reminds me of Mark Twain's celebrated 1897 quip that "the reports of my death have been greatly exaggerated." In the vein of Twain, *New York Times* columnist Peter Steinfels wrote that

> *On every side, one can read obituaries for the religious right. . . . Sometimes stated outright and sometimes between the lines is the hope that the decline of the religious right will ease what Americans have come to know as the culture wars. . . . There is no question that many evangelical Christians and conservative Roman Catholics have grown disenchanted with both the political agenda and what they see as the strident style of the organized religious right. Some have been convinced, by their own Scriptures and by new leaders, that poverty, human rights, genocide, sex trafficking and global warming must be no less matters of Christian concern than abortion, homosexuality and embryonic stem-cell research. Even more have reacted against their faith being enlisted in partisan politics. . . . But what will this retreat of the religious right mean for the future of the culture wars?* Caution is in order. Combat may wane, at least a little, at least for a while. But there are good reasons to doubt any lasting truce, let alone a real peace.[6]

His note of caution is prudent indeed. The prologue to this volume explains that the gene for theocracy is built into the RR's DNA. That gene drives the christianist passion that *government must act on behalf of the devout to impose the will of the divine on the doubters.* Though recent political events may for a time have nudged that gene from dominant to recessive, it nonetheless remains strong and tough. Based on his studies of the RR's political ambitions, Lee Marsden echoes Steinfels: "The death of the Christian Right as a domestic and foreign policy actor are greatly exaggerated. . . . [On the international front, they aim to] shape a conservative foreign policy agenda. As such they have no intention of leaving the world's stage any time soon."[7]

Although the RR may, for the moment at least, be somewhat restrained from sailing the ship of families full tilt backward into the past; it exerts a drag on that ship and prevents it from moving steadily forward into the future. Christianist political clout keeps the ship closely tied to yesterday's status quo. Consider, for example, the sobering reality that, on the very same day Barack Obama was elected U.S. president, christianists successfully spearheaded amendments to the constitutions of three more states banning same-gender marriage. The total of such states now stands at 29, with 26 of those coming since 2003.[8]

OVERVIEW

This book begins with the prologue followed by two major sections. Part I listens to some "Voices from the Not-Too-Distant Past." Part II suggests some "Ideas for Today and Tomorrow."

The prologue sets the stage for the entire book because it describes the "gene for theocracy" that pervades the RR. Christianists are adept at spinning myths in order to gain and hold political clout. One of its most hallowed fables says that our founders were Christians, that the United States was founded as a Christian nation, and that the founders' agenda for the Christian family was built into the fabric of our nation. Putting it far too politely, such notions are simply false. The prologue shows that, to the contrary, most of our founders were not Christian and feared lest any religion—including Christianity—might unduly influence their infant republic. They worried that what I call the gene for theocracy—which exists in most world religions—might somehow become dominant and undermine the cherished liberties they'd worked so hard to establish.

Part I argues that the changes among today's families are simply a continuation of long-term trends stretching way all the way back into pre-Revolutionary America.[9] Getting a handle on those trends helps us understand what's going on today. Chapter 1, for example, shows that changes in families began surfacing soon after the Europeans settled New England during the 1600s, and that's good news. It's good because change is a vital sign of life—no change, no life. Second, the changes are positive because many of us believe that families today are actually better than were our forebears' families. Which of us wants to jump into a time machine and join the families of previous centuries? A deafening silence compels us to say that most of the changes in families since those long ago days have indeed been beneficial. Our refusal to go back is most resolute if we happen to be black, a woman, or a poor white man or, for that matter, a younger person. Keep in mind that being poor during those good old days covered some 95 percent of the population.

For the most part, the long-term changes in families have tilted in a certain direction: they've tended to edge away from oppressive control over one's life by others. They've leaned instead towards greater liberty, freedom, and autonomy for the individual man, woman, and youth. Importantly, this autonomy has by and large been tempered by responsibility and accountability. In the main, it has not been hedonistic or narcissistic. To be sure, liberty occasionally descended into license, as it did in the late 1960s and early 1970s. But that proved to be the exception rather than the rule.

The term *evolution* is sometimes used as a metaphor to capture long-term social trends. This book, for example, pivots around the ongoing evolution of gender and work, human sexuality, partnering, and parenting. But the centuries-long evolution of those broad areas has not been mindless or random. Their evolution is no more the product of mere chance than were the political upheavals occurring in late 18th-century America. Driven by a quest for freedom, our founders rebelled against Britain, and installed a new republic. Western societies place enormous weight on the need for human freedom within the political and economic spheres. The sphere of families is no exception to this towering principle. Accordingly, the basic force impelling the long-term evolutionary trends in Western families is the quest by men, women, and youth for ever-increasing degrees of control over one's life—autonomy tempered, however, by responsibility.

Chapter 2 is about the changes in patterns of human sexuality also dating back several hundred years and extending throughout the 1950s. The gradual evolution of those patterns of sexuality eventually ran head-on into the counterrevolution mounted by christianists in the 1960s. I agree with those who say that when we cut to the chase, the RR is fundamentally about sexuality—hetero and homo alike.[10] And I would add that the christianists' view of sexuality is inseparable from their views on keeping women in their supposedly proper place—linking the two is as old as the Garden of Eden. Remove sexuality and women from the mix, and the christianist agenda droops rather limp and flaccid.

Part II steers our discussion into the present and future. Chapter 3 talks about women, men, and work. Central themes include the idea that work is at its core far more than money. Work also includes several intangible dimensions, most prominent of which is a sense of control over one's life—an awareness of one's autonomy or lack thereof. The point is made that autonomy rests in large part on economic independence.

Importantly, throughout the several millennia of the agricultural age, women and men worked side by side struggling from dawn to dusk to eke out a meager living. But the mid-19th-century rise of the industrial revolution removed large numbers of middle-class women for the first time in history from the sphere of economic or productive work. However, as we evolve into the information age, chapter 3 discusses something *old*: Is it time for women to assume once again their *historic* place in the world of work? Is it time for women to add—as did their foremothers—the *identity* of worker to their identity of mother? Likewise, chapter 3 discusses something *new*: Is it time for men to add the *identity* of father to their identity of worker? In short, what are some innovative ways for women and men alike to be autonomous persons and effective parents at the same time?

Chapter 4 pivots around the pros and cons of the staple christianist argument that marital sex equals moral sex. Outside of marriage, intercourse is, they say, immoral. We consider the obvious limitations of that view, particularly so for adults but also for youth and adolescents. Branding nonmarital sex per se as immoral cripples creative efforts to take the kinds of contraceptive steps necessary to prevent pregnancy, abortion, and sexually transmitted diseases (STDs), including HIV. Our entire discussion is immersed in the reality that all things sexual—including the tragic moral choice of abortion—are a glaring case in point of less advantaged citizens bearing an undue share of the burdens the RR imposes on society.

Chapter 5 explores the thorny question of partnering. Partnering includes marriage—both straight and gay. It also covers cohabitation, and what's known today as *the relationship*. Our discussion leads us to ask what historians mean by saying that after many centuries love has conquered marriage.[11] When all's said and done, love turns out to be indefinable. Nonetheless, in the late 20th and early 21st centuries, growing numbers of persons (youth in particular) have concluded that whatever else it is, love holds at its core Plato's ideal of profound emotional intimacy: *partners should be confidantes, or soul mates*. That is so whether the partners are straight or gay/lesbian. And because our culture celebrates and rewards marriage as the ultimate affirmation of love, marriage is both a status symbol and a cultural and civil right that cannot be denied legitimately to any couple—heterosexual or homosexual—seeking it.

Chapter 6 considers the question of parenting. The public schools (kindergarten through 12th grade, or K–12) alongside families are charged with the vital task of shaping America's children and youth. Since the 1960s, the RR has followed two strategies in its efforts to influence youngsters' education. One is its private academies, organized chiefly in reaction to the racial integration of the public schools. Not content with that, christianists have also attempted to gain control of what goes on within grades K–12. Most notably, they've been quite successful at imposing abstinence-only curricula. Although thus far less successful at imposing intelligent design (creationist) curricula, the RR keeps up a continual bombardment on evolutionary biology.

Youngsters from families that are less economically advantaged suffer most from both of those misguided and foolish crusades. Recently, some younger evangelicals have committed themselves to address the socioeconomic needs of persons who are less well off.[12] Hence, Chapter 6 wonders whether or not evangelicals might fulfill at least part of that commitment by resisting both of those christianist crusades to cripple less advantaged youngsters.

Finally, chapter 7 draws from the many ideas suggested throughout the book. The chapter integrates those suggestions into a coherent whole and explains how the four broad areas of families (gender and work, sexuality, partnering, and parenting) overlap to a considerable degree. Tweaking any one of those areas invariably brings about adjustments in or more of the others. A prime example of how these four areas interlock pivots around the issue of women's autonomy. Creating social policies and programs designed to cultivate a woman's autonomy requires not only a certain perspective on work, it also calls for a particular outlook on sexuality, partnering, and surely on parenting. The coherent whole that emerges from the intertwining of these four broad areas consists of 10 principles aimed at enhancing the human development of persons in families. Taken together, those principles give rise to an image or picture of families that we might call *progressive*. I call it progressive because it entails the creative blending of liberal ideals (e.g., freedom and growth) with conservative ideals (e.g., responsibility, accountability, and order).

A PROGRESSIVE APPROACH TO FAMILIES: AN ALTERNATIVE TO CHRISTIANISM

Recently, more and more people of goodwill (some profess faith, others not) are beginning to view themselves as political and social progressives rather than as conservatives or liberals.[13] New York Governor Nelson Rockefeller called himself a conservative while seeking the 1964 GOP presidential nomination. At that year's national convention he warned that his beloved party was "being taken over by 'a minority wholly alien to sound and honest conservatism.'"[14] A year earlier, he'd called those aliens the "radical right."[15] The latter was in fact the forerunner of today's RR, which is as alien to "sound and honest conservatism" as was its 1960s life form.

Although Rockefeller did not define "sound and honest conservatism," *Atlantic* editor (and conservative) Andrew Sullivan does. He worries that the classic meaning of *conservative* has (just like the equally classic term *liberal*) gotten drowned out by the RR's corrosive political style. While the L word is now tainted, Sullivan argues that the C word is badly misunderstood. He believes that because the media, politicians, and especially christianists have no idea what *conservative* actually means, they mangle it beyond recognition. The christianist lust for power, he argues, disgraces and discredits the very idea of the term *conservative*.

The principal differences between the conservative and liberal perspectives stem, he says, from their views on the *pace* of social change, but not the *fact* of it. A conservative does indeed honor tradition and believes in the past. Nonetheless,

> *Tradition is not a static entity. Although conservatism leans toward regretting change and loss, it is not wedded to the past. It never seeks to return to a golden age or distant past.*[16]

And, in another place, Sullivan remarks that the conservative

> *accepts change as an integral part of human organization and society. What distinguishes conservatives in the sense I prefer from liberals is a residual respect for what has been, a desire to understand it before changing it.* But change it conservatives will.[17]

But before embracing change, a conservative must be convinced that change offers something better. Change simply for the sake of change, believes the conservative, might in fact make things worse. Hence, the conservative is deeply suspicious of efforts to modify things—especially by government. The conservative tends to believe that if left to her own devices, the individual may rise to the numerous challenges of life and, eventually, overcome them.

Liberals share with conservatives a profound passion for individual freedom, and a fervent desire that each person should be able to develop his talents, gifts, and abilities to the fullest extent possible. However, they differ over the role that external supports might play to facilitate changes that enhance personal freedoms.[18] For example, during the 1950s and 1960s liberals argued that legal segregation placed severe limitations on black people to be all they could be. In order to facilitate the development of blacks, liberals took the lead in abolishing laws limiting black freedoms. They also insisted on establishing new laws aimed at facilitating black liberties. Today, segregation has morphed into a nonissue. Sullivan says that the genuine conservative gradually accepts the reality of change—in this case, integration—and learns not only to live with it but eventually to embrace it.

A progressive approach to families draws on and seeks to blend the best of liberal ideals (freedom, exploration, growth, development, change) with conservative ideals (responsibility, accountability, duty, order, stability, continuity). A progressive image stands, first, in sharp contrast to the christianist (nonchange, traditionalist, reactionary) image.[19] Second, it differs just as markedly from the self-indulgent, irresponsible liberal perspectives of the 1960s and early 1970s described in chapter 2. Hence, a progressive image of families is superior both to the christianist and the hedonistic or narcissistic approaches. It is a cut above both because it aims to empower 21st-century persons trying to figure out how to do the right thing when it comes to gender, work, sexuality, partnering, and parenting. On the one side, progressives strongly favor freedom for the individual to grow and develop. Indeed, human and social health requires autonomy in order to flourish. But on the other side, one's freedom must be balanced with an appreciation for the importance of tradition and social continuity. In the realm of families, freedom must be tempered with a keen sense of responsibility to other persons (adults, youth, and children) and to the society as a whole.

Sullivan himself personifies this balanced and nuanced approach to changes in families. Alongside being conservative, Sullivan is a practicing Roman Catholic and openly gay. He is a "fervent, passionate crusader . . . for gay marriage . . . he is [thus] crusading for a radical change in the way we define the most fundamental unit of human society."[20] As the new century wends its way, it is likely that growing numbers of Americans will be as hard to pigeonhole as Sullivan. As citizens become increasingly aware of the thorny complexities inherent in the issues facing contemporary families (homosexual marriage is but one example), the folly of swallowing snake-oil remedies—whether from christianists or anywhere else—will grow ever more apparent. A progressive approach to families is not a cure-all—it is basically a process for solving problems—a process living at the core of the traditional American way of life since the 18th century.

NOTES

1. Sullivan 2006.
2. Mohler 2000.
3. Kinnaman and Lyons 2007.
4. Wallis 2008.
5. Dionne 2008.
6. Steinfels 2008, italics added.
7. Marsden 2008:253.
8. "States with Voter-Approved Constitutional Bans on Same-Sex Marriage, 1998–2008." www.prwresearch.org. To be sure, by late 2009 six states permitted same-sex marriage, at least for the time being.
9. Wood 1992; Coontz 2005.
10. Herzog 2008; Goldberg 2009.
11. Coontz 2005.
12. Wallis 2008.
13. Kazin 2008. And see progressiverevival.com, "Faith, Values, and Politics for the 21st Century."
14. Martin 1996:83.
15. Martin 1996:80. The term "Radical Right" had appeared, for perhaps the first time, in Lipset 1955.
16. Sullivan 2006:268.
17. "Conservative and Liberal Brains," Andrew Sullivan, September 12, 2007, italics added, http://andrewsullivan.theatlantic.com/the_daily_dish/2007/09/conservative-an.html
18. Smith 2007; Wolfe 2009; Beinart 2006a, b.
19. See O'Beirne 2006 for a frightening example of what Sullivan means by non-change, traditionalist, and reactionary.
20. Brooks 2006.

Prologue: Our
Not-So-Christian Nation

I have opponents in this race who do not want to change the Constitution. But
I believe it's a lot easier to change the Constitution than it would be to change
the word of the living God. And that's what we need to do is amend the Consti-
tution so it's in God's standards rather than trying to change God's standards
so it lines up with some contemporary view of how we treat each other and how
we treat the family.[1]

While in hot pursuit of the 2008 GOP presidential nomination, Governor Mike
Huckabee declared that the U.S. Constitution should conform to God's standards. Earlier, John McCain had said that God was already on the side of our
constitution. McCain asserted that "the Constitution established the United
States of America as a Christian nation."[2] McCain's comments appeared several
weeks after the First Amendment Center released the results of its 2007 survey showing that most Americans agreed with him: the center reported that,
"Sixty-five percent of Americans believe that the nation's founders intended
the U.S. to be a Christian nation and 55% believe that the Constitution estab-
lishes a Christian nation."[3]

Rick Green "says the poll doesn't mean a majority favors a 'theocracy' but
that the Constitution reflects Christian values . . . 'I would call it a Christian
document, just like the Declaration of Independence.'"[4] Green speaks for a group
called *Wallbuilders*. His is one of several christianist groups attempting to re-
vise history and thus fool unsuspecting citizens.[5] Such groups aim to make

history say what they believe *should* have happened, as opposed to what actually *did* happen. The groups claim they are

> dedicated to presenting America's forgotten history and heroes, with an emphasis on the moral, religious, and constitutional foundation on which America was built—a foundation which, in recent years, has been seriously attacked and undermined.[6]

Although Green said that a "Christian nation" is not the same thing as a theocracy, he didn't bother to define either term. Nor did the researchers from the First Amendment Center define "Christian nation" for their respondents. The introduction to this book noted that christianists aim to impose their views about families on the rest of us via legal and/or political means. I added that the gene for theocracy is built into the RR's DNA. That gene drives the christianist passion that *government must act on behalf of the devout to impose the will of the divine on the doubters.* Does that qualify as a definition of theocracy?

At one point in time, Ralph Reed (one of the RR's early, influential leaders) declared that the RR aims to replace our degenerate culture with "a thoroughly Judeo-Christian culture."[7] But at another time, Reed seemed to backtrack because he "explicitly denied that America is or should become a 'theocratic state or unicultural society.'"[8] The most extreme Christian theocrats are called Reconstructionists, and they believe that "Christians have a mandate to rebuild or reconstruct all of human society."[9] Rather than using the label *theocratic,* they prefer instead to speak of a *theonomic order.* Their blueprint for rebuilding America (and other societies) is based on the biblical laws of Moses, including death by stoning for lawbreakers (women in particular, and sometimes children).

Christianists vary among themselves regarding the scope of their theocratic ambitions for America.[10] Nonetheless, virtually all of them agree on the following set of bogus ideas: *First,* our founders established the United States as a uniquely Christian nation. *Second,* our founders believed that Christian values (as defined by the RR) should govern American families. *Third,* our founders believed that healthy families result in a strong America, and christianists say that both our families and our nation were strong through the 1950s. *Fourth,* since the 1960s our families have declined and so has America. *Five,* to make America strong again, we must rebuild strong families based on traditional moral values. We must, in other words, restore all facets of the traditional family that prevailed in the 1950s.

Accordingly, christianists are determined to use political and legal muscle to impose their image of the family on the United States, just as some Islamic extremists intend to mold Muslim nations according to their vision of what a

good society should be. Sullivan describes christianist ambitions as a "theo-
conservative project."[11] To be sure, any label that's even remotely akin to *theocracy* terrifies many citizens by conjuring up horrific images from the past—a
past I describe below. Owing to universal fears of a theocratic nightmare, most
RR leaders (like Reed or Green) shy away from any hint that their ultimate
goal is to establish any such thing as a theocracy. Accordingly, they tend instead
to employ bland labels to cloak their objectives, such as Green's use of the be-
nign phrase "Christian America." When, for instance, Pat Robertson sought
the 1988 GOP presidential nomination, he announced that "God's plan, ladies and gentlemen, is for his people to take dominion."[12] He also declared
that Ronald Reagan's 1980 election as president had been the "direct act of
God. . . . The Republican takeover and reversal of direction in this country is
no coincidence."[13]

There seems little doubt that christianists believed that the 2004 reelection
of George W. Bush was indeed a "direct act of God," and that they were finally
poised to "take dominion." Not only was the RR convinced that a thoroughly
Christian America was at long last in their sights, but also several political an-
alysts seemed to agree. Michelle Goldberg wrote about the apparently unstoppable "rise of Christian nationalism."[14] Randall Balmer wrote the scary words
"How the Religious Right . . . Threatens America."[15] Dan Gilgoff terrified us
by describing "How James Dobson, Focus on the Family, and Evangelical America Are Winning the Culture War."[16] At the time, however, no one anticipated
Bush's precipitous decline and with it the rapid deceleration of the RR's forward speed.

Though christianists may be down they are by no means out, as noted in
our introduction. They're not even slinking quietly away. Last time I looked, the
RR remained unchallenged on the moral high ground of what families are all
about. While its capability to harm Americans (especially the less advantaged)
might be held in check temporarily, it remains a potentially virulent force. Although the gene for theocracy that drives it may now be somewhat recessive,
the gene has not been and almost certainly never will be exorcised. Thus, as I
see it, in order to undercut and discredit the RR's take on families it is essential
that we punch a hole in its fabrication that America was founded as a Christian
nation complete with Christian family values.

THE AMERICAN GOOD NEWS: INVENTING THE FUTURE

Newsweek editor Jon Meacham pulls no punches: "The problem with [the chris-
tianist] reading of history is that it is *wrong*."[17] While christianists dream of
restoring a past that never was, Meacham says that the American good news

is instead all about inventing a better future—both spiritually and materially. Our public religion, he says, has always been forward-looking—never backward-looking. Another historian adds that Thomas Jefferson "was never more American than when he told John Adams in 1816 that he liked 'the dreams of the future better than the history of the past.'"[18] It is quite accurate to conclude that most of our founders were indeed *religious* persons. But, by the same token, it is simply false to assert as does the RR that they were evangelical Christians and thus handed us a ready-made Christian culture.[19] Though they believed in God, they successfully resisted every effort to make America a Christian nation.

Rather than being Christian, most of our founders were known as *deists:* they believed in a supreme being who transcends the ordinary limits of time and space.[20] God is, moreover, beneficent and created the universe along with its physical laws. Those laws enable the cosmos to proceed in an orderly and predictable manner. In the same way, they said, God created the social laws that govern human society. Deists, however, rejected Christian teachings such as the trinity, the virgin birth, eternal damnation and hellfire, an error-free Bible, and the divinity of Jesus.[21] In 1819, Jefferson used an actual pair of scissors on his King James Version of the four gospels and physically "cut out miracles and signs or declarations of Jesus' divinity."[22] Today, we call his work the "Jefferson Bible."

Deism was a product of the Enlightenment—a movement that swept across Europe and America during the late 17th and 18th centuries. One of the most influential Enlightenment figures was the British thinker John Locke and our founders were in fact his disciples.[23] Thus, the Declaration of Independence was a Lockean and *not* a Christian document. Like other deists, Locke believed in God but argued that "Reason must be our last judge and guide in everything."[24] Locke and our founders believed passionately in human reason as opposed to written revelation (e.g., the Bible or Koran).[25] Deists also asserted that reason is superior to and is the ultimate judge of all ecclesiastical authority, which they viewed as pretentious. Despite rejecting the ultimate authority of both the Bible and organized religion, they believed that reason emanates from God. Accordingly, God created humans and expects them to use reason as the basis for inventing societies that optimize human freedom, promote personal growth, and are marked by social justice:

> The God of the Declaration is a divine force that created the universe, endows all men with human rights, and is an actor in the drama of the world he made. . . . It was this God who became the God of America's public religion.[26]

The eminent 17th-century British physicist Isaac Newton (acknowledged by many as the father of modern science) was a well known deist. And so was Benjamin Franklin: "He believed in a divinity that he called the Supreme Being, a term much used in his day. I think he was comfortable with God. He would have asked God, 'How did you put electricity up there in the clouds?' He must have considered God a fellow scientist."[27] Because Franklin's sister Jane was evangelical, the two had frequent and spirited (though good-natured) disagreements over religious matters.

Given their deism, including their faith in the power of reason, our founders took great care *never* to insert the terms "Christian" or "biblical" into either the Declaration of Independence or the U.S. Constitution. Their strategy greatly distressed some Christians who at the time were spearheading efforts to insert a statement into the constitution declaring "Jesus Christ as the source of religious liberty."[28] Jefferson later wrote that he and his colleagues rejected that and similar assertions on the grounds that they wanted America's religious liberty to "comprehend within the mantle of its protection, the Jew and the Gentile, the Christian and Mohammedan, the Hindoo and Infidel of every denomination."[29]

In 1797, the United States and the Muslim government of Tripoli were having serious disputes that could have led to war. But our senate crafted, and President John Adams signed, a treaty with Tripoli that averted bloodshed. One of the clauses of their treaty stated that "America bore no 'character of enmity against the laws, religion, or tranquility of Musselmans,' for [the United States] was 'not, in any sense, founded on the Christian religion.'"[30] This treaty further highlights the fact that the first Americans were entirely convinced that the United States is *not* a Christian nation as do the comments 15 years later of the president of Yale College. In 1812, he complained bitterly that the Christian view of God was left out of the earlier debates on how to compose America's new constitution:

> "Thus," said [Yale] President Dwight, "we commenced our national existence . . . without [the Christian] God."[31]

A media event featuring those favoring a Christian nation versus those who believe in our founders' public religion occurred at the start of the 2007 Congress. Newly elected Representative Keith Ellison chose to swear his oath of office on the Koran. Representative Virgil Goode objected, claiming that Ellison is required to take his oath on the Bible, even though Article 6 of our constitution states that "no religious Test shall ever be required as a Qualification to

any Office or public Trust under the United States."[32] Ellison responded graciously saying, in the manner of Jefferson, that what unites us all is our shared
loyalty to our Constitution. Ellison added an eloquent and moving depiction
of America's public religion—a description that our founders would have ap-
plauded because it overrides all sectarian perspectives: "Muslims," he said, are
"here to support and strengthen America, [and] they are nurses, doctors, husbands, wives, kids who just want to live and prosper in the American way."

Notwithstanding the complaints of Dwight, Goode, and other christianists,
our founders' primary objective was to expand—not curb—personal liberties.
They believed, as do most Americans today, that the best possible society is
one in which every effort is made to develop each person's potential to the fullest extent possible. This faith, says Meacham, is the essence of the American
gospel, that is, its good news. It follows that our founders were not prepared
to tolerate efforts by any sectarian group—including the Christian churches—
to impose on others any of its particular ideas regarding families.

In a 2006 speech, former Georgia governor and U.S. Senator Zell Miller
warned that unless Americans "reclaim our lost heritage . . . moral scurvy will
overtake the nation."[33] Miller and other RR leaders are fond of spinning fairy
tales about what he called the "uncompromising integrity and spirituality of
[our] founders."[34] Was Miller, I wonder, thinking of Alexander Hamilton, who
was at the epicenter of America's very first sensationalized public sex scandal?
Hamilton, who was married, confessed in 1797 to an ongoing adulterous affair
with a married woman named Maria Reynolds.[35] Or was Miller thinking perhaps of Benjamin Franklin, who in 1730 married and "established a respectable
household to which he could bring his illegitimate son William," the fruit of
one of his many sexual liaisons?[36]

Or might Miller be thinking perchance of Thomas Jefferson, who prior to
his marriage made an "offer of sexual companionship to a neighbor's wife,
Betsey Walker? When it came to light, he admitted it and apologized."[37] Following our Revolution, the recently widowed Jefferson lived in Paris represent-
ing the new U.S. government. From 1786 until his return to the United States
in 1789, he carried on an affair with a married British woman named Maria
Cosway.[38]

Audiences worldwide got to see what one reviewer called their "invigorating
romance" portrayed in the 1995 film *Jefferson in Paris*.[39] The film also turned its
spotlight on an issue with vastly more serious implications for our infant republic, namely, Jefferson's "thirty-eight year affair with his slave Sally Hemings,
half-sister to his late wife."[40] That his relationship (begun in Paris) with Hemings supplied him with "lasting contentment" adds unbearable irony to the

stance that Jefferson and most of our other "uncompromising and spiritual" founders took towards African slavery.[41]

THE ANCIENT GENE FOR THEOCRACY

The chief reason our founders adamantly refused to allow America to be a Christian nation was their faith in Reason as the ultimate governing principle of the universe. The second major reason they said no to Christianity or any other religion was their reading of history. They knew all too well what happens when *any* single religion exercises control over government. The landscape of the Europe that they knew all too well was soaked with the horrific bloodshed perpetrated by Christian theocracies. Our founders were painfully aware of the horrors and untold sufferings that Catholic and Protestant theocracies alike had rained down on Europe in the name of God for hundreds of years, and they sought to steel their infant republic against any repetition of such horrendous follies.[42] Closer to home, they had firsthand knowledge of the suffering caused by those American colonies that had resorted to legal and political means to impose their religious views on unbelieving citizens. Those colonies had flirted with theocracy, and our founders were utterly determined to preclude even the slightest possibility that their new republic would ever pursue such perilous flirtations.

While growing up, I sat through numerous sermons and lectures describing the gradual transformation of Christianity from a despised and persecuted sect into a formidable and feared political force. In an effort to strengthen his hold on political power, the Roman Emperor Constantine issued his momentous Edict of Milan in the year 313. His edict permitted Christians for the first time ever to safely exit their catacombs—their underground hideaways. They were suddenly allowed to venture forth into the sunshine and to practice their faith openly—free at last from the terror of being drawn and quartered and then burned or devoured by lions.

It may seem surprising to learn that some of the preachers I listened to couched the Christian route to political power in negative terms. It was regrettable, they informed us. To be sure, the earliest Christians did not approve of what they saw as the corruption of Roman culture. Nonetheless, agitating for political power to change society was simply not on their radar screen. Their strategy was instead to get people saved and to wait patiently for the bodily return of Jesus from heaven. When he returned, their persecutions would be ended and they'd no longer be forced to breathe the polluted cultural air around them.

The edict, however, altered their strategy. As their persecutions ended Christians enjoyed, for the first time ever, a certain degree of respect and status. Furthermore, they got the beginnings of political influence: "Within a century, Christianity and the Roman Empire were fused tightly together."[43] But observers reasoned that as the status and influence of Christianity increased, its spiritual fervor began to decrease; for if the church could, through political means, get Romans to behave outwardly like Christians, why bother with the hard work of trying to get them saved?

Those anxieties notwithstanding, the gene for political influence got implanted into the Christian church during the fourth century, and it's been part of its DNA ever since. Having once tasted the elixir of political power, all too many Christians have, to one degree or another, lusted for it from that time to this. During the centuries following the edict, the Roman Catholic Church developed into the official religion of Rome and most other European nations. In effect, those nations became *theocratic,* that is, a state ruled by officials that claimed to be divinely guided. Catholic Church clerics leaned on monarchs and insisted that their religious values should be written into the laws of the state, and woe to anyone who violated state laws because they were one and the same with God's laws.

As a quid pro quo, the Catholic Church declared solemnly that monarchs ruled according to God's will—the divine right of kings (and queens). And woe to anyone foolish enough to dispute God's will in such a grave matter! In short, a religion that began as a fiercely persecuted sect—barely hanging on by its fingernails to the hope that Jesus would soon return and get its oppressors off its back—morphed into the relentless and unforgiving persecutor of any and all deviants and heretics. Anyone whose behaviors or public statements veered from divine laws was at risk of a wide range of tortures and all too often death. The gene for theocracy was not simply present in their DNA—it had become dominant. Indeed, by the mid-11th century some Catholic thinkers argued that "it was the pope who wielded supreme power, even above that of an emperor."[44]

Does the notion of supreme power have an eerie ring to it? Does it sound like Mike Huckabee saying that God's law is above the Constitution? Does it sound like John McCain saying our Constitution makes us a Christian nation? Does it echo a person interviewed by Florida Public Radio in spring 2008 while he and his peers were demonstrating in Tallahassee against laws allowing abortion? He told the reporter we must obey the "higher laws" of God regarding abortion rather than man's laws. Our founders were exceedingly vexed about the gene for theocracy precisely because of this notion of supreme power. That phrase implies that those who exercise power in the name of God have the right to compel others to obey *by any means.* In its extreme form, *any means* includes stripping citizens of their rights, torture, imprisonment, and even death.

Our founders could look back in time to see that Christians had in fact employed any means to compel obedience to God. Christians had done so in four different settings—the Crusades, the Inquisition, the Holy Wars, and finally within certain American colonies. Peering some 200 years into the future it would not have surprised our founders—though it would have troubled them—to see, for example, that some christianists opposed to abortion bombed clinics, harassed, and even murdered physicians in the name of God.[45] Equally disheartening to our founders would be the fact that, in the name of God, some of them want to stone women and children to death for violating God's laws. More broadly, our founders would be profoundly distressed, I believe, with any attempt to impose the christianist agenda by legal and/or political means.

THE CRUSADES AND THE INQUISITION: BY ANY MEANS

There seemed little doubt that Pope Urban II was basking in his supreme power when in 1096 he ordered the First Christian Crusade to take back the Holy Land from the infidel Muslims who had, he said, occupied Jerusalem contrary to God's will. It turned out to be the "largest and most ambitious military operation launched from Western Europe since the days of the Roman Empire."[46] Nonetheless, after some half-dozen additional crusades spanning over 300 years, the only firm outcome was that hundreds of thousands of Christians and Muslims alike (including women and children) died from sickness, exposure, starvation, and the sword. The church's efforts to impose its supreme power on others had exacted a high price in blood and treasure with nothing good to show for it.

The crusades against the Muslims were the first example of Christian leaders exercising their supreme power by any means—including violence. The second example of their supreme power evolved as the crusades were winding down. Growing weary of oppressing the Muslim outsiders, Catholic leaders started looking around for insiders—Europeans—to impress with their power. The first group they targeted was Christian heretics—persons suspected of deviating from church teachings. To sniff out their heresies, the church established a judicial procedure in the 13th century that evolved gradually into a permanent institution called the Holy Office of the Inquisition.[47] Before he became the current Pope Benedict, Cardinal Joseph Ratzinger was in charge of the Office of the Inquisition, though it had a much less odious label.[48]

Today, the closest we've come to the Inquisition are the secretive U.S. government agencies that pursued, detained, and extracted information by dubious means from alleged terrorists.[49] Then as now, the suspects (heretics) are assumed to be guilty until and unless they can prove their innocence. Then as now, officials used torture on their suspects. Inquisitors also had the right to put suspects to death. The most infamous example of the Inquisition's supreme power and miscarriage of justice occurred in 1633 when it condemned Galileo to life imprisonment for asserting that the sun—not the earth, as the church taught—is the center of the universe. Indeed, only the intercession of powerful friends saved him from being burned at the stake.

The second group targeted by the Inquisition was Jews. The Spanish Inquisition begun in 1492 is notorious for the brutality inflicted on Jews. They had the choice to emigrate out of Spain, be tortured until they converted to Christianity, or be put to death and their family's wealth seized. Targeting Christian heretics as well, the Spanish Inquisition is one of the most barbarous examples in history of the cruelty that humans are capable of inflicting on other humans in the name of God. The 2002 film *Inquisition* is set in the Spain of 1680 and is based on a Dostoevsky short story *The Legend of the Grand Inquisitor.* Alongside detailing the brutality of the Inquisition, it gets into the head of the Inquisitor and tries to fathom how such inhumanity is possible. The 2006 film *Goya's Ghosts* (directed by Milos Forman) portrays the horrors of the Inquisition in late 18th-century Spain. It shows that the famous painter Goya was being investigated by the Inquisition because his etchings portrayed in gory detail how the church had tortured and brutalized Spanish citizens.

As contemporaries of Goya, our founders were no doubt well aware of the horrors occurring in Spain, just as they knew all about the evils of several hundred years of Inquisitors using "any means" to compel obedience to God. Jonathon Kirsch calls it "Terror in the Name of God."[50] Surely our founders found the Inquisition as abhorrent as the crusades. Both series of events helped to convince them that the gene for theocracy was part of Christianity's DNA, and that their task was to prevent it from becoming dominant—to keep it as recessive as possible. And it was to that end that they designed their new republic— one in which Christianity would be free to flourish but never to exercise any kind of supreme power.

A CASE OF GENETIC CLONING AND THE (UN)HOLY WARS

There is yet a third page of history that helped persuade our founders of the dangers inherent in establishing a Christian nation. As Martin Luther, John Calvin, Henry VIII, and other Protestant reformers strode onto the European stage in the early 16th century they complained bitterly that the Roman Catholic Church had forsaken God's truth. Eventually, those and other reformers withdrew from the Catholic Church and invented their own theocratic establishments, though each with a different style. In effect, the gene for political power got cloned: previously, there'd only existed one Christian theocracy—Roman Catholic. Now, there were several species of Christian theocracies (Lutheran, Calvinist, and Anglican) in places such as Switzerland, Germany, the Netherlands, Scandinavia, and England. Although the Protestants differed sharply among themselves over many issues, they were firm in their shared conviction that any species of Protestant theocracy was better than the Catholic variety.

Because every theocracy is convinced it has a corner on God's truth for all humankind, it simply cannot under any circumstances tolerate any other group claiming (falsely, of course) that it instead is *the* genuine theocracy. At first, neighboring Catholics and Protestants contented themselves with merely hurling epithets at one another: *you are blinded by your church's satanic teachings; you're a heretic who deserves to burn in hell.* It wasn't too long, however, before the verbal assaults worsened into violence. Roving bands of either Protestants or Catholics attacked and sometimes killed one another—on occasion driving whole communities from the ancestral lands that their blood families had farmed for centuries. Slowly, the violence escalated into the gruesome European holy wars (both civil and cross-national) of the 16th and 17th centuries that ultimately sucked in nations such as France, Spain, the Netherlands, England, and Germany.

During the 1560s, for instance, the French Catholic theocracy fought three civil wars with its Protestant Huguenot citizens. Although the combatants signed an official truce in 1570, the government sponsored a covert operation against the Huguenots in Paris on August 24, 1572.[51] Called the *St. Bartholomew's Day Massacre,* French soldiers and citizens reportedly slaughtered some 70,000 Huguenots beginning in Paris and spreading across France. Following the massacre, many Huguenots fled France for Protestant countries such as Switzerland. As the French/Catholic persecutions continued off and on throughout the next century, many more Huguenots escaped to America. Finally, those centuries of ghastly violence by all sides in the name of the one true Christian God reached a bloody apex in the English Civil War, resulting in the Protestant beheading of their Catholic king, Charles I in 1649.

All parties were keenly aware of the fact that the wars they'd fought were not simply about religious doctrines or personal piety, but about social, political, and economic power. Governments battled within and across national boundaries, using God's will as a justification for their violence. Both sides claimed that the bloodshed they inflicted was a just or holy war, and each invoked the name of their one true Christian God to justify their killing. Each side believed that its dead soldiers went to heaven, but that the dead soldiers (who believed they were the true Christians) on the other side went to hell. The ever-increasing efficiency of the technology of warfare (e.g., artillery) took an enormous toll of soldiers and civilians—losses never before experienced or even imagined.

Today, most of the world's citizens are horrified, and rightly so, by Islamic violence in the name of God. Few Christians, however, would presume to pull up their skirts in righteous indignation as did Pope Benedict XVI when in 2006 he approvingly cited a 14th-century description of Islam as "evil and inhuman."[52] Though the Pope may not wish to discuss it, the hands of our Christian forebears are deeply stained with blood from the ambitions of earlier theocracies determined to impose a religious and political order that was one and the same. And those gruesome images never strayed very far from the minds and hearts of our American founders.

THE PEACE CHURCHES: SUPPRESSING THE GENE FOR THEOCRACY

The most prominent exception to the indictment of evil and inhuman Christians is found in the Peace Churches—known in the 16th century as Anabaptists. Today, they are the Quakers, Brethren, Moravians, and Mennonites (including the Amish). Like the preachers of my earlier years, the Anabaptists believed passionately that using political means to impose any sorts of religious views on others was an aberration from God's truth, and they worked very hard to exorcise that demon from within their own religious communities. Although they acknowledged that the State (whether Catholic or Protestant) had a legitimate sphere, "Anabaptists categorically denied that the magistrate [State] had any right to exercise authority in spiritual matters."[53] Needless to say, the theocracies that engulfed them were outraged with Anabaptist dissent from prevailing religious beliefs and their resistance to the state's efforts to enforce those beliefs: Protestant leaders regarded them with "alarm and abhorrence."[54] Consequently, those theocracies launched a series of violent and centuries-long persecutions of the Anabaptists.

The ruling Christians were surprised to discover that the violence they directed against the Anabaptists was greeted by nonresistance and nonviolence; Anabaptists sometimes called themselves "defenseless Christians."[55] Despite the fact that their fellow Protestants and Catholics alike inflicted horrendous violence on them, Anabaptists did not respond in kind. The nonviolence practiced by Gandhi and by Martin Luther King, Jr., owes a great deal to the Anabaptists. They believed that Jesus and his apostles commanded the first Christians to practice nonviolence, and the Anabaptists reminded the theocrats of their day that until Constantine, Christians had refused to serve in the Roman military. However, because conscription was not introduced until much later (i.e., the French Revolution and Napoleonic Wars) the Anabaptist refusal to bear arms (i.e., pacifism) was not at that time the major cause of their persecutions. Instead, they suffered owing to their stout refusal to conform in any way at all to the dictates of any theocratic state regarding matters of faith and conscience.

In order to escape the violence that other Christians inflicted on them, many Anabaptists fled to North America. Most famous of these was the Quaker whose picture on the oatmeal box is known to every American—William Penn. In any event, we must agree with historian Peter Brock that the Anabaptist suppression of the gene for theocracy was both extraordinary and historic: "Here, indeed, existed in embryo the modern ideas of the separation of church and state."[56] The centuries-long drive to bury once and for all the archaic notion that the state is beholden to any distinctive religious ideology began with what today are called the Peace Churches. They shoved the gene for theocracy well into the furthest recesses of their Christian DNA. No doubt our founders were well aware of and strongly influenced by the Anabaptist example. They vowed that within their new republic, the gene for theocracy must be kept deeply buried once and for all.

COLONIAL AMERICA: A MIXED BAG OF RELIGIOUS INTOLERANCE AND LIBERTY

Throughout our 200-year colonial period, some Christians were content that the gene for theocracy should remain recessive. Others, however, were only too eager to make the gene just as dominant as it had been in Europe, and our founders were entirely familiar with the sufferings they'd imposed on their fellow immigrants. The pains resulting from the theocratic-like patterns they'd established in certain American colonies were, in our founders' minds, derived from the same gene as the untold human miseries inflicted by European theocratic Christians.

To be sure, apart from the late 17th-century Massachusetts witch burnings, most of the time most of the colonies had not actually murdered religious dissenters in the name of their Christian God. Nevertheless, except for Rhode Island, Delaware, and Pennsylvania, each of the colonies had established one or perhaps several denominations. Establishment meant (at the least) that each citizen had to pay taxes to support the favored religion(s) even though that citizen held a different religion or none at all. More ominously, it meant that the colony had the legal right to discriminate against persons who dissented from their religion, and sometimes to persecute them as well. Dissenting Christians were sometimes "forbidden to evangelize [and] attendance at the established church was sometimes required, expressions of disrespect toward ministers were often forbidden, and blasphemy could be punished by death."[57]

Maryland offered our founders some valuable lessons on how difficult it is to navigate the perilous mine fields away from tyranny over the human mind and toward freedom of religious expression. Maryland was founded originally as a haven for European Catholics suffering at the hands of Protestants. Despite its Catholic roots, the colony passed the 1649 Toleration Act allowing all Maryland citizens the freedom to practice any and all varieties of the *Christian* religion. Although not as generous as Rhode Island, which granted every person the liberty to practice any (or no) religion, the 1649 act is nonetheless viewed as one of the threads eventually woven into the First Amendment of the U.S. constitution.

Nevertheless, subsequent events in Maryland must have struck our founders with the extreme fragility of any effort to ensure freedom from tyranny over the human mind. In 1650, Maryland's resident Puritans overthrew its government and outlawed both Catholicism and Anglicanism. By the end of that decade, however, the Anglican colonial government finally quashed the Puritans and reestablished the Toleration Act. But by 1688, the Anglican colonial government effectively undermined the Toleration Act and, ironically enough, Catholicism was outlawed in Maryland until after the American Revolution.

WE THE PEOPLE AND OUR FOUNDERS: ADDING IT ALL UP THEN AND NOW

Our founders were, in sum, deeply and painfully aware both of the ghastly horrors of religious bloodshed in Europe, and of the religiously based cruelty of some Americans against Americans—all in the name of the one true Christian God. Our founders must have thought it deplorable that some Christians who'd fled the Old World to escape fierce persecutions had, in their turn, hounded other Christians (and non-Christians) in the New World. Our founders added up their colonial experiences, the holy wars, the Crusades, and the Inquisition. The sum total equaled their conviction that America must *not* be a Christian—nor any other sectarian—nation. Or, as Barak Obama put it during a 2009 press conference in Turkey: "We do not consider ourselves a Christian nation or a Jewish nation or a Muslim nation. We consider ourselves a nation of citizens who are bound by ideals and a set of values."[58]

Our founders were unreservedly determined *not* to repeat the grievous actions of the European and colonial American Christians. They refused to allow their republic to retain any vestige of tyranny over the human mind and spirit. Thus, the very first amendment to our constitution reveals their eagerness to plumb the uncharted and murky waters of freedom from religious strictures— liberties they perceived as beneficial both to politics and faith alike.[59]

> *Congress shall make no law respecting an establishment of religion, or prohibiting the free exercise thereof; or abridging the freedom of speech, or of the press; or the right of the people peaceably to assemble, and to petition the Government for a redress of grievances.*

Although our founders were not so naïve as to think they could entirely eradicate the gene for theocracy, they hoped ardently to dispatch it once and for all into a permanently recessive state of dormancy. And, to an admirable extent, they've succeeded. Although we've had our share of religiously based political conflicts, the United States has never been wracked by the religious repression and bloodshed that once devastated Europe and which today saps the blood and treasure of societies around the globe. Nonetheless, I have little doubt that if our founders were alive today they'd fear that the gene for theocracy is not as recessive as it ought to be. Despite the RR's recent setbacks, our founders would perceive evidence among christianists of certain traits that marked both the European theocracies as well as their colonial offshoots. Specifically, it seems to me that our founders would be appalled by the christianist obsession to impose its family agenda on the rest of us.

If it is prudent to ask how far Islamic activists are willing to go to reshape their societies, it is equally wise to ask how far christianist leaders are willing to go in their efforts to restore the family patterns and features of yesterday. Would the extremists among them go so far as to imitate the bizarre zealots in Margaret Atwood's 1985 novel (*The Handmaid's Tale*) and stage a military coup in order to impose their agenda for families? Probably not, though I agree with Goldberg that christianist leaders would do everything short of violence to achieve and hold political power.[60] Am I, however, *convinced* that their leadership would *never* resort to violence as a means to grab and hold political power for its own ends? I wish I could respond yes, but in all honesty I cannot. I am not aware that the gene for theocracy has as yet been modified in order to excise from it a certain obsessive conviction: if one acts in the name of their one true Christian God, one may do *whatever it takes* to force on the rest of us a society and family made in the image of their God.

NOTES

1. Former Arkansas Governor Mike Huckabee, as reported by Domenico Montanaro on MSNBC: "Huck, the Constitution and 'God's Standards,'" January 15, 2008.

2. Meacham 2007.

3. First Amendment Center, www.firstamendmentcenter.org, September 24, 2007.

4. From an interview with Andrea Stone, 2007: "Most Think Founders Wanted Christian USA," *USA Today,* September 5, 2007.

5. Goldberg 2006a.

6. Please see www.wallbuilders.org; www.coralridge.org.

7. Ralph Reed, 1996, "We Stand at a Crossroads," *Newsweek,* May 13:28. Reed's ideas are elaborated in greater detail by his 1996 book.

8. Cited in Martin 1996:364.

9. Martin 1996:353.

10. Meacham 2006:217ff; 232ff; Goldberg 2006a:6ff.

11. Sullivan 2006:73ff.

12. Martin 1996:268. Also see Palmquist (1993) as an example of an overtly biblical theocrat.

13. Martin:268.

14. Goldberg 2006a.

15. Balmer 2006.

16. Gilgoff 2007.

17. Meacham 2006:233.

18. Wood 2006:115.

19. Brookhiser 2006:62ff. See Kowalski 2008:21, and Wills 2007, for the same argument.

20. Meacham 2006; Wills 2007.

21. Kowalski 2008:58; Weisberger 1958:6ff

22. See "The Jefferson Bible—The Life and Morals of Jesus of Nazareth Extracted Textually from the Gospels." Compiled by Thomas Jefferson. Edited by Eyler Robert Coates, Sr. /www.angelfire.com/co/JeffersonBible/.

23. Kowalski 2008:13.

24. Kowalski 2008:13.

25. Hyland 2003.

26. Meacham 2006:75.

27. Claude-Anne Lopez 2000.

28. Goldberg 2006a:32.

29. Goldberg 2006a:32.

30. Brookhiser 2006:62–63.

31. Goldberg 2006a:44.

32. Phillips 2006.

33. Baptist Press 2006, "U.S. Headed toward Moral Scurvy, Zell Miller Warns," October 10. www.bpnews.net. (Formed in 1946 by the Southern Baptist Convention, and supported with Cooperative Program funds, Baptist Press [BP] is a daily international news wire service.)

34. Baptist Press 2006, "U.S. Headed toward Moral Scurvy, Zell Miller Warns," October 10.

35. Brookhiser 1999:97–100.

36. Chaplin 2006:51.

37. Ledgin 2000:2.

38. Ledgin 2000:2.

39. Janet Maslin, *New York Times,* March 31, 1995.

40. Ledgin 2000:2.

41. Ledgin 2000:2.

42. Martin 1996; Meacham 2006; Cohen 2007.

43. Madden 1999:1.

44. Madden 1999:6

45. Martin 1996:xxx; Wicklund 2007; Press 2006. And see the 2006 film, *Luke of Fire.*

46. Madden 1999:17.

47. Kirsch 2008.

48. Kirsch 2008:208.

49. Kristof 2008c. And see Kirsch 2008:254ff.

50. Kirsch 2008.

51. Kelley 1972. For an engrossing fictional account of some of the social and personal consequences of that particular religious bloodshed, see Tracy Chevalier, *The Virgin Blue* (1997).

52. "The Pope's Words," 2006, Unsigned Editorial, *New York Times,* September 16.

53. Brock 1968:4.

54. Brock 1968:4.

55. Brock 1968:5.

56. Brock 1968:4.

57. Martin 1996:372.

58. Lind 2009.

59. Martin 1996:374–75.

60. Goldberg 2006a.

Voices from the
Not-Too-Distant Past

Families in Flux versus the Myth of a Golden Age

Christianists are superb spinmasters. One of their favorite fables is that America began as a Christian nation. Another fairy tale is about the traditional family. To be sure, people have always lived, loved, and survived in families of one type or another, and they've surely embraced and honored their family traditions. But the truth of many different family traditions in numerous cultures over many thousands of years is not what Christianists want us to think about when they speak piously of The Traditional Family. They don't want to bore us with messy facts about the varieties of families any more than they want to confuse us with the fact that most of our founders were deists and not evangelical Christians.

Spinmasters are terrific at conjuring 30-second sound bites. Picture the following video clip of a man and a woman strolling in a lovely countryside: she's gazing adoringly into his eyes—a boy holding his hand and a girl holding hers. Accompanied by heart-tugging music the voiceover cites a 1990s religious right (RR) political organizer:

> [We] have a desire to put America back on its feet in a righteous order, [we] truly believe that God and family are very important to the future of America. [We] have dreams and memories of long past. If [some of us are] too young, they remember their parents speaking of it. If they're my age, they remember the days when they could walk the streets and not worry, when people cared about one another, and when there was not all this divisiveness. There wasn't violence on TV,

there weren't lyrics in music that said the opposite of everything you believe.
We're wanting to go back to those days. Are we ever going to get totally back? I
don't know, but I do know that a lot of people care about that. And that is really
the make-up of Christian Coalition: people like that.[1]

Christianists want us to believe that the traditional family is like a towering
mountain of solid granite that God made some six to eight thousand years ago.
They tell us that a mountain cannot change and neither does the traditional family. Despite its being ageless, they say that a half a century or so ago some self-
indulgent fools began chipping away at the mountain—trying to destroy its
beauty and integrity. It's now time, say christianists, to put an end to their hare-
brained schemes and restore the mountain—the traditional family—to its former pristine golden-age state.

Repeating that fiction endlessly adds believability to the RR's claim that its
agenda is the only moral game in town regarding families. And the sad fact is
that christianists don't have to work very hard to keep citizens in fairyland. For
some time, studies have shown that many Americans are woefully uninformed
even about U.S. history.[2] When it comes to the history of families around the
world, they're even more in the dark. I can testify that before I began seriously
studying families, I believed the mountain myth. Based on my own experience
as a professor, I would say that many of today's college students remain equally
clueless. Regardless of their religious faith or lack thereof, many citizens take
it for granted that the early 20th-century traditional family has been around for
as long as humans have lived on the earth.

If the mountain imagery is fatuous, what's a better way to conceive of families? A more perceptive metaphor is, I believe, that of a grand historical novel
like Leo Tolstoy's *War and Peace*. The drama unfolds over many decades—set
in the midst of the monumental events convulsing 19th-century Europe. The
reader comes to know and care about a large cast of complex characters struggling to make sense of the chaos happening around them. Their lives follow
a series of unpredictable and unforeseen twists and turns. The reader never
knows what to expect next, other than feeling that as the story continues it
deepens her insight into both the madness and the resiliency of the human
condition.

That, in my view, is the truest way to think about families: Replace the granite mountain with a fluid drama whose characters somehow survive in the midst
of the social, political, and economic forces raging around them. Over the past
400 years American families have, say historians Steven Mintz and Susan Kellogg, "undergone a series of far-reaching '*domestic revolutions*' that profoundly

altered [them]. . . . The claim that [families are] an . . . island of stability in a sea of social, political, and economic change is largely an illusion. . . . The American family has changed dramatically over time."[3] People have indeed lived, loved, sacrificed, and cared for their families. But the flip side is that some persons have dominated, exploited, and inflicted dreadful wounds on spouses, children, sibs, or parents. Thankfully, most people learn from their mistakes. Over the course of many centuries people are, through painful trial and error, learning how to craft better families. In my view, today's families are better, say, than families of 2,000 or 200 or 100 or 60 years ago.

Contrary to the RR's scary pessimism that families are tumbling down a slippery slope, I take a more optimistic view. The central storyline about families in Western societies, and now in some developing countries, is that most of the time they are moving in an upward trajectory and thus getting better. That is particularly so for families that are economically advantaged. Throughout many centuries, there's been a long-term trend away from oppressive control by others (family members, outsiders) over one's life. Replacing it has been the trend toward greater liberty, freedom, and autonomy (tempered by responsibility) for the individual man, woman, and child. More persons of both genders from varied racial/ethnic groups have greater opportunities than ever before to grow into all they can possibly be. One of the outcomes is an expanding pool of persons able to make meaningful contributions to the public household—the greater good.

Given that the imagery of a fluid drama is the most accurate way to think about families, chapter 1 briefly describes four episodes excerpted from that saga. The episodes take place in 18th- and 19th-century America, and each one illustrates our central story line—oppressive control versus increased liberty. The first two episodes are revolutions—they move with the tide of history. But the last two are *counter*revolutions—they move against the tide of history.

DOMESTIC REVOLUTION 1

The Patriarch and His Household: "Honor Thy Father . . . "

At the close of the 1600s, Cotton Mather was the most influential clergyman and theologian in the colonies. Among his many achievements, he was noted for "helping to excite the hysteria" resulting in the 1692 Salem, Massachusetts, witch trials and hangings where "twenty people and two dogs were executed."[4] In his numerous writings, Mather complained bitterly about the "degeneracy" of colonial America—especially in the realm of family values.[5] By *degeneracy* Mather meant two things. First, compared with the children of the early 1600s, the offspring of the late 1600s had become less obedient to their parents. Second, wives had become less obedient to their husbands.

Throughout prerevolutionary America, obedience was far and away the most significant family value of all. Disobedience to authority was a sure sign of moral decay, as well as an indicator of cultural degradation. Although it's tough for a 21st-century person to wrap his head around it, Mather and other leaders were just as fiercely anti–family disobedience as today's christianist leaders are passionately anti-homosexual or anti-choice in terms of abortion. Influential figures like Mather worried a great deal about the disobedience of offspring and wives because he and other leaders perceived it as a threat to the viability of America: in that "patriarchal world . . . such slippage in family authority threatened chaos in the larger social order."[6] They believed that social order happens when every citizen has a clear idea of the time-honored rules for everyday life. The rules govern what a person is supposed to do and when and how to do it.

When asked who gets to decide the rules, the churches said that God decides. God (who is male) gives his rules to the king (or queen). Almost all the Christian churches in the American colonies proclaimed the divine right of kings—the notion that God appoints their ruler.[7] The monarch then passes on God's rules to the male aristocracy. Those privileged males then forward the rules to the male commoners. The commoner then conveys God's rules to his wife and children and his hired hands (maids or ploughboys). God commands each level in the chain of command to obey the level(s) above it. Hence, the monarch must obey God (but no one else), and so on, until we finally reach the hired hand who, being at the bottom of the chain, must obey virtually everyone else. The 18th-century citizen curious enough to enquire *why* God set up this chain of command would be informed that

> Order is Heav'n's first law; and this confest
> Some are, and must be, greater than the rest,
> More rich, more wise.[8]

But if the citizen complained that such a chain didn't seem at all fair, she would be reminded that it has a lot going for it:

> The inequalities of such a hierarchy were acceptable to people because they were offset by the great emotional satisfactions of living in a society in which everyone, even the lowliest servant, counted for something. In this traditional world "every Person has his proper Sphere and is of Importance to the whole."[9]

Of the two types of mounting disobedience, Mather and others were much more anxious about offspring rejecting parental authority than they were about wives challenging the rule of their husbands. Although wifely challenges were germinating at about the same time, their insubordination took much longer to come to full flower. Recall that the Ten Commandments say nothing about wifely obedience. They do, however, demand that children honor their parents.[10] St. Paul defined honor as obedience and observed that this commandment guarantees a payoff—obey your parents and, he says, you'll live a long and happy life.[11] For thousands of years, Jews and Christians alike took the Fifth Commandment as seriously as any of the others. The American colonists were no exception to the divine rule of surrendering to parental authority. Their deference was not, however, based altogether on their piety or moral fiber—particularly so for families that were not religious. *Obedience to parental authority was bound inextricably to the ownership of land.* That economic reality meant that submission of the offspring occurred in a drastically different social and economic world. It was like living on another planet when compared with today's 21st-century Western society.

First, of all, when we think about today's children obeying parents, we think of persons up through the age of 18. But among prerevolutionary parents and children there was no magical cutoff point at all. The offspring were obliged to submit to their parents as long as they lived.

Second, when we talk about the family, we customarily picture what social scientists call the 19th- and 20th-century immediate or nuclear family—husband, wife, and dependent children. In sharp contrast, when the term *family* was used within the agricultural context of colonial America, it referred primarily to the entire set of blood kin—the extended family. During the colonial era, each nuclear unit resided typically in its own dwelling (small cabin—often one room). Occasionally it took in an unmarried relative. Sometimes, a hired hand (male or female) might also reside in the cabin or in a nearby barn. Less common but not unknown was the boarder. Neither kin nor workers, boarders paid to stay either permanently or temporarily in a cabin or barn.

Third, depending on how much land was available, the cabins of nuclear units were frequently situated nearby the cabins of other nuclear units with whom they were blood-linked. Hence, at that time, "the family" meant the whole network of blood kin consisting of nuclear units living in cabins situated nearby one another—all engaged in a shared agricultural enterprise. And when I say "all" I mean everyone: adults of both genders married and unmarried, children of all ages, as well as hired hands, laboring from dawn to dusk at their divinely appointed tasks and struggling to wrest a living from a fickle environment.

Fourth, the term *household* was also in common usage at that time. Most often, household referred to the entire cluster of cabins containing several blood-linked nuclear units, in addition to any number of unmarried kin and workers. Household thus equaled all the blood kin and their workers.

Five, and fundamental to everything else,

> *everyone [no matter their age] in the household [whether one dwelling or several]
> was dependent on the will of the father or master (the terms were indistinguish-
> able). The family was, in fact, not simply those living under one roof but all
> [including workers] those dependent on the single head . . . the patriarch.*[12]

The patriarch was the eldest male of the entire extended family or household that resided and worked a certain land area. *Economic dependence on and subjection to him is the essential key to understanding colonial families.* The prevailing pattern at that time was, say, for a midlife father to own a certain amount of acreage. He was likely to have been his father's eldest son and had thus inherited the land from him. The patriarch's younger brother(s) might possibly reside on the land in his cabin with his wife and children. Likewise, the patriarch's eldest son (next in line to inherit the land) would also reside in his cabin with his wife and children on his father's land. The patriarch's younger son(s) might also live on the father's land—perhaps with a wife and children in his own cabin or perhaps with his brother or father. Indeed, "the colonists believed that society [as a whole] was little more than a collection of [these sorts of extended] family households."[13]

Furthermore, Americans firmly believed that God demanded that everyone in the entire household must obey their patriarch in everything. Although each father was typically the decider within the confines of his own nuclear unit, the patriarch was the decider-in-chief. He could, if he chose, overrule his brothers and sons even on matters internal to their own nuclear unit. The rationale for his considerable power was simple: the patriarch was acting in God's name to preserve order within the extended family/household. Because society consisted of such households, each patriarch was doing his bit to ensure that the larger social fabric of which they were a part would be strong and stable.

The allegiance of kin members to their patriarch rested ultimately on the fact that he owned the land on which they lived and worked. That reality was just as powerful in the 18th century as it was when the Ten Commandments were first devised by the ancient Hebrews. Each person in the household relied on the patriarch for economic survival. Anyone refusing to conform to his wishes ran the risk of being cut off from his or her livelihood. To be sure, some men defied their patriarch and tried to make a go of it anyhow. The young Ben Franklin, for instance, disobeyed his older brother's wishes to serve his household as a printer's apprentice. He ran away and eventually became an independently wealthy merchant. But Franklin, we're told, was a genius, and for every person like him (or like Alexander Hamilton—born to a poverty-stricken, unmarried, Caribbean woman) there were many other thousands of men and some women who, after defying their family patriarch, ended up destitute or worse. As St. Paul had warned, their disobedience led indeed to an unhappy life.

Nevertheless, the picture I've painted is not a still life. Beyond its narrow Atlantic strip America was a vast expanse of wilderness waiting, thought the colonists, to be tamed. The degeneracy that distressed Mather and other christianists sprang from the reality that a son or brother could in fact defy his patriarch and go almost anywhere else to farm his own land. This trend of ever-increasing economic *in*dependence from the patriarch got even stronger as the 18th century wore on and more and more Americans moved farther and farther west. Alongside farming, growing numbers of young men were, like Franklin, testing their mettle at becoming merchants within America's growing cities and towns.

In short, 18th-century colonial America was by no means static. Change was happening within the economic sphere of society. The ancient pattern for survival was no longer the sole game in town. The God-ordained, vice-like grip held by the patriarch on the economic well-being of his family and workers was being pried loose ever so slowly. An alternative means of livelihood, or game, was emerging in which an ambitious man could make his living either on his own land or in the commercial life of the towns (and sometimes both)—quite apart from his father or older brother(s). John Adams was, for instance, a highly respected late 18th-century Boston lawyer and, in addition, he and his remarkable wife/partner Abigail successfully managed their own farm.[14]

Social scientists have long noted that people change their behaviors prior to changing their values. For example, if a poll had been taken in the mid-18th century, most people would likely have told the pollster, "I believe in the extended family style, and I believe that offspring of all ages should obey their patriarch." Citizens would have embraced such family values even though more and more of them were in fact behaving in precisely the opposite fashion.

Social scientists have also observed that when a gap opens up between what persons say they believe and what they actually do, people eventually close the gap by changing their values to fit how they behave. For example, if a second poll had been taken at the end of the 18th century, it would have shown that Americans were gradually changing their family values. Rather than believing that God wanted them to live out their life within the bosom of the extended family style, they were starting to feel that God wanted them instead to live their life within the nuclear family style. Instead of believing that God wanted them to bend to their patriarch's will throughout their entire lifetime, they were beginning to feel that God wanted them instead to place limits on the degree to which they should obey their parents.

Oddly enough, a series of religious revivals called the Great Awakening spread across the colonies throughout the 18th century and encouraged Americans to change both their behaviors and their values. Historian Gordon S. Wood wrote,

> The religious revivals became in one way or another a massive defiance of traditional authority. . . . Revivalists urged the people to trust only in "self-examination" and their own private judgments, even though "your neighbors growl against you, and reproach you."[15]

The central theme of the revivalists' message was the born again experience.[16] Prior to that time, most Christians were simply mainstream Protestants—they believed in God and did not question the authority of their church to instruct them on the chain of command. But the evangelists criticized the mainstream churches. Evangelists warned that the churches were leading their parishioners astray by not making the new birth the centerpiece of religion. The revivalists preached that being born again ushers one into a personal relationship with Jesus. To cultivate their born-again new life, converts were exhorted to study the Bible and *interpret for themselves what Jesus was saying.* If one's study of scripture leads one to believe, say, that *God wants me to live in a nuclear family style,* so be it. Likewise, if the Bible and my prayers lead me *to question the authority of my father,* so be it.

What was happening was that "The individualistic logic of Protestantism was drawn out further than ever before."[17] But the new family style and new family values would have made no sense whatever apart from the shifting agricultural and commercial opportunities stimulated by an expanding frontier. The overriding fact is that the colonists wanted the freedom to explore those emerging material opportunities even though it meant setting aside the traditional family. The individualism they were embracing had of course been part of Western thought long before Protestants came on the scene. Freedom from any sort of control over mind and body was first championed by the pre-Christian Greek thinkers.

Ironically enough, the individualism being cultivated by mid-18th-century American evangelicals was quite compatible with the Enlightenment political ideals that were then influencing the deists and other non-Christians, including our founders.[18] Deists believed that reason is the ultimate judge of past traditions, past writings, and past ways of doing things. Though more restrained, the evangelicals began to understand that they could use their minds to judge and perhaps set aside previous interpretations of the Bible, earlier church teachings, and former ways of doing the family.

The practical result was that deists and evangelicals became curious bedfellows indeed. Each found itself at odds with christianists arguing that human and social health spring from conformity to tradition and obedience to authority. Deists and evangelicals argued instead that human and social health require the freedom to grow and thus to change. Moreover, deists and evangelicals alike argued that God builds the elements of freedom, growth, and change into both humans and society. Finally, both camps argued that social order does not arise out of static conformity to the past. They said that order happens instead when citizens feel a sense of social justice. And social justice comes about when the affected parties participate in the creation of new values and new ways of behaving.

Many historians agree that this fusion of individualistic ideas—emerging from both the Enlightenment and nonconformist Protestantism—was one major force helping to spawn America's rebellion against King George III. In particular, this fusion justified the colonists' rejection of the divine right of kings. Most Americans buried the traditional belief that God had appointed George as the patriarch-in-chief of all his subjects. Similarly, just as it was no longer the moral thing to do to give unquestioning obedience to George, it was no longer the moral thing to do for adult children to submit to the authority of the eldest male in their family—whether their own father, uncle, older brother, grandfather, or whomever.

DOMESTIC REVOLUTION 2
The Husband and His "Dutiful" Wife

Wives, submit yourselves unto your own husbands, as unto the lord.[19]

So wrote St. Paul, and the churches taught that the wife's subordinate place in the chain of command had both a theological and a political justification. Theologically, "the relationship of man and woman in Christian marriage was the same as that between Christ and His Church."[20] Politically, "The first duty of a wife was to obey her husband since this relationship was understood to parallel that of king and subject."[21] In effect, she learned that obeying her husband is the very same thing as obeying Jesus. Lest that seem a bit abstract, she was also taught that obeying her husband is the very same thing as obeying her king and his magistrates.

Either way, the wife was on the receiving end of her husband's commands, and the practical justification for that one-way street was precisely the same as it was for the authority held by fathers over their offspring—*social order*: the chain-of-command must be unambiguous. Though a husband and wife might disagree over something, someone must make the final decision about what or what not to do. If a wife pushes her husband too far, stalemate and confusion could emerge and/or the wrong steps might be taken. Disorder and chaos would surely result. When family members don't know what to do, and/or they do the wrong thing, or fail to do the right thing, then decline and decay invariably set in. And as decay creeps into some families, their bile quickly spreads to others. Eventually, the decay among increasing numbers of families infects the society as a whole, and thus its very stability is in doubt.

Despite dire warnings that wifely disobedience would lead to social disorder, the same 18th-century individualism gnawing away at the patriarch's control of his offspring was slowly undermining the husband's authority over his wife. The Quakers were probably the first religious group to reinterpret the Bible so as to do away with the subordination of women. The Quakers discovered Bible verses proving it was God's will that among born-again Christians the genders should be equal both in and out of marriage.[22] Despite that powerful challenge to an ancient Christian tradition, every colonial woman faced a huge obstacle in her pursuit of the freedom to determine her own destiny—a barrier not faced by her husband, sons, or brothers.

Any man electing *not* to conform to his patriarch's wishes had the option to rent or buy land elsewhere, and/or to try his hand at being a merchant. He had entrée into the new economic game. The new game made it possible for growing numbers of men to achieve economic independence. As crass as it may sound, autonomy requires money and it's hard to imagine the freedom to shape one's own destiny without it. However, virtually no 18th-century woman had the option to achieve the same level of economic self-sufficiency as men. Women were by and large shut out of the new game. Nonetheless, historians have accumulated evidence showing that some 18th-century wives were inhaling the individualism filling the air around them. As a result, some of them began to chafe under the authority of their husbands. As a further result, marital conflict, wife-beating, adultery, and desertion became more evident.[23] But even if a wife left her husband—with or without her children in tow—and somehow managed to escape his rule, what was she to do? Where could she go? How could she support herself apart from a man?[24]

Very few women (or men) of that period could read or write, and among the privileged women who could read, only a tiny handful had ever studied anything beyond the Bible.[25] That handful, however, can be credited with sparking what we today call the feminist movement. The most significant Enlightenment figure was the late 17th-century British philosopher John Locke, on whose reasoning Jefferson drew deeply to write our Declaration of Independence. Locke argued that every human being has certain "inalienable rights" including the most basic right of all—the freedom to determine one's own destiny. If asked, most of our founders would have agreed with women thinkers of the day such as Mercy Otis Warren and Catherine Macaulay that this right applies as much to women as to men.[26] The most outspoken of those thinkers was Warren, also known as the conscience of the American Revolution.[27] Despite their keen sensitivity to the justice of women's freedoms, our founders were preoccupied with breaking away from King George, and intent on securing their own political and economic liberty. Hence, they reckoned that it was not in their best interest to add the fight for women's autonomy to their crowded agenda—it could come later if at all.

The goals of those early feminists were described cogently in 1792 by the British thinker Mary Wollstonecraft (mother of Mary Wollstonecraft Shelley, author of *Frankenstein*) in her *Vindication of the Rights of Women*.[28] The elder Mary argued that women should be educated in order to pursue the emerging mercantile and professional opportunities of the time. Her argument was that education was a prerequisite if women were to participate in the new economic game and thus gain the means necessary to shape her own destiny. Wollstonecraft justified her ideas by arguing that education and professional status would "help single women and widows better support themselves, as well as help married women become better wives and mothers."[29]

The sharp tension between what our founders knew to be the right thing (supporting women's autonomy) and their reluctance to do anything about it is plain to see in the numerous letters exchanged over many years between John Adams (who was often away from his family for months and even years at a time tending to the care and feeding of his new republic) and his remarkable soul mate (who also happened to be his wife and manager of their farm), Abigail Adams. In March 1776, she wrote to John while he was in Philadelphia devising the Declaration that he and his colleagues should "'remember the ladies'" as they debated independence from Britain.[30] She urged him to "be more generous and favourable to [women] than your ancestors [had been]. Do not put such unlimited power in the hands of the Husbands." Abigail reminded John of his own earlier assertion that "all Men would be tyrants if they could."

Abigail Adams belonged to that tiny handful of women thinkers who believed that the cause of American independence should be linked together with greater rights and autonomy for women. Abigail good-humoredly warned John that if women were not given their rights, "we are determined to foment a Rebelion, and will not hold ourselves bound by any Laws in which we have no voice, or Representation."[31] Though John responded with equal playfulness, he did not trivialize the significance of what Abigail was saying. It is crystal clear that he and his cofounders "took her position seriously."[32] Nonetheless, "The cause of women's rights made no overt gains in the Revolutionary era, and no rebellion was fomented."[33]

THE DIE OF FAMILY FREEDOMS WAS CAST

Despite the fact that the "cause of women's rights" was blocked, the die of family freedoms was nonetheless cast during the 18th century. The individualism spreading across the colonies saturated not just the political and economic spheres, but the sphere of families as well. As our culture began edging away from traditional family values, increasing numbers of persons felt the changes were positive. Citizens slowly came to believe that offspring should be free to pursue their own economic interests and free to choose their own spouse. They also agreed that the wife should, to some degree, be free to assert her individualism and to insist that her husband take her interests into account while deciding what was best for their family. Male offspring were, of course, much more likely to get what they wanted than was a wife or daughter. The son or brother could obtain his own land and/or become a merchant. But the wife or daughter had no comparable access to the economic means necessary for either type of independent action.

Nonetheless, if a poll had been taken among early 19th-century Americans, the majority would likely have responded that, compared to 100 or 200 years earlier, America's families had indeed been upgraded. Everyone, except the christianists among them, would probably agree that things had gotten better—not worse. Men had much more freedom to shape their own destiny, women slightly more. Older family traditions (patriarchal authority and the extended family style) were coming under severe scrutiny and newer traditions were emerging. Importantly, the changes in families—though excruciatingly painful for many persons—did *not* result in social chaos or cultural decay—the sky was not falling!

DOMESTIC COUNTERREVOLUTION 1
The Christian Slave-Owner and the Marriages of His Slaves

> *Slaves, be obedient to them that are your master.*[34]

The two revolutions discussed previously shifted Americans away from older, religiously based traditions and toward increased liberties—especially among younger persons. However, the next two *counter*revolutions swelled up *against* the tide of history and led to a *reduction* of liberties (at least for a while). The first reduction occurred among slaves as soon as they arrived from Africa. The second reduction occurred among white, middle-class married women during the mid-19th century.

To me, there is little doubt that the christianist argument that our founders handed us a pristine Christian culture is demolished entirely by, among many other things, the founders' insertion of slavery into our Constitution. How could slavery conceivably square with "establishing justice" or "securing the blessings of liberty"? And as if that were not enough, the family values and behaviors imposed on black slaves by their owners (white Christians and non-Christians alike) could not have been any more degraded or degrading. American (Christian) slavery was much more brutal and dehumanizing than the milder forms of Roman (pagan) slavery familiar to St. Paul.

Chapter 6 of this volume talks about William Wilberforce—the late 18th-century British politician who was influential in ending the Atlantic slave trade. While some Christians like Wilberforce believed that God wanted Africans to be free, most American Christians held fiercely to what historian D. G. Mathews called the "Evangelical Slaveholding Ethic."[35] Simply put, most Southern evangelicals believed that God had entrusted them with African slaves in order to help them, namely, to elevate them from their benighted savagery "to a 'high moral plane.'"[36] Or, as one South Carolina Baptist preacher put it, "We who own slaves . . . honor God's law in the exercise of our authority."[37]

The divine right of slaveholders meant that they had total control over every facet of the life of their slaves—including their families. And the slave-owners' treatment of African families is without doubt the final nail in the coffin of the christianist argument that America's families have, over time, gotten worse rather than better. Many Christians at the time believed that God had ordained slavery and they held the biblical evidence to prove it.[38] Throughout the 18th and early 19th centuries, American culture was influenced by a Christianity that for the most part bolstered the practice of slavery. (The Quakers were a notable exception. They'd always opposed African slavery, and were in the forefront of the abolitionist movement.) That amalgam of Christianity with slavery included a horrendously savage twist on marriage that was unbelievably bizarre. It seems creepy to realize that today's christianists—the self-appointed champions and protectors of marriage—claim an historical tie to some of the very Christians that once ravaged it.

Although no Southern state permitted legal marriage among slaves, white Southern Christians frequently used a public ceremony of pair-bonding (masquerading as marriage) as a shrewd strategy to buttress their own economic self-interest.[39] Most owners favored the practice of public pair-bonding because they believed it discouraged slaves from running away. Marriage for whites was, they said, established by God—a holy union of one man and one woman. But for blacks, pair-bonding was devised by white slave-owners to satisfy their economic greed. Although the following is taken from Lalita Tademy's account of early 19th-century Roman Catholic Louisiana, a similar pattern existed throughout the Protestant slave states as well.

Typically, a slave owner in the Cane River (Louisiana) vicinity co-opted a priest into composing some sort of a special bonding ceremony for their slaves—in this case Clement and Philomene:

> *You [says the priest], Clement, do now in the presence of God and these witnesses, take Philomene to be your wife; Promising that so far as shall be consistent with your relation which you now sustain as a servant, you will perform your part as a husband toward her* . . . only so long as God shall continue your and her abode in such places as you can conveniently come together . . . *[Philomene vows likewise].*[40]
>
> *I then [says the priest]*, with the consent of your masters and mistresses, *do declare that you [are] husband and wife*, so long as God shall continue your places of abode as aforesaid; and so long as you shall behave yourselves as it become servants to do: For you must both of you bear in mind that you remain still, as really and truly ever, your master's property, and therefore it will be justly expected, both by God and man that you behave yourselves as obedient and faithful servants . . . for the time being.[41]

The religious right grouses that many of today's marriages are little more than temporary deals dissolved at the whim of their contractors. Be that as it may, the marriage concocted for slaves by their Christian owners was based shamelessly on the avarice of their owners rather than on any pretense of spiritual blessings for the couple or their children. It was the absolute embodiment of a most horrific bargain except that the couple had no voice whatever in its permanence. Slaves were informed that their owners (guided by God) decided when it was in the economic self-interest of the owners either to keep the partners together or to sell one or both of them (as a pair or separately). God also guided their owners to sell some or all of their children, if need be. How could a despised slave presume to debate almighty God?

In short, the historic Christian culture to which christianists implore us to return sanctioned an extraordinarily perverse take on the families of African slaves. Emancipation forced white Christians to relinquish slavery and blacks were free (at least formally) to follow the same family values and styles as whites.[42] Once they possessed those freedoms, black Americans seized every opportunity to try to make their families better than they'd ever had a chance to be under the heavy yoke of slavery.[43]

In a 2006 speech, former Georgia governor and U.S. senator Zell Miller warned that unless Americans "reclaim our lost heritage . . . moral scurvy will overtake the nation."[44] Given what we've just seen, the christianist claim that America's family values have been in freefall since the days of our founders is at best sheer rubbish. At worst, it is gross deception. As measured by increased personal freedoms for whites *and for blacks in particular,* family values have, over time, gotten healthier and not sicker. And, though christianists resist it vigorously, that inexorable movement toward greater freedoms—blended with responsibility—is not going away any time soon.

DOMESTIC COUNTERREVOLUTION 2

Sentencing the Middle-Class Mother to "True Womanhood"

Like an invading conqueror, the 19th-century Industrial Revolution overran the economic, political, and family spheres of British and American society. Compared with the limited commercial opportunities of the prior century, the factory system offered seemingly infinite economic possibilities. And, as 19th-century economic horizons brightened, the severe 18th-century wound inflicted on the traditional authority of males over their youth proved fatal.

In sharp contrast, the 18th-century hurt inflicted on the traditional authority of a husband over his wife was not fatal until the mid-20th century. One reason it took so long was because an unforeseen obstacle got in the way. The barrier was a significant social change advertised as giving women greater opportunities than they'd ever enjoyed before. The reality was, however, precisely the opposite. The 19th century imposed a unique limitation on the freedoms of middle-class women—one that had never before existed among the vast majority of women anywhere in the world. I said earlier that changes in families have over the centuries tended to move in the direction of greater liberty. By and large that's been true, though sometimes social change may actually shift people in a reverse direction—against the tide of history—as in the case of marriage under slavery. And that's exactly what happened to mid-19th-century American middle-class women.

We might describe the numbers of younger 18th-century Americans forsaking traditional family values as a gentle stream. But the longer the 19th century wore on, the more those numbers became a rushing torrent. Joining the large numbers of Americans leaving the countryside for the urban factories were ever-increasing masses of European immigrants. All were bent on the same goal that became known as the *American dream*—gaining material wealth alongside personal prestige and middle-class status. At first, women and children who had for millennia labored on farms and fields alongside their husbands and parents did the obvious thing by working with husbands and parents in the factories. Throughout history, the traditional pattern had been for women to work at productive labor alongside their men. Hence, there was no reason why women should not carry this ancient tradition with them into the industrial age. And that is in fact what happened in both Britain and America during the early years of the 19th century as working-class women, men, and children alike performed arduous manual labor in the dark, dirty, and dangerous factories.

The atrocious conditions of 19th-century factories are well known. Safety was an unheard-of commodity during the 12–14 hours that workers toiled with little respite. Children in particular suffered mightily—frequently maimed or worse. The meager wages of all family members were pooled in their frantic search for survival. It soon became apparent that as long as men and women remained on the factory floor they'd be excluded from the American dream— just as if they'd remained landless farm workers. The most rewarding parts of the new economic game were being played, not on the factory floor, but within the offices and boardrooms of business and management. Hence, increasing numbers of males began to leave the floor for the boardroom aiming to become successful and middle-class.

The big question is why intelligent and ambitious women were then forbidden to accompany their men on the journey from factory floor to business boardroom. Virtually all married women were denied the chance to compete for either the tangible or intangible satisfactions of work that drew men into the world of business. The ancient family value of wife-submission that had been weakened slightly in the 18th century was actually strengthened during the 19th century. That reversal of the past was in part a reaction to the staggering changes taking place as the United States underwent its steady metamorphosis from an agricultural to an industrial society:

> *In a society . . . where fortunes rose and fell with frightening rapidity, where social and economic mobility provided instability as well as hope, one thing at least remained the same—a true woman was a true woman. . . . Anyone [who] dared to tamper with the complex of virtues that made up True Woman-*

hood was damned immediately as an enemy of God, of civilization, and of the Republic.[45]

Clergy preached and politicians proclaimed that if women got educated and played the new economic game as fiercely as men, the level of social confusion already present in 19th-century America would become unbearable. Because children would suffer from parental neglect, the whole of U.S. society would then be plunged into unimaginable disarray. The inevitable result would be widespread social decay and the demise of the nation.

Accordingly, religious and civic leaders argued that for the sake of children and country the wife must submit to the will of God and her husband. And so was born what Barbara Welter calls "The Cult of True Womanhood."[46] For centuries, wealthy women had slaves or nannies to care for their children while they pursued their own interests. Throughout the remainder of the social ladder—among the 95 percent of the population toiling the land—mothers had for centuries given themselves over every day to nonstop productive activity. The survival of their family—nuclear and extended—demanded it. Children too—almost from the time they could walk—labored on the land alongside older siblings, kin, or workers—all of whom paid at least some attention to the children's well-being.

During the 19th century, newly affluent middle-class men pulled their wives out of the factories and kept them out of the boardroom. Many of those men could have afforded nannies to care for their children—just as wealthy men had done for centuries. That practice would have provided middle-class mothers the option to participate in the newer forms of productive labor, just as 95 percent of mothers had for centuries participated in the older forms. Instead, girls and women were informed that there is an allegedly unique bond—both spiritual and psychological—between the mother and her child. Neglecting that bond would do irreparable damage to the child and eventually destroy the entire society. The specter of disorder and decay was once again paraded by clergy and civic leaders insisting on the traditional value of wife-submission. This occurred while they conveniently ignored the equally traditional value of the historic participation of mothers in productive labor.

Hence, the true woman had no choice but to devote herself utterly to the cultivation of this supposedly special mother-child bond—for the well-being of both child and society. The middle-class woman was informed that her unique biology not only bends her towards motherhood, but it also makes her too pure to sully herself competing with men in the sordid and ugly world of commerce and politics. The true woman was thus set on a pedestal towering far above the baser concerns of men.[47] That entire package was sold to her in the guise of freedom: By laying aside the burden of productive labor, the middle-class woman was told that for the first time in history, she was finally free to pursue the essential identity given her by God—the true woman!

A STILL, SMALL VOICE OF DISSENT

Hence, any yearnings felt by 19th-century women to compete in the new economic game were sabotaged by this novel twist—the image of the true woman that remained more or less intact until the 1960s. Though frustrated, some educated 19th-century women were by no means content to renounce the individualism inherent in the glowing promises of the American dream. Some privileged though mostly single women were chafing under the inequality and injustice they were forced to endure when compared with men. They felt that a woman should be as free as any man to shape her own life—to pursue the American dream.[48]

Interestingly enough, it was the abolitionist cause that brought together a number of women arguing that both genders and all races should have equal opportunities to fulfill their own destiny. During the early 19th century in both Britain and America, most abolitionists of both genders were also feminists. Elizabeth Cady Stanton and her colleagues were the heirs of the feminist thinkers from the previous century—Warren, Macaulay, Adams, and Wollstonecraft. The ultimate goals of abolitionists and feminists were identical—empowerment and self-determination for every human being—regardless of skin color or gender. The U.S. constitution denied both women and blacks the right to vote, and feminists believed that the first step toward self-determination was gaining that right. In 1848 at the historic Seneca Falls (New York) Convention, Stanton proclaimed her famous "Declaration of Sentiments" applying Jefferson's earlier phrases to women. In describing the plight of women that Jefferson had ignored, Stanton appealed to the same God as he—the God of America's public religion. And just as he'd used God to justify political revolution, Stanton too used God to validate justice and empowerment for women:

> *We hold these truths to be self-evident: that all men and women are created equal; that they are endowed by their Creator with certain inalienable rights. . . . Now, in view of this entire disfranchisement of one-half the people of this country, their social and religious degradation—in view of the unjust laws above mentioned, and because women do feel themselves aggrieved, oppressed, and fraudulently deprived of their most sacred rights, we insist that they have imme-*

> *diate admission to all the rights and privileges which belong to them as citizens of the United States.*

Unfortunately, all too many Americans think that women's lib oozed up from the swamp in the 1960s and was all about bra-burning and pot-smoking. Quite the contrary is true. The struggle against women's second-class status in society has its roots in that most ancient of all struggles—the "fight against tyranny over the minds and bodies of the powerless in nation after nation."[49] Our founders viewed the American Revolution as a fight against political and economic tyranny. Abolitionists saw their struggle as a fight against racial tyranny. Feminists viewed their struggle as a fight against gender tyranny.

Nineteenth-century and early 20th-century feminists were known as suffragists because they thought that once women got the right to vote, they would then be able to pass legislation that might achieve gender equity. However, they disagreed among themselves as to precisely how voting would bring about that equity. Some, though not all, agreed with Wollstonecraft, and with the influential thinker John Stuart Mill, that women should be allowed to participate in the new game on an equal footing with men.[50] Nonetheless, all of them concurred that gender equity was entirely *incompatible* with any concept of true womanhood, and they did all they could to excise that novel and ill-conceived family value from American culture. They did not, of course, succeed and their ultimate objective was thus deferred until the 1960s.

THE GOLDEN AGE MYTH

In his 1995 address to entering freshmen and their parents, Stanford University President Gerhard Casper told his listeners that perhaps the most celebrated of all golden age myths was devised by the Greek poet Hesiod around 800 B.C. Hesiod asserted that at some earlier point in time which he called the golden age,

> *the mortals lived "as if they were gods, their hearts free from all sorrow . . . and without hard work or pain, no miserable old age came their way. . . . They took their pleasure in festivals and lived without troubles."*[51]

Alas, lamented Hesiod, the golden age soon deteriorated into the much less advantageous silver age, followed thereafter by the dreadfully pernicious bronze age in which he and his peers lived. Regrettably, as if life wasn't bad enough already, Hesiod predicted that far more ghastly conditions lay ahead of his fellow citizens. The onrushing and relentlessly decadent iron age would soon erupt and get so evil, corrupted, and foul that

a time would come when "children, as they are born, grow grey on the temples,
when the father no longer agrees with the children, nor children with their fa-
ther, when guest is no longer at one with host, nor companion to companion,
when your brother is no longer your friend as he was in the old days."

Recently, I came across a modern-day Hesiod:

There is a growing wave of secularism sweeping America's culture and schools.
An entire generation is being raised to accept immorality and materialism. At
the same time, moral relativism has made huge inroads into our culture. Add
to this widespread, rapid drop in biblical knowledge, and you have perhaps the
most serious threat ever facing our nation.[52]

The fact is that there has never been a golden age in which families, and the
people who lived in them, were both stationary and better off than many of us
are right now. Instead, families are and always have been a drama in action—
an ongoing evolution marked by constant change. Families have "undergone
a series of far-reaching *'domestic revolutions'* that profoundly altered [them]. . . .
The claim that [families are] an . . . island of stability in a sea of social, political, and economic change is largely an illusion. . . . The American family has
changed dramatically over time."[53]

The story of American families is inseparable from the political and economic story of our republic. Not long after they arrived, our Euro-American
forebears began to lean increasingly on reason as the basis for fashioning, not
just their political and economic worlds, but the world of families as well. In
the process of doing so, older traditions were set aside and newer ones carved
out. Within each of those three worlds, the goal has been to achieve greater
freedom tempered by responsibility. The ideal of America's public religion has
been that every person should be able to develop his or her potential to the fullest degree possible, while at the same serving the greater good of our society.
Although the long-term evolution of families has been marked by repeated fits
and starts, the main story line is that we're a bit closer to that ideal than we were
400, 200, 100, or 60 years ago.

NOTES

1. Cited by Martin 1996:367.
2. Examples of such studies can be seen at "College Students Show Poor Knowledge of History, Civics," *The Chronicle of Higher Education*, September 18, 2008. Katherine Kersten from *The Center of the American Experiment* stated that a 2001 study by
the U.S. Department of Education revealed that "57 percent of high school seniors—

soon-to-be voters—actually score below basic [information] on their knowledge of U.S. history. These students neither know the basic facts about our nation's heritage nor understand their importance" (*Minneapolis Star-Tribune,* June 9, 2002). I know of no studies reporting that citizens, regardless of their age, have at a least a "basic" grasp of U.S. history—much less of European or world history.

    3. Mintz and Kellogg 1988:xiv, italics added; see Shorter 1975.

    4. Kowalski 2008:29.

    5. Wall 1990:1.

    6. Wall 1990:2.

    7. Wood 1992:18. The idea appears in St Paul's letter to the Romans, 13:1ff.

    8. Wood 1992:19.

    9. Wood 1992:19; caps and italics in original.

    10. Exodus 20:12, KJV.

    11. Ephesians 6:1–3, KJV.

    12. Wood 1992:44.

    13. Wood 1992:44.

    14. Butterfield et al., 1975, and see the 2008 HBO film, *John Adams.*

    15. Wood 1992:145.

    16. The best known revivalists were Jonathan Edwards and George Whitfield. See the preface for a brief summary of what evangelicals mean by the born-again experience.

    17. Wood 1992:145.

    18. Meacham 2006; Wood 1992:217ff.

    19. Ephesians 5:22, KJV.

    20. Schuking 1970:32.

    21. Wall 1990:10.

    22. R. Larson 2000:21. See St. Paul's letter to the Galatians, chapter 3.

    23. Lantz 1976.

    24. Chapter 3 shows that despite laws and traditions dictating inequality, the economic realities were such that the farmer could no more survive apart from the farmer's wife than she could make it apart from him.

    25. Peril 2006.

    26. Basch 1986; Brookhiser 2006:147ff.

    27. Weatherford 1994:364–65.

    28. Wollstonecraft 1792/2001.

    29. Peril 2006:20.

    30. Butterfield et al., 1975:5.

    31. Butterfield et al., 1975:5.

    32. Butterfield et al., 1975:5.

    33. Butterfield et al., 1975:5.

    34. Ephesians 6:5, KJV. The word translated *servant* in the King James Version more accurately means *slave,* as the context shows.

    35. Matthews 1977:136.

    36. Matthews 1977:136.

37. Matthews 1977:136.

38. Cheatham and Stewart 1990; Matthews 1977.

39. Cheatham and Stewart 1990:179ff.

40. Tademy 2001:128, italics added.

41. Tademy 2001:128, italics added.

42. Scanzoni 2000.

43. Scanzoni 1971.

44. Baptist Press, October 10, 2006, "U.S. Headed toward Moral Scurvy, Zell Miller Warns."

45. Welter 1978:313.

46. Welter 1978; McHugh 1999:35–59; Scanzoni 2000: 28ff.

47. Kraditor 1968.

48. Rosenman and Klaver (2008) describe a number of scenarios in which some 19th-century century women were rebelling against true womanhood.

49. Rossi 1970:4.

50. Rossi 1970.

51. Casper 1995.

52. Michael J. Easley, president of Moody Bible Institute, from a fund-raising letter sent in May, 2008.

53. Mintz and Kellogg 1988:xiv, italics added.

Chipping Away at Sexual Traditions: Pre-1960s

We just saw four episodes drawn from the drama of ongoing changes in families. Two moved with the tide of history—two against it. Plainly, American families have never been closeted within some sort of fanciful and idyllic golden age. America started changing almost as soon as the first Europeans got here, and our families have kept pace. Neither has human sexuality stood still. It is in fact impossible to disentangle the ongoing social evolution of sexuality from continuing changes in families. To help us see how closely the stories are entwined, we turn to several episodes drawn from the drama of how we think about and actually do our sexuality. Revolutions 3, 4, 5, and 6 are in synch with the tide of history. *Counter* revolution 3 aims to swim against the tide of history.

DOMESTIC REVOLUTION 3

Making Pleasure the Purpose of Marital Sex

> [A] frightful and fundamental immorality . . . an utter and pitiful failure in sense of perspective.[1]
>
> —*President Theodore Roosevelt, 1903*

Roosevelt's surprising target was the bourgeoning middle classes identified in chapter 1—privileged Americans feasting on the bounties of the 19th-century century industrial revolution. He denounced their growing embrace of a new and shameful idea—"family limitation." During the agricultural age, the notion that marital sex was all about reproduction fit perfectly with the idea that lots of children were good for families—nuclear and extended. Children were desirable because they were an economic asset—they supplied extra hands for the dawn-to-dusk labors required of everyone.

But once the children of middle-class families were pulled from the factories, they ceased to be economic assets. Instead, 19th-century children were seen as a status symbol for the true woman. Catherine Beecher (sister of Harriet Beecher Stowe) argued that just as the status of a good husband was based on his ability to provide, the prestige and esteem of a good mother was based on her capability to produce high-quality children.[2] Quality meant several obvious things—physical health, emotional and psychological well-being, getting along with others, good manners, doing well in school, skills in gender-appropriate activities (sports for boys, sewing and music and dancing for girls), and so forth. It did not take the good mother too long to realize that a reduction in family size might help simplify her task; concentrating her finite time and energies on a smaller number might boost her chances to make each one a high-quality child, thus enhancing her own prestige. Precisely the same logic applied to her family's finite economic resources: having fewer children meant more dollars to invest in each one, thereby increasing the chances for a high-quality child and thus greater prestige for the mother.

Chapters 4 and 5 explain that long ago marriage was invented to produce children and thus heirs for the husband. Men—married or single—seeking sexual delights visited prostitutes or, if well off, kept a concubine or mistress.[3] That traditional family value (marital sex equals reproduction) was based on the ideal of expansion—more is better. The Bible supported that ideal by stating that "Children are an heritage of the Lord . . . Happy is the man that hath his quiver full of them."[4] In pre-Revolutionary America, his quiver was bursting because "families commonly had eight or ten children."[5] But by 1900 "the average number of children per family was closer to three." That number, however, masks an important fact: advantaged families (middle- and upper-middle-class) were having fewer children than the average. But poor and working-class families (native-born whites, blacks, immigrants) were having substantially more children than the average.

On both sides of the Atlantic, a new family value—*limitation*—was gradually replacing the traditional family value of *expansion*. The new value was acquiring a vise-like grip on advantaged families. A new goal—high-quality children—required middle-class families to value and practice a new behavior—family limitation. But Roosevelt called it "race suicide," and many clergy and politicians agreed with him.[6] In their view, family limitation was indeed a "frightful and fundamental immorality." There was, in addition, something else lurking in the background that ramped up their disgust and revulsion over family limitation, namely, the means for getting there. Given that only a handful of married couples thought sexual abstinence a good idea, the most realistic means for limiting children was to use artificial methods of birth control.

Any device (e.g., condom, diaphragm, pill) made by humans aimed at preventing conception is judged artificial. The Roman Catholic Church did and still does condemn artificial methods as sinful. The church does, however, allow the rhythm or natural (God-given) method. Until the mid-20th century, many evangelicals shared a similar viewpoint.[7] Catholics and some evangelicals felt that artificial methods were tainted, dirty, vile, and beneath contempt. When my first wife and I were married, we refrained from using any methods because we, like our evangelical peers, believed that doing so reflected lack of faith in God to provide for each heavenly blessing He might send our way. I must admit, however, that the advent of a child within 11 months of marriage drastically altered our beliefs about artificial methods.

Though the notion first gained wide public acceptance during the 19th century, researchers tell us that humans have, in way or another, always tried to limit family size—even prior to the dawn of recorded history.[8] The big problem facing our ancestors was that the technical features of their methods were abysmal—they could at most expect only minimal success at limiting births. But that situation changed dramatically during the early 19th century as the Europeans began experimenting with a range of birth control methods that significantly increased a couple's chances of success. Prior to the 19th century, the "upper, more privileged classes" were the persons most likely to know about and be able to pay for contraceptives, whatever methods might be in vogue.[9] However, throughout the 19th and early 20th centuries, the expanding middle classes in Europe and America took full advantage of the increasingly sophisticated methods of contraception that became widely available. Norman Himes calls this development the "democratization" of birth control.[10]

Unfortunately, less advantaged persons either did not know about the newer methods, or if they did, could not afford them. Hence, they kept on having many more children than did privileged families. When Margaret Sanger and other founders of the birth control movement in America tried to rectify that injustice by establishing contraceptive clinics for poor women, they were maligned as immoral and as vile criminals. For example, in October 1916 Sanger and her colleagues were charged with violating a New York law that "made it a misdemeanor for anyone to 'sell, lend, or give away,' or to advertise, loan, or distribute, 'any recipe, drug, or medicine for the prevention of conception.'"[11]

Despite the law and the strictures of traditional religion, privileged 19th-century century Americans were crafting a new ways of thinking about and doing marital sex. Owing to the spread of effective contraceptive methods, marital sex was, for the first time in history, detached from having babies. Sex apart from fear of an unwanted pregnancy became a reality among millions of middle-class couples. But if marital sex and babies were no longer bound up together, why then bother with marital sex? While husbands had always sought sexual delights elsewhere, sexual pleasure had typically not been in the cards for wives. *Passionlessness,* not the vain quest for carnal delight was, says historian Nancy Cott, the stamp of a virtuous wife.[12] But passionlessness slowly faded away during the late 19th and early 20th centuries as the bond between sex and babies got unglued. Given that babies were no longer the inevitable outcome of marital sex, pleasure became increasingly important. For instance, it gradually dawned on couples that the wife was indeed entitled to be sexually pleasured by her husband. The next ideal that slowly came into play was that the husband should begin to look to his wife as the chief—if not the sole source—of his sexual bliss. In effect, middle-class couples were creating a new set of family values in which pleasure for both genders gradually became the preeminent rationale for marital sex.

Today's evangelicals, by the way, take this new family value very seriously indeed. Central to their campaign to promote sexual abstinence among unmarried persons is their assurance of unimaginable sexual ecstasies awaiting patient souls once they finally wed their one and only. Some years ago, University of Chicago Professor Martin Marty coined the offbeat phrase "fundies in their undies" to capture the fascination that evangelicals typically display regarding the hoped-for delights of marital sex. A recent example of their continued absorption with the arcane mysteries of matrimonial sensuality is *Naked and Not Ashamed—How God Redeems our Sexuality.*[13] Another is *Real Sex—The Naked Truth about Chastity.*[14]

DOMESTIC REVOLUTION 4
Connecting Single Persons with Halfway Sex

> *I don't know. And there is nothing to guide us. And if everything is so nebulous about a matter so elementary as the morals of sex, what is there to guide us in the more subtle morality of all other personal contacts, associations, and activities? Or are we meant to act on impulse alone? It is all a darkness.*[15]
> —British Novelist Ford Madox Ford, 1915

Ford's novel focused on two privileged couples who had indeed tasted the once forbidden pleasures of passionate marital sex. Still, several of the four spouses seemed to be teetering on the edge of seeking sexual delights outside the marriage bed. The broader theme in which Ford sets his characters is one that concerned many clergy, writers, and social critics during the early 20th century. Observers became aware that traditional sexual norms were in fact gradually losing their grip on the hearts and minds of younger persons on both sides of the Atlantic. The quest for sexual pleasure for both genders within marriage was but one example of the evolutionary developments occurring regarding sex long before the 1960s. But Ford and other observers wondered aloud if the flaking away of ancient, though repressive, sexual traditions was perhaps a mixed blessing. Is it possible, Ford and others worried, that society might be perched on the edge of some sort of yawning sexual abyss?

THE ROARING TWENTIES: THE ECSTASY OF VIOLATING TABOOS

Following the assault against the ban on marital sexual bliss for both genders, the next taboo to come under siege was the prohibition of sexual pleasures among unmarried persons. Compared with the 1960s, the 1920s challenges to traditional values were modest though significant because they planted the seeds that came to full flower four decades later.[16] In 1919, the United States (spurred on by the christianists of that era) ratified the 18th amendment to our Constitution, which prohibited the "manufacture, sale, or transportation of intoxicating liquors." Prohibition was, however, dead on arrival. The ban on drinking was a failure because many younger (and older) citizens were discovering the high that comes from the very act of violating a taboo. Prohibition initiated them into the tantalizing satisfactions of indulging in a forbidden pleasure alongside the enjoyment of the booze itself.[17]

During the 1920s, drinking together in public bars and dance halls became one of the new, and scandalous, behaviors being invented by younger, privileged women and men alike. Both genders likewise took up cigarette smoking in public. Young men and women drank together and danced with abandon to the newest crazes derived from sensual forms of popular music (e.g., jazz and blues) hitherto unknown to most white citizens. They also listened together to that tantalizing music on a mysterious new invention—the phonograph. Later on in the decade they listened and danced together to the new music via the magic of wireless radio. Perhaps the most captivating invention of all was the marvel of (silent) moving pictures. Youth attended theaters in droves to see beautiful, scantily clad women embrace and passionately kiss handsome, virile men. Youth watched the larger-than-life characters on the screen fall in and out of love, endure sexual unfaithfulness and heartbreak, and try to cope with the travails of romance and marriage.

Single women (like their married sisters) had long been thought to exist on a pedestal towering above the vulgar male driven by his coarse passions.[18] If she remained unsullied in heart, mind, and body, a single woman would one day be fitted to discharge her noble and God-given mission of motherhood. Nevertheless, growing numbers of single and privileged 1920s women were discovering that being elevated above the nitty-gritty of life excluded them from a great deal of its fun. Respectable women were, for the first time ever, gaining entrée to a whole new way of life that seemed exotic and deliciously wicked.[19]

Women's naughtiness was also expressed in the daring fashions of the day, and by a marked increase in their shocking use of cosmetics. The 19th-century century Victorian styles covered up as much of a woman's body as possible in order to hide her natural attributes: loose-fitting dresses extended to her ankle, sleeves went to her wrist, and collars to her neck. In sharp contrast, form-fitting 1920s fashions were designed to show off female curves and features. Women threw away their corsets, and skirts rose to the knees or just below. Sedate Victorian hair styles gave way to a series of smart fashions, the most prominent of which was called bobbed hair. Women's chic hair styles symbolized the growing corruption of American womanhood, prompting one well-known (and rather dour) fundamentalist preacher to write a book condemning America's sexual and gender decay—*Bobbed Hair, Bossy Wives, and Women Preachers.*[20]

DATING: BRIDLED LUST

The joy of violating taboos rose to a blissful high when young, white, middle-class men and women started to breach sacred sexual customs that preachers and parents told them came from the Bible. To be sure, apart from evangelicals, most citizens today would view their sexual transgressions as quaint, innocent, and amusing.[21] But during the 1920s, the whole of respectable society on both sides of the Atlantic was shaken up by this next step in the long-term social evolution of sexuality *prior* to marriage. No one, by the way, held up a banner saying *let's set aside our traditional values and come up with new ways for women and men to do their premarital behaviors.* Instead, younger single persons—in the pursuit of pleasure—simply started behaving differently from their parents and grandparents. Quite apart from any public discussion of its morality they gradually began to set aside traditional courtship customs in favor of a new set of customs called "dating."[22] Though critics charged that the new behaviors showed clear evidence of moral and cultural decay, genuine social change was happening.

The sole objective of elaborate 19th-century century courtship rituals was to get a spouse. The severe courtship customs that Jane Austen described so vividly in her 1818 novel *Persuasion* remained more or less intact throughout respectable society at least till the onset of World War I (1914). The parents of respectable single women were very much a part of those rituals. And sometimes the men's parents were too. Parental involvement was based on the premise that although she was sexually naïve, he definitely was not and was thus likely to steal her virginity, thereby compromising her honor. Once she'd lost her honor to a man he'd have no incentive whatever to marry her and, what is more, no other respectable man would have her either.

Hence, to guard against that horrific possibility, family members were seldom entirely absent whenever a courting couple was together—whether on the family's front porch, or in the parlor, or at a community or church event. If they continued courting, her family (usually her father) asked him if his intentions were honorable. That is, *do you intend to marry her and to keep her a virgin until you do?* Sometimes the man would request her father's approval for his daughter's hand in marriage. In either case, if all parties were convinced that the couple's marriage was assured, an engagement was announced and soon thereafter a date set. The 2006 film *Miss Potter* (featuring Renée Zellweger as the famed author of the *Peter Rabbit* books) is an entertaining way to get a handle on both the subtlety and force of late 19th-century courtship customs.

Prior to her engagement, a respectable woman did not allow any gentleman to kiss her. Following their engagement the couple might be permitted to kiss tenderly (not French-kiss) in a quasi-private setting, though still never far from the purview of an alert chaperone. From an evangelical perspective, their light kissing did far more than help protect her virginity. It ensured the moral purity (of the woman in particular, but also of the man) which was something quite distinct from sexual intercourse. Intercourse between engaged persons was decidedly *not* the issue. At that time it never appeared anywhere on the radar screen. Instead, the issue was something quite different though of course related—it was purity, or cleanliness of one's mind, heart, and feelings. Purity meant that a single person should be free from all lustful thoughts and feelings until the marriage bed.[23] The engaged couple was expected to be morally pure by refusing to do anything (passionate kissing, fondling "privates") that might arouse lustful thoughts or wicked feelings of any sort. The notion of

mutual sexual arousal was viewed as inherently immoral for single persons—
whether engaged or not.

In sharp contrast, enjoying the sensual pleasures of lust was the *first* major
objective of dating as practiced from the 1920s to the mid-1950s. Lust's great fa-
cilitator was the automobile, which by the 1920s had become an essential fix-
ture of the middle-class American household. From "modest kisses on the front
porch to ardent French-kissing in the back seat" was how some observers portrayed the transition from courting to dating.[24] Terms such as necking (kissing
passionately from the neck upward) and petting (fondling of breasts and genital
areas) became common parlance. During the previous courtship era such behaviors were banned outright because they were thought to be the foreplay that
led inevitably to intercourse. Necking and petting were unique behaviors that
married persons alone had the right to do. Women who willingly consented to
such outrages (even if engaged) were thought to be the moral equivalent of the
fallen woman.

Despite the sexual arousal that such foreplay was bound to stimulate, intercourse was still not a culturally legitimate option for respectable dating couples
of the 1920s onwards. No matter how heavily they petted, they were not free (officially at least) to go "all the way." Dating was, in effect, lust reined in. It was primarily the woman's task to ensure that the couple ceased petting before they
went too far. Although his foot might be on the gas pedal, hers must, as one wag
put it, be on the brake.

That was so because a *second* objective of dating was identical to the sole aim
of courtship, namely, getting a spouse. Among women, marriage remained as
vital to their existence and identity as it ever had been. Hence, she could not afford the reputation of being an easy or loose woman. Gentlemen did not marry
the women they slept with. Although the 1920s upset many conventional ways
of doing things, it did not shatter the ancient double standard: gentlemen slept
with loose women and prostitutes, but never with a potential spouse. Unlike
the more public nature of courtship, dating was almost entirely private. That
forced a respectable woman seeking a good match to rely on her own wits to
curb men's animal passions—her family was nowhere to be found on the back
seat helping to guard her virginity. Because the petting partners typically kept
their clothes intact, going all the way was easier to avoid during the 1920s than
it became later on. But by the early 1950s, abstinence got more difficult because
petting couples were starting to touch each other's naked flesh.[25] The final in-
stallment in the saga of bridled lust was called *technical virginity,* which at first
meant that the couple practiced either oral sex or mutual masturbation.[26] After a
while, technical virginity also came to include penetration of the woman's anus

by her partner's penis. One might say that technical virginity was a sort of missing link between several decades of reigned-in lust and the 1960s—a time when bridling anything seemed a very un-cool thing to do.

The upshot is that the youth of that era were inventing social change. Since the 1920s, American society has been in the process of disentangling itself from traditional notions of premarital purity. It would be difficult if not impossible today to find a nonevangelical railing against necking and petting. A nonevangelical might be reluctant to state publicly that necking and petting are good, but would argue that such innocent behaviors are a nonissue, doubtless adding that it's far more vital to address the urgent (and not unrelated) issue of vaginal intercourse owing to its potential for unwanted pregnancy. Equally urgent are the links between a range of sexual practices and socially transmitted diseases (STDs), the most appalling of which is HIV/AIDS.

Among single evangelical youth, however, the story was and is not so simple.[27] Insisting on sexual purity in the midst of a society that no longer valued purity placed post-World War II evangelical youth in an untenable situation. (Today, evangelical youth find themselves in an even far more vulnerable position.[28]) My first-ever encounter with adolescent evangelicals ignoring Christian teachings on sexual purity occurred as a young teen attending a party sponsored by peers who came from our church's leading families. For the first time in my life, I learned about and actually played Spin the Bottle and other kissing games. As I recall, the games caused me a great deal more embarrassment than lust, but before long I discovered that evangelical youth enjoyed being naughty just as much as did the unsaved kids around us.

I later became very much a part of an evangelical adolescent crowd in and around Chicago in which necking and petting in parked cars were routine activity. We sensed that our parents and church leaders suspected what was going on but chose conveniently to look the other way. Since we were not allowed to drink, smoke, play cards, attend movies, or dance, we could at least have a little fun by "making out." However, among all adolescents (saved or not) the official line drawn in the sand by dating couples of the 1920s remained visible through the late 1950s—vaginal intercourse was *verboten*.

Nevertheless, despite Christian and cultural proscriptions, research showed that throughout the first half of the 20th century there were perceptible increases in the proportions of U.S. women admitting to premarital vaginal intercourse.[29] One report, for instance, revealed that during the Great Depression of the 1930s vaginal intercourse became increasingly common among the growing numbers of engaged couples who could not afford to marry.[30] However, no serious public and overt challenge to the formal (and legal) ban on fornication was mounted until the 1960s. Although everyone knew that mere mortals were frequently too weak to obey it, the formal ban remained part of American culture.

DOMESTIC REVOLUTION 5
Uncovering Sex in America: The Prophet Kinsey

The quest for sexual delights had subverted traditional family values, first, among middle-class married couples and, second, among respectable single persons. Despite those trends sexuality in America was, as late as the 1950s, still shrouded in a cloud of pious darkness—the less said about it the better. But Alfred C. Kinsey brought sexual pleasures out into the open for all to see and onto the table for everyone to discuss. If Columbus discovered America, Kinsey uncovered sex in America.

During the 1940s and 1950s, the world's leading gall-wasp scientist turned sex researcher managed to do something that no one had ever done before. Although critics like Sigmund Freud had faulted traditional views of sexuality, their critiques never penetrated the imagination of the everyday citizen. But Kinsey did precisely that. He was thus a towering figure in the long-term social evolution of sexuality. His two classic books (*Sexual Behavior in the Human Male,* 1948; *Sexual Behavior in the Human Female,* 1953) were explosive best sellers.[31] Hundreds of thousands of hardback copies were sold in the United States and abroad in addition to the rights for several foreign translations. That he continues to intrigue Americans some 50 years following his untimely death was demonstrated by the 2004 film *Kinsey* featuring Liam Neeson and Laura Linney. The following year, the Public Broadcasting System (PBS) produced its own dramatic account of Kinsey's life, work, and legacy.

Curiously enough, never before or since were two earnest tomes bought by so many, read by so few, and yet stirred so much public outcry. The books had no lurid pictures and only a handful of citizens actually managed to read them. They were jammed with dry statistics and plagued by a tedious writing style. But ever since the escapades of Alexander Hamilton the media understood that sex sells! Hence, every major U.S. magazine (*Time, Life, Newsweek, Collier's, McCall's, Redbook*) carried lengthy accounts of his lurid research (including photos of Kinsey and his staff and family), as did virtually all of America's newspapers. The newly emerging medium of television was stuffed with stories describing his work, his colleagues, his conventional Midwestern American family, and his home base at Indiana University-Bloomington. The upshot of such an immense media blitz was that virtually every American citizen, along with many persons around the world, learned about Kinsey and his shocking research. However, the vast majority of got their information secondhand:

> *Kinsey's reputation (even with scientists) rested on what had been written about him by reporters and journalists, many of whom had only themselves skimmed the book.*[32]

Although public reaction to the 1948 *Male* volume was fiercely negative, it was a picnic by comparison to the firestorm unleashed by the 1953 *Female* report. While Americans had been barely

> *able to take Kinsey's terrible language about the appalling [sexual] activities of men, about American womanhood they could take neither the language nor the activities. American womanhood masturbating, having orgasms, pre-marital sex, extra-marital sex, sex with each other . . . This simply could not be American womanhood.*[33]

Americans did not, in short, did not take kindly to the fact that a goodly number of our pure women had in fact leapt from the pedestal erected for them by 19th-century men. The uproar that Kinsey's *female* book provoked throughout Moody Bible College (where I was then a student) was considerable indeed. Because students were allowed to read newspapers (though not watch TV) we had a pretty good idea of what was going on. But school officials were frantic to protect us from learning too much. They did not want their naïve charges being corrupted by and falling victim to the corrosive effects of such foul garbage. Their fears were, however, groundless because virtually all of us were persuaded by the scathing and ceaseless assessments of Kinsey being made by influential religious spokesmen.

Billy Graham, for instance, though admitting he'd never read the *Female* (or the *Male*) volume, was nonetheless eager to comment on the salacious second-hand press reports being universally circulated. Like many other religious leaders and politicians Graham pontificated:

> *The book will teach young people how to indulge in premarital relations and get away with it. It will teach [them] terrifying perversions they had never heard of before. It is impossible to estimate the damage this book will do to the already disintegrating morals of America.*[34]

But what sort of massive destruction had Kinsey actually rained down on American society? And what did Graham propose to do about the tsunami of evil threatening to engulf us? Kinsey and his associates had in fact done nothing other than peel off the plain brown wrapper that enclosed the sexual lives of ordinary American women and men:

> *He'd pulled the shades and opened the closets, he'd cleared the cobwebs and aired the attics. He dusted, did windows, and it was the greatest, noisiest spring-cleaning sexuality ever had.*[35]

Kinsey did nothing more depraved than to uncover the reality that sizeable proportions of men and women were in fact seeking sexual delights in ways contrary to the prevailing traditional family values of the time.

It is intriguing to note the similarities between Kinsey and several influential artists of the late 1940s and 1950s. These included Tennessee Williams, Jimmy Dean, Marlon Brando, Elvis Presley, Marilyn Monroe, and Jack Kerouac and the *Beat Generation*.[36] They confronted respectable middle-class citizens with essentially the same message as Kinsey, each in his or her own way. Each artist was restive with the hypocrisy symbolized by the brown wrapper, that is, the deafening silence that muffled Americans' sexuality. Like Kinsey, they sought to get beneath Americans' façade of respectability and shake things up by exploring the normal sexual passions, behaviors, and relationships of everyday citizens. Elvis's audience was of course American youth, and his music celebrated the normality of their sexual feelings and encouraged their expression.[37] Taken together, those artists anticipated the typical fare—both good and bad—of today's TV, film and movies, theatre, popular music, and literature.

During the 1950s, Western societies no longer imprisoned or banned artists whose work supposedly undermined public morals as was done, say, in Shakespeare's time. Likewise, 1950s scientists had less to fear from theocratic regimes than did the 17th-century Galileo whom the Roman Catholic Church threatened to burn if he did not recant his heresy that the sun is the center of the universe. Notwithstanding, a few U.S. congressmen did in fact worry aloud that Kinsey's research was part of the international communist conspiracy to destroy America. Indeed, if torture had still been permitted in the 1950s, they would no doubt have set Kinsey's feet to the fire.

Unlike the artists who could be dismissed because they were prisoners of their personal demons, Kinsey, like Galileo, claimed the mantle of science for his work. He argued that he'd used sound scientific methods to discover the actual sexual behaviors of Americans. Although some scientists criticized his methods, the fact is that no subsequent social science research has undermined his fundamental conclusion that beneath the façade of conformity to prevailing sexual norms, a great deal of secret sexual nonconformity was going on among Americans.[38] Furthermore, at least some of that nonconformity later morphed into overt practices now followed openly by growing numbers of citizens. One of the most prominent of these practices is cohabitation—publicly acknowledged fornication.

Kinsey was—like today's AIDS researcher—a scientist on a mission. He grew up evangelical but became deeply resentful of what he viewed as the sexual repression inflicted on him by his religion. The instrument of that oppression was his tyrannical father—a lay preacher who stood for everything Kinsey despised. Kinsey believed that prevailing religious/cultural norms had caused him enormous suffering, and he did not want any other human being ever again to experience the unspeakable anguish he'd endured. Alongside being a rigorous scientist, one could say that Kinsey was also a prophet in one of the two senses of that term as used in the Old Testament. A prophet not only *foretells* the future but also *forth-tells,* that is, critiques the present. In that second sense, a prophet challenges the prevailing political and cultural climate and urges citizens to practice a more authentic and honest style of life.

And that was precisely Kinsey's prophetic role. He believed that sexuality is a natural and wholesome part of being human, and that a healthy society is composed of human beings free to celebrate sexual pleasures. Such persons, he argued, practice their sexuality in an honest and authentic manner. He challenged the religious establishment of his time to set aside its obsession with silencing sex and covering it up. Sexuality, he believed, should become a topic of open and frank dialogue, as with any other serious topic. He hoped that our society would gradually learn to become comfortable with sexuality by enjoying its delights and celebrating its beauty. His ultimate goal was to confront and change Americans' beliefs and values about sexuality. Sexuality, he believed, is a good thing that everyone should enjoy as fully as possible.

THE PROPHET'S DARK SIDE

Regrettably, Kinsey had a dark side—in his case, one that belied his lofty ideals regarding authentic sexuality. When I became a professor at Indiana University (IU) in the mid-1960s most of my senior social science colleagues had either known him personally (he'd died in 1956) or knew of him through other faculty who'd known him well. My colleagues were, like virtually everyone else in America, convinced that although his research was incendiary, his personal and family life was quite prosaic. Several colleagues reminisced fondly about attending his classical music concerts held each Sunday evening. Kinsey, it turns out, was an accomplished classical musician as well as an expert gardener. The concerts were held either inside his house or in his huge and ornate flower garden that he himself tended with great care and devotion. As far as I could tell, my colleagues' perception of Kinsey as scientist, serious musician, and floral connoisseur was the prevailing campus image, and those few persons who knew otherwise were not talking. That included the social scientist Paul Gebhard (one of his closest associates) with whom I became professionally acquainted.

Indeed, it was not until the late 1990s that two widely circulated biographies revealed to the world that there was a whole lot more to Kinsey's private life than most of us had ever before imagined.[39] The 2004 film conveys Kinsey's fundamental blind spot in a scene where two of his principal male colleagues (Gebhard and Clyde Martin) get into a fistfight at Kinsey's IU research facilities. Their brawl is not over the fact that Gebhard is sleeping with Martin's wife Alice. They're fighting because Martin accuses Gebhard of stealing his wife's affections. Kinsey stumbles onto the melee, pulls them apart, and admonishes them for their schoolyard foolishness. He then drags Martin into his private office to scold him for letting his rage with Gebhard spin out of control. To defend himself, Martin erupts into a fierce denunciation of Kinsey and blames him for his squabble with Gebhard. Martin charged Kinsey with being obsessed with the biological aspects of sexuality and thus oblivious to its psychological and social dimensions—especially the green-eyed monster of jealousy.

It turns out that Kinsey encouraged his colleagues and their spouses to have sex (both hetero and homo) among themselves. Moreover, Kinsey and his wife were active participants in what eventually became a "group of interacting open marriages, in which others occasionally joined."[40] Most of the in-group's researchers and their spouses took part, though some spouses opted out. The in-group's situation was not unlike the carefully orchestrated sexual patterns practiced by the 19th-century Oneida Colony—with Kinsey (rather than John Humphrey Noyes) being the maestro.[41] During their filmed office encounter, Martin blurted out that Kinsey was deluded by imagining that the sole function of sex is to experience pleasure. In effect, Kinsey grossly oversimplified the profound nature of human sexuality by ignoring the range of complex emotions attached to it. Although he fully shared Kinsey's objective of undoing centuries of religious and social sexual repression, Martin argued that they were equally obliged to come up with something new to replace the antiquated norms and customs they were undermining.

Notwithstanding Martin's cogent arguments, Kinsey maintained their in-group's open-marriage patterns, though he did order Gebhard to cease his covert affair with Alice Martin, which he did at once.[42] Surprisingly, though Kinsey was anything but conventional when it came to sexual practices, he was as traditional as any evangelical about marital stability. Because he believed that marriage is for life, he did not take kindly to the possibility that the Martins might divorce on account of the Martin-Gebhard affair. As do evangelicals, Kinsey believed that divorce undermines the family, which he like them viewed as being the foundation of a stable society.

Curiously enough, one of the rationales Kinsey offered his colleagues and close friends for his version of "open marriage" is that it serves as a pressure-release valve: an open marriage might, he said, help offset the predictability and tedium of having to sleep for decades with the same person. Greater sexual variety, he implied, could keep persons in their current marriage, thus reducing divorce rates. Needless to say, the general public knew little and cared less about his arcane logic regarding open sexuality and marital stability. Citizens were instead totally mesmerized by Kinsey's sensational revelations of the naughty (if not perverse) sexual behaviors of American women and men.

THE 1950s AS A SEXUAL WATERSHED

Though Clyde Martin feared that Kinsey and their in-group were teetering on the brink of sexual narcissism, the men behind two other eventful 1953 publications seemed untroubled by such anxieties. In the same year that Kinsey's *Female* volume appeared, Hugh Hefner's *Playboy Magazine* published its first issue, featuring among other things nude photos of Marilyn Monroe. Rounding out the trilogy of 1953 publications calling into question prevailing sexual ideals was the first James Bond novel written by Ian Fleming and published initially in Britain and then in America.[43] Though traditional values regarding sexuality had been evolving for some time, the 1950s turned out to be a defining moment in the ongoing social development of sexual beliefs and behaviors on both sides of the Atlantic.[44]

Plainly, christianist leaders are confused when they identify the "corrosive sixties" as the onset of America's moral scurvy.[45] Had they done their homework and consulted say, Billy Graham, their spin would be quite different. He could have told them that things had been going to hell in a handbasket at least as far back as the late 1940s. Though Graham saw America flirting with damnation prior to the 1960s, how did the ordinary citizens feel who were actually doing those things? Did they in fact believe they were paving their own path to perdition? Or did they instead believe they were experimenting with a more interesting life—as had Noyes and his followers a century earlier? Did they think anything at all? Was it simply a matter of doing things that felt good? Did they see any reasons *not* to do them?

Why then do christianists point to the 1960s as the decade when an eruption of foul moral evils spewed forth and engulfed an upright American society? Long before the earth explodes geologists tell us that tectonic plates far below the earth's surface are forever shifting. But until their imperceptible motion results in an earthquake, most citizens get on with their everyday life, blithely unaware of what's happening underneath their very feet. Kinsey, *Playboy, Bond,* Elvis, and the Beatniks notwithstanding, the predominant cultural symbols of the 1950s were solidly in place—TV sitcoms such as *Leave It to Beaver, Ozzie and Harriet, Father Knows Best, I Love Lucy, The Honeymooners,* and others. Variety shows such as *Ed Sullivan* and *Lawrence Welk* were equally powerful symbols of sweetness and light, as was President Dwight Eisenhower himself. Evangelicals, along with most other citizens, had no idea of the ferment churning just below the surface.

The critiques of America's sexual patterns by Kinsey and others were, relatively speaking, understated. Even Elvis eventually came to be seen as the cute though mischievous boy next door. By comparison, the 1960s launched a broad frontal assault not only on the sexual sphere itself, but also on the nuclear family style and on the roles that wives and husbands had played since the mid-19th century.[46] Even though Kinsey was well ahead of the curve when it came to the social evolution of human sexuality, he seemed oblivious to the social evolution of gender and families. Given his views on marital stability, we may only guess as to what his reaction might have been had he lived to see the 1960s.

DOMESTIC REVOLUTION 6

Disconnecting Women's Sexual Intercourse from Marriage

Demands for greater sexual freedoms were but one part of a larger mosaic of liberation movements erupting in the 1960s. Each movement was derived from core American values—social justice, self-determination, and autonomy. The most prominent of those 1960s eruptions was, of course, the black civil rights struggle.[47] There was also the women's movement, the student movement, and the gay/lesbian movement. The backdrop for those civil rights struggles was the antiwar (Vietnam) movement. Mixed into this boiling cauldron of battles for expanded liberties was President Lyndon Johnson's War on Poverty. He envisioned it as a struggle to release poor people from the age-old scourge of economic deprivation. A society free from that curse would truly be, he said, a *Great Society.*

Freedom and liberty, innovation and change—those were the heady themes of the 1960s/early 1970s. Many citizens were caught up by the high tide of a liberalism holding out the promise of greater social justice and individual opportunity for a broader range of citizens than ever before in our history. Believe it or not, the 1960s liberals (rather than the incipient RR) virtually controlled the marketplace of using moral values as a legitimate means to influence politics:

They held the moral high ground. There is no doubt that the freedom movements of the time were driven by the sorts of lofty moral values expressed by persons such as Johnson, Martin Luther King, Jr., and New York Senator Robert F. Kennedy.[48]

High-sounding moral values notwithstanding, many Americans were troubled by and uneasy over what they perceived to be a dark underside to the passionate cries for freedom and justice.[49] Ordinary citizens were apprehensive over the excesses of the counterculture and dismayed by the drug scene—especially the hard stuff. A number of persons, Billy Graham included, felt intimidated by civil disorders that disrupted the normal routines of thousands of law-abiding citizens and led often to mass arrests. Citizens were especially troubled when the protests spiraled horribly out of control and resulted in the destruction of businesses, public buildings, and residential neighborhoods.

Most appalling of all was the violence and injury that sometimes accompanied marches and demonstrations in certain cities and on some university campuses.[50] I happened, for instance, to be visiting my parents during the same week as the 1968 Democratic national convention being held in Chicago just a few miles from their apartment. The initially peaceful student protests outside the hall against the Vietnam War soon degenerated into violent confrontations with the Chicago police (seen on TV around the world) in the streets and parks nearby the hall. I can still envisage the indignation in my father's face over what he perceived to be the students' intolerable and unconscionable behavior. I silently listened to him express his anger over the students' alleged assaults on law and order. I suspected that many other working- and middle-class citizens around the United States were feeling as furious as he with a liberal government that would permit what they perceived to be intolerable damage to the social fabric.

Despite the misgivings of large segments of the populace, liberation advocates opened all the stops—no holds were barred when it came to the scope of the changes they explicitly proposed. One shift in particular upset a lot of ordinary citizens: contrary to the implicit understandings of prior decades, lust became *unbridled*—unrestrained sexual passion was publicly touted as a good thing by the spread of rock and roll music and by the innovative films, plays, and novels of the decade. *If it feels good, do it,* was a common slogan of those years. Saving intercourse for marriage was thought to be as naïve as the idea that the world is flat. Having sex and losing one's virginity was for both women and men alike viewed as a mark of emancipated adulthood.[51]

Throughout history, men's sexual adventures had of course never been restricted to marriage. Gradually, women's sexual intercourse too got detached from marriage—just as it was among men. As a result, the term *premarital sex* morphed into a rather quaint notion, as did the expressions necking, petting, and going all the way. Sexuality gradually worked its way out from under the mantle of marriage and evolved into a distinct sphere of society with its own social patterns, values, and behaviors. Youth were having sexual intercourse simply because they wanted to enjoy it, not because it had anything at all to do with babies or with getting and/or keeping a spouse. Moreover, just as the automobile had facilitated making out during the 1920s–1950s, federal approval of birth control pills in 1960 greatly assisted the newly emerging patterns of intercourse-on-desire.

"REMEMBER THE LADIES"

Although the ideal of women's equity with men had been around since our Revolution, it never managed to gain much traction—apart from women finally gaining the vote in 1920. The 1960s changed all that. On one level, advocates sought to wipe out the ancient sexual double standard that what was okay for men sexually was not okay for women. But on an equally profound level, advocates also sought to transform the 18th-century dream into reality—gender equity in both the workplace and the homeplace. It was high time, said the advocates, to "remember the ladies," as Abigail Adams had phrased it in 1776.

Advocates argued that the United States must at long last take seriously Stanton's words in her 1848 Seneca Falls Declaration that all men *and women* are created equal. The last vestiges of the injustices against women that our founders permitted during the 18th century must be finally and decisively remedied, said the 1960s advocates. Likewise, the legacy of the 19th-century invention of true womanhood must also be set aside. One important step toward achieving those objectives was included in the 1964 Federal Civil Rights Act: discrimination was prohibited not only on the basis of race and national origin, but also on the basis of sex.

DOMESTIC COUNTERREVOLUTION 3
The Religious Right Is Spawned

It was bad enough that evangelicals had to contend, first of all, with the evolving views of sexuality that exploded all around them everywhere they turned. They were just as appalled by the emerging ideas of gender equity being thrust on them and on their children. But evangelicals were struck with special horror when sexuality and gender equity got bundled together in what gradually came to be known as "alternative lifestyles."[52] Unlike the bridled lust of earlier dating customs concealed from public view, and quite different from the discreet behaviors of Kinsey's in-group, women and men were suddenly flaunting their innovative patterns of living, loving, and having sex (even having children) together. Cohabitation was but one item on a long list of those new and shocking lifestyles. Most disturbing of all to evangelicals was the fact that advocates were shamelessly declaring that their humanist lifestyles were actually *healthier* for adults, children, and society than were the allegedly repressive family patterns of previous decades.[53]

The excesses of the 1960s were like a perfect storm, that is, a set of social circumstances coordinated to trigger a ferocious blast of pent-up forces. Growing numbers of ordinary citizens found themselves unable to shake the uneasy feeling that the family was under siege.[54] The Huns and the Visigoths were at the gates threatening to overrun everything that many citizens held sacred and dear. The world-renowned anthropologist Margaret Mead described the eruptions occurring within the spheres of sexuality and gender as a mixed bag.[55] On the upside, she praised youth for aiming to develop their human potential to the fullest extent possible and thereby contribute to the greater good. She agreed that many traditional family and sexual customs had outlived whatever usefulness they might once have served.

But on the downside, Mead uttered a warning that escaped me entirely when I first read her essay in 1967. Viewed through today's 20/20 lenses, it's clear that her caveat was prophetic, perhaps even clairvoyant. However, as far as I can tell, no one at the time fully appreciated the fact that a significant social action creates a vigorous *reaction*:

> *The introduction of radically new styles of [family and sexual] behavior may engender* counter-revolutions *that may be ideological or religious in character . . . [The] most intense efforts might be made to nullify the effect of innovations in life styles. . . . [Their] aim . . . might well be to refocus attention on the home, limit sexual freedom, curtail the individual development of women, and subordinate the creative capacities of the individual adult.*[56]

Mead reasoned that some citizens would perceive transformations in the behaviors of women and men as signs of social deterioration and moral weakness—and not as indicators of growth, strength, and health. Even as she wrote, christianists were already on the march determined to obliterate the emerging lifestyles from the American landscape.

To blunt the christianist march, Mead urged a strategy that was lost on me and I suspect on most of her readers. Because they occupied the moral high ground at that time, most liberals felt it was inconceivable that any reactionary social or political movement could ever dislodge them. From the liberals' exalted vantage point a ragtag group like the RR—dedicated to replacing the present with the past—could never become a serious threat to their moral and political supremacy. But Mead was not so naïve. To guard against the seductive appeal of an idealized golden age, liberals should establish what she called "socially responsible protections during the transition stages in the development of new styles of behavior."[57]

Mead placed the issue of balance squarely on the liberals' lap. The new, exhilarating freedoms that people were enjoying must, she said, be held in some sort of equilibrium with personal responsibility. As far as I can tell, her plea for balance never got through to liberals or anyone else for that matter. Instead of sensing that Mead had it right and then figuring out what families might look like if responsibility and freedom were placed side-by-side, liberals focused almost exclusively on further expansion of personal freedoms. Determined to escape the restrictions and hypocrisies of past decades, liberals failed to grasp the importance of building responsibility and obligation into those new behaviors.

Regrettably, Mead was not terribly specific about the types of "socially responsible protections" she had in mind. The closest she came was by drawing from her fund of lifelong experiences doing field research among tribal societies. The model Mead described was similar to, though different from, what chapter 1 called the extended family style of pre-Revolutionary America. Mead was well aware that the ancient kin-based extended family could never be resurrected in postindustrial societies. She suggested instead that we should invent new arrangements that might serve as today's equivalent of the old-time blood kin. Such equivalents have been called *fictive kin* and I discuss them in chapter 6.[58] Fictive kin would, Mead said, be designed to balance responsibility and protection with the emerging freedoms of the 1960s. The fact she was vague about what fictive kin might look like should not deter us from the major theme she hammered home. Her premise was that healthy families do not develop by a cut-and-paste job of imposing the past onto the present. Nor do they stem, she argued, out of a conviction that because I'm a free human being I can do whatever I want. Both extremes, she asserted, are quite unacceptable.

THE INITIAL CLASH OF THE CULTURE WARS: SEX EDUCATION

The "seismic shift in sexual attitudes and behavior" of the 1960s was repulsive to many evangelicals: "They could not approve of what they saw happening. Some dared to hope they could stop it."[59] The christianist counterrevolution was in part sparked by the efforts of liberals to introduce family life and sex education into grades kindergarten through 12 (K–12). The religious right felt that liberals wanted to use the schools as a Trojan horse to indoctrinate our children into their wicked and corrosive lifestyles.

During the 1950s and early 1960s, several prominent organizations such as the National Education Association and the American Medical Association "publicly endorsed the idea of sex education in the public schools."[60] Advocates were concerned that in the wake of the many changes in sexual behaviors occurring at that time, America's youth lacked basic information about human sexuality and reproduction, including contraception. Advocates hoped that the information might help reduce the chances that youth would be infected with STDs such as syphilis and/or gonorrhea, and/or that girls might get pregnant. They were, in effect, echoing Clyde Martin's concern that contemporary understandings of personal and social responsibility regarding human sexuality must be formulated. Those new understandings were designed fill the vacuum left by the evaporation of traditional values regarding sexuality.

During the mid-1960s a new organization was created to do precisely that— The Sex Information and Education Council of the United States, or SIECUS. Public opinion polls showed that "most parents were in favor of school-based programs to help prepare their children for *responsible* sexual behavior in the changing social climate."[61] But a strange thing happened as SIECUS started paving our way into the brave new world of responsible sexuality. A minority of citizens—most evangelical, some not—reacted fiercely to what they viewed as an attempt by libertines and communists to brainwash their children. Those christianists denounced the lifestyles emerging around them as rotten, perhaps even satanic, and they believed that SEICUS aimed to promote those heinous lifestyles via their sex education courses. Accordingly, christianists were not about to allow our children — and with them our entire nation—to be sucked into such repulsive and unspeakable evils.

The upshot is that starting with the late 1960s and persisting into the present, the christianist minority has been able to thwart meaningful sex education in most American school districts.[62] The minority discovered that if it became well-organized and vocal enough it could either eliminate or neuter sex education programs throughout K–12. It did so by intimidating and/or electing school board members sympathetic to their cause. It also threatened principals and teachers with being fired. The upshot of their efforts is that today most family life education programs, where they exist at all, are tepid indeed. For the most part, contemporary programs are limited to promoting the merits of abstinence from vaginal intercourse.[63] The religious right has been successful in wrangling federal dollars to support those programs by spinning the issue

entirely away from the original evangelical concern that sex among singles is
sinful because they're unmarried. Instead, christianists now wrap the issue
in a secular package by asserting that sexual intercourse undermines adolescent health. *Ergo,* every true American must endorse programs that teach
abstinence-only.

The RR's political success in gutting sex education in America got christianists back onto the political track for the first time since their early 20th-century
forebears had imposed prohibition on Americans. This very first taste of blood
by a new generation of christianists caused them to think the unthinkable: if
they could not make society into their own image by getting lots of people saved,
they at least proved they could control an important part of society via political
action.[64] After all, said some christianists, despite the thousands of souls that
Billy Graham had won to Christ, America just keeps on getting worse and
worse. What had Graham ever accomplished that measured up to the practical
importance of eliminating sex education from American schools? Weren't all
Americans a whole lot better off by excising such vile programs from K–12?
Religious right leader Jerry Falwell at first refused to get into politics because
he believed that preaching the Bible was God's sole means of changing society.[65] But Falwell later abandoned his earlier stance when he saw that political
action was in fact much more effective than preaching when it comes to changing society.

DEFEATING THE EQUAL RIGHTS AMENDMENT

If suppressing sex education placed christianists squarely on a political track,
their decisive triumph over the Equal Rights Amendment in the 1970s and
1980s propelled it onto the express lane. No sooner had women gained access
to the ballot box in 1920 when activist Alice Paul drafted ERA. She based it on
our Fourteenth and Fifteen Amendments, which guarantee equal rights to all
citizens regardless of race. ERA failed, however, to pass Congress when it was
first introduced in 1923. It was then reintroduced but failed every year thereafter
until Congress finally approved it and sent it to the states for their ratification
in 1972:

> Section 1. *Equality of rights under the law shall not be denied or abridged by the*
> *United States or by any state on account of sex.* Section 2. *The Congress shall have*
> *the power to enforce, by appropriate legislation, the provisions of this article.* Sec-
> tion 3. *This amendment shall take effect two years after the date of ratification.*

For a half-century, the ERA had more or less languished—not going away
but not going anywhere either. Just as sex education advocates were utterly as-

tonished by the RR's successes in stifling their agenda, the ERA's supporters were totally blindsided by the massive turbulence ERA stirred up after Congress finally approved it. The ERA (alongside *Roe v. Wade* in 1973) was another significant catalyst for the early formation of today's christianist movement. During the late 1960s and 1970s a loose collection of evangelicals and others were calling attention to America's alleged headlong plunge into moral chaos.[66] The congressional passage of the ERA confirmed their worst fears about America's moral rot.

Opposition to the ERA was spearheaded by a charismatic Roman Catholic attorney named Phyllis Schlafly. Her anti-ERA movement was the lightning rod attracting an array of groups convinced our society was plummeting down a slippery slope. As the several groups united in opposition to the ERA, they congealed into a potent political force that by the early 1980s buried the ERA at the states' level. But perhaps even more important, having tasted political blood for the second time they set out to hunt down still more prey. Defeating the ERA and the insidious message it carried was a sure sign that the new kid on the block had to be reckoned with. The growth of the christianist movement was finally in high gear.

Although the actual words of the ERA are mild enough, its opponents claimed it would lead to unspeakable wickedness such as unisex toilets, homosexual marriages, and women in combat. Falwell allowed as how evangelicals believe not just in "equal" but in "superior rights for their women."[67] "Superior," he explained, meant that men are obliged to open doors for women, help them put on their coats, and provide for and defend them. In addition, he said that the ERA "degrades womanhood," because it forces women into combat. However, that series of lame excuses for opposing the ERA cannot in my view begin to explain the fanatical feelings held by its opponents. If the ERA were reintroduced into Congress today, there seems little doubt christianists would oppose it even more ferociously than they did decades ago. That is so even though unisex toilets are everywhere, and Iraq-II showed us—in excruciatingly painful terms—that some women (including mothers) are willing to kill and be killed or maimed.[68] Nor, as I see it, is homosexual marriage the fundamental issue. Were it to be officially banned, christianist opposition to the ERA would still remain as fierce as ever.

Clearly, something much more fundamental is at stake than anxiety over any specific matter. It seems to me that the ERA arouses in its opponents a firestorm of fervent opposition owing to what it symbolizes. Christianists perceive the ERA to be an official seal of approval—an *imprimatur*—on the long-term evolutionary changes occurring in both families and in sexuality ever since the

18th century—changes that finally came to a head in the 1960s. Christianists loathe the ERA because they view it as the people's public stamp of approval on the belief that it's okay for humans to the creators and arbiters of what is good, bad, or indifferent within the spheres of sexuality and of families. Schlafly and other christianists seized on the ERA as a means to draw a line in the sand: *We shall allow the moral scurvy of U.S. society to proceed no further. We shall not permit the ERA to signal the headlong plunge of America into debauchery and oblivion.*

NOTES

1. Cited by Kennedy 1970:47.
2. Weisman 1992:87; McHugh 1999.
3. Acton 1870/1968.
4. Psalm 127:3–5, KJV. There is a present-day evangelical group with a Web site (quiverfull.com) that in fact still follows this philosophy.
5. Kennedy 1970:42.
6. Kennedy 1970:42.
7. Spitzer and Saylor 1969.
8. Himes 1963/1970:3.
9. Himes 1963/1970:210. Italics in original.
10. Himes 1963/1970:210.
11. Kennedy 1970:83–84.
12. Cott 1979.
13. Scott 2008.
14. Winner 2005.
15. Ford 1989:14.
16. Allen 1997; Currell 2009.
17. Leeman 1989; Munger and Schaller 1997.
18. Kraditor 1968.
19. Soland 2000.
20. Rice 1941.
21. McCulley 2004.
22. Bailey 1989; Scanzoni 2000.
23. McCulley 2004.
24. Bailey 1989; Allen 1997:364–65.
25. Reiss 1960; Bell 1966.
26. Reiss 1960.
27. McCulley 2004.
28. Goodstein 2006.
29. Reiss 1960.
30. Modell 1989.
31. Kinsey et al., 1948, 1953.
32. Gathorne-Hardy 2000:394.

33. Gathorne-Hardy 2000:395, italics in original.
34. Graham 1953.
35. Elkin 1983.
36. Gathorne-Hardy 2000:400.
37. Rohter and Zito 1977.
38. Martin 1996:101.
39. Gathorne-Hardy 2000; Jones 1997.
40. Gathorne-Hardy 2000:168.
41. Gordon 1978.
42. Gathorne-Hardy 2000:247.
43. Lindner 2003.
44. Halliwell 2007; Halberstam 1993.
45. Bauer 1986.
46. Spates 1976; Gitlin 1993.
47. Gitlin 1993.
48. MacAfee 2008.
49. Gitlin 1993.
50. Gitlin 1993.
51. Allyn 2000; Regnerus 2007:85.
52. A comprehensive list and description of those lifestyles may be found in Macklin and Rubin 1983. Also see Scanzoni 1972, 2004.
53. Otto 1970.
54. Lasch 1977.
55. Mead 1967.
56. Mead 1967:874, emphasis mine.
57. Mead 1967:874.
58. Mead 1967:873; Stack 1974; Scanzoni 2000.
59. Martin 1996:100.
60. Martin 1996:101.
61. Martin 1996:102, italics added.
62. Martin 1996:102ff; Luker 2006.
63. Freedman 2006a.
64. See my preface to this book, note 3.
65. Martin 1996:69–70.
66. Mansbridge 1986.
67. Martin 1996:163.
68. Alvarez 2009.

Ideas for Today
and Tomorrow

Work and Parenting for Men and Women: Something Old, Something New

In 1971, the Institute for Advanced Christian Studies (IFACS) sponsored a conference to consider an evangelical response to the liberation movements of the 1960s described in chapter 2. The IFACS was not, however, interested in sexual or drug liberation; it was instead intrigued by something else. Some liberation movement organizers (mostly upper-middle-class, white males) wanted "liberation from work."[1] They spoke of dropping out from what they perceived to be the rat race for material success that had grown up in the United States since the end of World War II. Disillusioned by the vacuous symbols of conspicuous consumption that captured America in the 1950s and 1960s, they sought a simpler way of life uncomplicated by a pervasive and insidious materialism.[2]

The leaders of the IFACS were, to be sure, just as appalled as those youth over the materialism gripping America. But they were equally distressed by their solution—what youth called *tuning out of work*. The leaders countered that dumping work is not an acceptable option. Work or vocation, is they said, essential to being fully human, and not merely because it's necessary for survival. Work, said the leaders, has two faces, one of which is of course material and tangible. But the other face of work is nonmaterial, intangible, and intrinsic—perhaps even spiritual but not in any sectarian sense. Work is spiritual in the sense that it is built into that part of our humanity that lies beyond the material realm. Both faces of work are equally critical, and the conference organizers assigned me the task of developing a perspective on work that blends information from the social sciences with insights from Christianity.[3]

THE SPIRITUAL FACES OF WORK

Privileged 1960s white men hoping to ignite a mass movement of youth flee-ing the world of work bumped up against several insurmountable barriers. The most formidable was the fact that most women and blacks had been shut out of the labor force. Their ambitious goal was to get themselves into the world of work—not escape something they didn't have. Equal access to paid labor came to be seen as a woman's fundamental right. However, it became apparent at once that women workers earned fewer dollars than men. The media were filled with stories showing that though more and more women were entering paid labor, they earned on the average only 70 percent as much as men.

The upshot of that intense media spotlight on income differences was that women's work was framed using the mindset already in vogue for men: total at-tention was fixed on the material or tangible face of work. Very little, if any, no-tice was paid to its intangible or spiritual face. And today, not a great deal seems to have changed. When I ask graduating college seniors of either gender what's next after college, their typical response leans almost entirely toward the material side of work: "Well, I'm not sure, I just want to make lots of money." Similarly, a successful, midlife, middle-manager woman told me recently that "I work in or-der to get the money to do the things I *really* want to do."

But it was not always so. The spiritual or innate rewards of work are high-lighted by something called the Protestant ethic. Max Weber, an influential early 20th-century German social scientist, noted that the 16th-century Protestant re-formers taught that the work of every person—laity and clergy alike—is a special vocation or calling from God.[4] In God's eyes, the blacksmith, farmer, or midwife has just as sacred and exalted a vocation as the celibate monk translating the scriptures from Latin into the everyday language of the people. Work, said the reformers, is in and of itself a divine calling of the highest order. The reformers added that as one serves God by fulfilling his or her vocation—whether as mid-wife, farmer, seamstress, or stonemason—one serves one's fellow human be-ings at the same time. One becomes part of something bigger than oneself by contributing to the greater good of society.

To be sure, ever since humans have been around and long before the reform-ers, people understood that work has a spiritual as well as a material face. In short, one does not have to believe that work is a calling from God to appreciate the enormous significance of its innate or spiritual benefits.

THE PLEASURES OF SOLVING PROBLEMS

The first built-in pleasure of work is the chance it offers to confront problems, puzzles, or challenges and then to solve, master, overcome, or get the better of them. During the agricultural age, for instance, the cultivation of soil and crops (as well as the maintenance of livestock) required constant thought and problem solving by the farming partners—husband and wife alike. And once harvested, thinking and problem solving were likewise demanded in order to manage their crops and livestock: How much should they store in order to meet their own survival needs? How much should they barter or sell in order to get the items they did not grow? Though often painfully frustrating, extracting a livelihood from the reluctant soil offered many satisfying and fulfilling experiences. Indeed, the more daunting the challenges they faced, the greater the partners' opportunities to be creative problem solvers and to sense at least a bit of control over their hostile environment.

Today, the world of sport offers familiar examples of the joys and frustrations of working hard to overcome awesome challenges. Recall, for instance, the films we've all seen of resolute mountain-climbers. Some 95 percent of the film is devoted to the arduous series of problems the team faces as it struggles upward—coupled with their successes and failures in trying to solve those challenges. The climbers derive enormous satisfactions from conquering those never-ending tests of their problem-solving capabilities. The last 5 percent of the film shows that it's great fun to arrive finally at the summit, and when they do everyone smiles, waves, and hugs. But the viewer also picks up a tinge of sadness among the climbers because their exciting adventures are at an end—at least for a while. And we also sense that the climbers look forward eagerly to doing their adventures all over again by testing their skills on yet another mountain. In short, what's often said about travel surely applies to work as well: *The journey, not the arrival, matters.*

THE SATISFACTIONS OF ECONOMIC INDEPENDENCE

Though the spiritual and the material dimensions of work are distinct, they are also partnered. For example, a second built-in pleasure of work is a sense of economic independence or self-sufficiency. But in order to gain that feeling of independence and control of one's life, a person must either be working or have some other source of income. Economic independence means that person is able on her own (apart from the inputs of anyone else) to provide basic personal material needs (not necessarily wants) as well as those of any dependents. Let's say, for example, that a person has a job at Wal-Mart enabling her to supply the material needs of both herself and her child. Because she is economically self-sufficient, she's aware that she is in control of this vital part of her life. And that sense of accomplishment is, she discovers, enormously fulfilling and satisfying.

THE SATISFACTIONS OF SELF-RESPECT
AND THE RESPECT OF OTHERS

That feeling of accomplishment is satisfying to her, not only in and of it-self, but also because it opens the door to yet another built-in reward of work. And that is a sense of esteem, or regard, or respect—I am an okay person. Respect includes both the esteem she holds for herself and the good opinion in which she is held by persons (family, friends, and co-workers) who matter to her and whose judgments she values. The respect in which she is held—by herself and by others who mean a lot to her—stems from the fact that she has accomplished no small thing: she is demonstrating that she is indeed a self-sufficient person.

THE JOYS OF AUTONOMY

Despite her self-sufficiency, it gradually dawns on her that she possesses an array of talents and abilities that are not being used by her current job and, in-deed, never can be. In effect, she realizes that there's an important part of her life over which she is not in charge, and over which she has no control. Accordingly, she feels less independent, or autonomous, than she ought to be and wants to be. Because she's unable to fully cultivate all of her abilities she feels blocked from growing into everything she could possibly be—her human development is being held back.

In hopes of overcoming that lack of control and to gain a stronger sense of autonomy, she starts taking classes at her local community college. Her long-term objective is to get the sort of education that will open doors to occupations quite different from her present job. She wants to work at something that might enable her to cultivate the entire range of her talents and abilities. She seeks the intrin-sic or spiritual satisfactions that arise from something beyond self-sufficiency— *as basic as that is*. She wants the intensity of joy that stems from the awareness that she's taking charge of her life in ways that go beyond money. She seeks, in other words, to broaden and deepen the scope of her autonomy.

THE PLEASURES OF SERVICE TO OTHERS

Today, we hear a lot about youth taking a year or two off from school or career in order to serve humanity via groups like the Peace Corps or Teach for America.[5] The pitch used to entice applicants is similar to military recruiting: "Our society has given you a lot. Isn't it time you gave something back?" After being hit with the stick of obligation, potential applicants are then offered the carrot of spiritual satisfactions: "Just think how great you'll feel in your heart by making a difference in the lives of others." Making a difference in the lives of others is known also as serving the greater good or contributing to the public household.

Although those are admirable ideas indeed, I must say again that the reformers did *not* make a sharp distinction between activities that contribute to the public household *versus* one's everyday work—contributions to one's private household. They believed instead that, ideally, every man and woman (and boy and girl) should conceive of his or her everyday work as a vehicle for serving others and oneself *at the same time*. They argued that God obliged each person to contribute to the well-being of others via everyday productive labor.

To be sure, the ideal of "my work as making a difference in the lives of others" was much more readily understood back then than it is today. Most persons (such as the farming couple) were busily engaged in producing food that kept others alive. Likewise, citizens that assisted in the production of food (the blacksmith, wheelwright, or harness-maker) also contributed to the public household. Finally, the link between one's vocation and the welfare of others was quite obvious for the physician, clergy, or midwife.

THE "REAL" TRADITIONAL ROLES OF WOMEN AND MEN

In 1981, the RR got a bill introduced into Congress called the Family Protection Act. Though never passed, its ideals are nonetheless alive and well throughout christianist circles today.[6] The bill's sponsors declared that one of its primary goals was to prohibit the use of federal monies to pay for educational materials that promote feminist values. Instead, federal dollars should only teach about "'traditional families' and the role of women 'as historically understood.'"[7] Historically understood, indeed! Christianists seem to understand very little prior to the mid-19th-century cult of true womanhood discussed in chapter 1.

The christianist grasp of gender is as spotty as that of a student of mine who used the phrase "woman's traditional role" in her paper. I asked her to define it, and she said, "It means the way things have always been done." I suggested that as she revises her paper she should study some of the many accounts of women's productive work both inside and outside their dwellings prior to the industrial age.[8] She should understand that most women around the globe participated actively in the planting, cultivation, and harvesting of crops. She should also appreciate women's work in the making of pottery, clothing, carpets, food items, and so forth that were often sold in the local village marketplace. Some wives, moreover, worked as a seamstress, herbalist, or midwife.

Women did all that at the same time that they labored at spinning yarn for, and sewing, their family's clothing. They also participated in the care and

slaughtering of livestock, in the preservation of meat, in the canning and prepa-
ration of food, and in the distillation and storage of wine and whiskey. Those
had been the *traditional* roles of the great masses of women for at least ten
thousand years. I might have added that if the student sought a biblical account of an agricultural-age wife working from dawn to dusk at economically
productive activities, she could do no better than read about the "virtuous
woman [whose] price is far above rubies."[9]

I did suggest to her that for fun she might read Diana Gabaldon's 2005 historical novel, *A Breath of Snow and Ashes*. Gabaldon vividly depicts pre-Revolutionary
North Carolina farming communities, and shows how women's labors were essential to the fabric of everyday life—so vital in fact that apart from women's labor
their families (nuclear and kin) could never have survived. Throughout history,
traditional gender roles meant that "Most people had a two-person, married couple career that neither could conduct alone."[10] Women and men alike shared in
both the spiritual and material rewards of productive labor. They enjoyed both
the satisfactions of being skilled problem solvers and the material benefits that
accrued from their skills. Moreover, their productive work gave them a degree
of economic independence, earned them self-respect alongside the good opinion of others, enlarged their sense of autonomy, and provided the satisfactions
that flow from serving others:

> *Man and wife working a smallholding were partners in a way quite unrecognized
> by the hollow letter of the law. Centered in her home, her family and her work, still
> at this stage a holy trinity, three in one, a woman could be proud, self-sufficient,
> strong, and free. It all sounds too good to be true. It was.* And with the coming
> of the machine age, it was to be swept away as if it had never been.[11]

Miles' gloomy assessment notwithstanding, women's traditional gender
roles did not entirely vanish in the United States, even as late as the 1970s. During that decade, Sherry Thomas traveled 17,000 miles throughout rural America speaking with older women who were still and/or had recently been active
in farm work: "When women described the farm work they would say they
'helped.'"[12] However, when Thomas pressed them for details, it became quite
clear that they performed precisely the same sorts of tasks as their menfolk. (If
the woman had no man around, she did all the farm work by herself.) Thomas
remarks, "To call all this work 'helping' serves the useful social function of keeping male pride intact." Our cultural stereotype has been that "rural women are
'farmers' wives,' not farmers. Yet every woman I met and spoke with had been in
some way a 'farmer,' had done a vast array of jobs, had a multitude of skills." In

effect, Thomas took the wraps off the genuine article—the actual traditional roles of women as they'd been practiced in the West for millennia prior to the 19th century. And today, in parts of Africa, Asia, and Latin America those traditions still persist.[13] Throughout history, traditional women and men were full partners together in both the material and the spiritual sides of work.

INVENTING "RADICAL" FAMILY VALUES
FOR MIDDLE-CLASS WOMEN

The Protestants that settled North America during the 17th and 18th centuries were totally immersed in the idea that work is a sacred calling from God.[14] They readily understood that work has both a spiritual as well as a material side. Work, they believed, is its own reward as well as the means to economic survival. Moreover, both faces of work applied with equal force to both genders.

Nonetheless, chapter 1 noted that commerce was gaining importance in both Europe and pre-Revolutionary America. Growing numbers of men were discovering that the balance between the material and the spiritual sides of work was slowly shifting as compared to the days when agriculture was the principal setting for work. More and more, the commercial character of work was perceived as a means not merely to survive but also to thrive—perhaps even to get rich. The spiritual or intangible face of work was of course still present, but its material face loomed ever more prominent.

The early 19th century ushered in the industrial revolution and what Karl Marx called the "alienation of the worker" from his or her work. On both sides of the Atlantic, masses of citizens were fleeing the countryside for the cities. Men, women, and children alike took jobs in the new factories that sprang up from nowhere. To their horror, they discovered a shocking reality that neither they nor their agricultural forebears had ever before encountered: they stumbled into work that had been stripped almost entirely of any spiritual satisfactions whatever.

Because factory work was repetitive, dull, and tedious, it robbed humans of the intangible satisfactions of problem solving that, during the agricultural age, had supplied at least some opportunities for creativity and control over one's labor. Factory work was by contrast dull, monotonous, and mind-numbing. It was often dangerous as well—especially for children and women. Work had one purpose and one only—the meager wages doled out to the laborers. The tangible face of work had virtually blotted out its spiritual face. The masses of citizens (men, women, and children) were sensing a vast distance between the essence of their humanity and their work.

By the mid-19th century, growing numbers of men sought to escape the alienation and miserable wages of the factory floor by seeking their fortune in the

boardroom—the exploding universe of industry and business. Their prime motivation was undoubtedly material—to earn lots of money. At the same time,
they were keenly aware that entrepreneurial and managerial work also carries
with it numerous intangible satisfactions. This new type of industrial age work
offered them the same sorts of spiritual rewards their ancestors had enjoyed for
millennia—the pleasures of problem-solving, independence, respect, and autonomy. Only now they must apply their problem-solving skills to industry and business, not agriculture.

Compared with being an unskilled laborer who earned little money and got
even fewer intrinsic rewards, these white, upwardly mobile men formed the core
of an emerging middle class in both Britain and America that was relatively well
off.[15] Though a number of men had opportunities to make the transition from
factory floor to company boardroom, their wives were not so fortunate. The cult
of true womanhood described in chapter 1 lay behind a concerted effort to deny
women the chance to compete within their husbands' world of commerce and
industry. Because the middle-class wife was excluded from the marketplace, she
no longer had direct access either to its material or its spiritual satisfactions. Instead, she was informed that her husband would now supply her with material
goodies. She was also told that her children would be the life-spring of her spiritual rewards. In effect, those 19th-century Americans invented something radical—a new way of life that departed from all known traditional family values.
They called it the husband-provider marriage. By the mid-20th century, an eminent social scientist declared that new type of marriage to be the core of the normal American family.[16]

Hence, when christianists speak of traditional gender roles they in fact refer
to the recently evolved species—the Western, middle-class *urban* family—that's
been around for a scant 150 years. They seem oblivious to the fact that in the *rural* areas of America and Europe the genuinely traditional family that had existed since ancient times remained alive and well at least until the 1970s.[17] The
religious right also appears oblivious to the fact that in rural areas of today's developing world the genuinely traditional family of ancient times is still the predominant family style. A spokesperson for the Southern Baptist Convention
(largely christianist) named R. A. Mohler exposed the unawareness of most christianists as to how the vast majority of men and women once actually behaved
(and many still do). He wrote recently that the SBC is "off the scale of political in-
correctness. [We] insist on traditional roles for women."[18] In sharp contrast, the
SBC's most famous member, former President Jimmy Carter, announced in July
2009 that he was leaving the SBC for what he termed its "repugnant sexism."[19]

Mohler's anxieties about women's and men's roles are shared by certain
evangelical groups that, in the late 1990s, captured a lot of media attention: Prom-

ise Keepers, a group in which evangelical men learn how to play their God-given upper hand over their women in a benevolent manner.[20] At the same time, Promise Reapers is one of several complementary groups in which evangelical women learn how to acquiesce graciously to the hand they've been dealt—being submissive to men. The husband might, for instance, forbid his wife to hold a job because, he tells her, God commands that the husband should support his wife: "You must therefore stay home and tend to our children." The Promise-Keeper is, among other things, expected to be sexually monogamous so that his wife will not resent his authority. She will thus feel comfortable submitting to his wishes. But in 2009 the national press made much of the fact that GOP Senator John Ensign "admitted ... that he had 'violated the vows' of marriage by having an affair with a staffer. . . . A born-again Christian, Ensign has been a member of the Promise Keepers, a male evangelical group that promotes marital fidelity."[21]

It is curious indeed that the RR so easily dismisses what Christians once believed was God's traditional plan for both genders—namely, that women and men alike should do productive labor and thus reap both its spiritual and material rewards. Christianists turn a blind eye to the historical fact that, beginning with the mid-19th century, large numbers of middle-class women were, for the first time ever, ejected from productive labor. By the 1960s, the radical, non-traditional pattern of excluding married women from paid labor had been entrenched for some 100 years. During those decades, money and the things it bought (consumerism) morphed into the foremost motivation for work. Although some white, upper-middle-class men (along with artists and craftspersons) enjoyed its intrinsic features, most citizens focused almost entirely on the material face of work.[22] The spiritually based Protestant ethic had given way to its secularized revision known as the American dream.

BRINGING WOMEN BACK INTO THE MATERIAL SIDE OF WORK

Advocates in the 1960s aimed to bury the womanhood cult by establishing a two-way flow of traffic between homeplace and workplace: men would, they hoped, become as actively involved in nurturing children as women had been since the mid-19th century. That's when middle-class mothers began to assume the full range of responsibilities for children that, historically, had been shared with kinfolk, neighbors, and hired hands. Advocates reasoned that as men flowed into the homeplace, women would start flowing in the other direction. Ideally, they would get just as actively involved in the world of work as men had been for a hundred years.[23]

The 1960s advocates for women's interests sympathized with the privileged white males complaining about Americans' self-indulgent materialism. Still, it seemed to make sense for advocates to focus on the material side of work be-cause money was the mark of gender fairness most readily understood by the majority of Americans. If men earned $20,000 per year but women earned $14,000 (70%), or were being denied job opportunities altogether, women were obviously unequal with men. Federal and state civil rights legislation was de-signed to reduce the discrimination that kept women from having access to the same jobs and earning the same dollars as men.

The fatal flaw in the advocates' strategy was that money came to dominate the national conversation that Americans were having during the 1960s and 1970s about *reopening* the world of work to women. Voices such as Margaret Mead's connecting women with the spiritual features of work were few and far between:

> *We are so urgently in need of every form of creative imagination to meet the challenges already before us, it may well be worthwhile to work out better ways of drawing on feminine constructive creativity in social invention. We cannot afford to waste the talents of educated women. . . . We cannot afford to involve in social change half the world's population [men] without also involving [women] with the responsibility for making the necessary social inventions.*[24]

The strategy followed by most advocates—targeting money as the chief indicator of gender equity—was expedient and no doubt well-intentioned. Unfortunately, one unintended result of their strategy was that the spiritual faces of work—which had been growing steadily indistinct for a long time—were submerged even further within the subterranean reaches of the national psyche. Ignoring work's spiritual features generated several unfortunate outcomes, one of which festered into a painful sore.

Americans' virtual obsession with the material side of work created, for the first time in history, an almost adversary-like relationship between work and children. Subsequent generations of women and men alike have grown up fram-ing their discussions about work and children as being a no-win conflict between the material and the spiritual—the tangible versus the intangible. The flip side of saying that work is principally about money is to imply that children are about an intangible and loftier realm of life—the sphere of the intrinsic or spiritual. By comparison with the nobility of children, money—though vital—seems igno-ble. And because the source of money is work, it too ranks below children when reckoning what's important in the overall scheme of things.

The womanhood cult played no small part in convincing Americans that, as far as women are concerned, nurturing children should be ranked as a higher spiritual calling than the pursuit of work:

"If in becoming a mother, you have reached the climax of your happiness, you have also taken a higher place in the scale of being . . . you have gained an increase in power." . . . The mothers must do the inculcating of virtue [in children] since the fathers, alas, were too busy chasing the dollar. . . . It was his wife who "formed the infant mind as yet untainted by contact with evil."[25]

Until the mid-19th century, productive labor for both genders was viewed as a lofty and sacred vocation—a calling from God that is as noble and splendid as anything else in life, including the nurture of children. That ideal has, however, long since been abandoned. The matching ideal that work conveys essential spiritual rewards has likewise been deemphasized. Seen in that half light, the nurturing of children will inevitably trump productive labor left half-naked— shorn of its spiritual side. If persons actually believe that nurturing children is a higher spiritual calling than paid work, even mothers who cannot afford to stay home (either because her husband's earnings do not permit it or she is a solo mother) are likely to feel dreadfully guilty about, and apologetic for, their less worthy material pursuits.

A recent Pew study reported that among mothers working full-time in 1997, some 32 percent said that full-time work is "ideal for me," but by 2007 that percentage had dropped to 21. During that same period the percentage of full-time working mothers saying that part-time work would be "ideal for me" increased from 48 to 60. (The percentage saying that not working at all would be "ideal for me" stayed around 20.) The researchers add that "The lack of enthusiasm that mothers . . . have for full-time work outside the home isn't shared by fathers— more than seven-in-ten (72%) fathers say the ideal situation for them is a full-time job."[26]

MOTHERS' PERSISTENT WAGE GAP

Their feelings of regret and guilt over not being able to spend more time with their children no doubt contribute to those mothers' "lack of enthusiasm" for full-time work. Their lack of enthusiasm is further compounded by the fact that many of them encounter situations distressingly similar to those faced by women in the 1960s and 1970s:

Raised to believe that girls could accomplish anything . . . [today's] women have reached parenthood only to find they faced many of the same pay, equity and work-family balance issues that were being fought over decades before.[27]

Many of today's advocates are deeply frustrated because, despite five decades of trying to close it, the wage gap between the earnings of mothers (married and solo) and of men persists tenaciously. Researchers report that in 2005, "college-educated women between 36 and 45 years old . . . earned 74.7 cents in hourly pay for every dollar that men in the same group did, according to Labor Department data analyzed by the Economic Policy Institute. A decade earlier, the women earned 75.7 cents."[28] Most of the women at both points in time had one or more children.

Nevertheless, in sharp contrast to that all-too-familiar scenario, recent census reports comparing young women and men—virtually all of whom were either unmarried and/or child-free, and living in big cities—reveal an astonishing reversal of long-standing patterns: "In 1970, New York [City] women in their 20s made $7,000 less than [young] men . . . By 2000, they were about even. [But] In 2005, according to an analysis of the latest census results [women] were making about $5,000 more: a median wage of $35,653, or 117 percent of the $30,560 reported by men in that age group."[29] That same pattern of young (child-free) women earning more than young men was found in several other large U.S. cities—especially Dallas, where young women earned 120 percent of the earnings of young men.

Advocates believe that the steady progress of young women who are single and/or child-free in closing and now reversing the gender wage gap sets the chronic plight of mothers in bold relief. It appears obvious that alongside facing workplace discrimination, having a child places most women at severe economic disadvantage when compared with most men. To help drive home that point, MomsRising (an advocacy group whose objective is to reduce gender income disparities) produced a documentary film called *The Motherhood Manifesto:*

> *The film opens with one woman telling her friend that she and her husband have decided to have a baby. "Are you clueless?" the friend asks. "Don't you know what happens to mothers in America?" One thing the movie makes clear: It isn't good.*[30]

PRIVILEGED WOMEN DROPPING OUT OF PAID LABOR

Back in the 1960s and 1970s, advocates complained bitterly that married women lacked the liberty to pursue paid labor. They assumed that once women gained their freedom most would embrace it eagerly—and for many that's been so. What advocates did not foresee and could never have imagined is that some economically privileged mothers would eventually choose not to exercise that option. Their grandmothers fought for the right *not* to be confined to their home—they struggled mightily to escape the role of housewife. Nonetheless, some of their privileged granddaughters aim to revive the 1950s role of housewife and assign it a chic label—stay-at-home mom (SAHM).[31] The SAHM evolved out of the 1950s housewife role, which in turn had its roots in the 19th-century cult of true womanhood. While the true woman/housewife was defined by her house, the stay-at-home mom is defined by her children. (There's even a Christian CSAHM.[32])

Use of the term *mom* rather than *mother* seems to me no accident: *mom* conveys an extraordinarily sentimental aura—unique feelings of warmth, softness, coziness, serenity, and security. The impression is that Mom is shunning base materialism for the sake of her child. Mom is gladly and willingly making a material sacrifice for the emotional and psychological well-being of her child. Her self-denial marks Mom as a person of indisputable moral excellence. The implication is that Mom is endowed with a loftier degree of virtue than the woman (with children) who works for pay.

Though the reformers (and others) would likely disagree, one might concede that freedom of choice should include the liberty *not* to pursue paid labor. However, that lifestyle choice is not as simple as it sounds. First, there is no defensible reason why that same kind of lifestyle choice should not be open to men. And indeed we now read scattered reports about the SAHD or stay-at-home dad.[33] Second, the harsh and unspoken reality about the SAHM is that it rests on the foundation of economic privilege. When politicians praise America as being a middle-class society they imply that our middle class is a seamless cloth. The fact is, however, that the cloth is stitched together out of several quite dissimilar pieces.

Social scientists classify the smallest piece as the *upper*-middle-class. The UMC is the piece in which the SAHM is most likely to be found and the reason is obvious: this SAHM resides with a partner (husband or cohabiter) who is earning enough dollars to support their family's needs as well as its extras.[34] He is by himself able to maintain the family's desired level of consumption, which usually turns out to be quite affluent. As a result, while weighing the pros and cons of her lifestyle choice, the notion of material sacrifice rarely if ever enters the calculations of an UMC wife or partner. She seldom has to consider that one of the downsides of being an SAHM is having less money for the wide range of material things her family needs or wants. The SAHM is something that well-to-do women and men can buy just as they might buy any other prestigious status symbol such as a luxury car, a yacht, or a trophy house.

The chief reason he's able to provide such a prosperous lifestyle is that the UMC man typically has some type of high-paying profession (physician, lawyer, and so on). The UMC also includes men who hold a well-paying (often managerial) career in the corporate world, or perhaps in the nonprofit sector. The UMC additionally includes men who have their own relatively lucrative business, and UMC men usually perceive their work activities as a *career* and not merely as a *job*. Most of those men hold a college degree and often a graduate degree as well. Despite their many advantages, UMC men were not immune to the severe economic downturn of 2008/2009—a matter to which I return below. Even before the downturn, economists differed among themselves as to how many SAHMs actually existed during any given year.[35] Given that the downturn robbed some UMC men of their jobs, it seems likely that the numbers of SAHMs has inevitably shrunk. As those SAHMs see it, their husband's misfortune has regrettably forced them back into paid labor. One national analyst of family trends asks and answers the question this way: "Is the opt-out revolution coming to an end? It sure feels like it these days."[36]

Linda Hirshman describes the SAHM as "elite" because she typically has as much as education as (or sometimes more than) her partner.[37] The women's high status also stems from the fact that, prior to becoming an SAHM, most of them held UMC careers in either the professions or in the business world. In her book contrasting the SAHM with dual-career couples, Leslie Morgan Steiner opens a window into how UMC couples wrestle with the competing demands of career and parenting.[38] In rather poignant terms, her book sheds light on how some career women opt to abandon the struggle and stop out of their career path (for either a specified or unspecified period of time) in order to pursue full-time motherhood. And, in her 2007 book *The Feminine Mistake*, Leslie Bennetts also interviewed a range of SAHMs, focusing in particular on the sad outcomes that at times stemmed unexpectedly from their lifestyle choice.[39]

Just below UMC on America's social class ladder is the middle-middle-class, followed by the lower-middle or working class, followed by the lower class. The latter includes poor persons who either have a job (at least for the time being) or those who had a job but lost it. The further we descend on the rungs of America's class ladder, the less likely we are to find the dollars necessary to support an SAHM lifestyle.

Furthermore, bear in mind that the further we descend on the class ladder, the more likely we are to find solo-mothers. Solo-mothers are, of course, found at all class levels, and they have no choice but to enter paid labor. Some solo-mothers are well educated and able to earn sufficient dollars to maintain a comfortable lifestyle.[40] Some less privileged solo-mothers are able to provide a reasonably comfortable lifestyle, particularly if they have only one or two children. The poorly educated solo-mother has, of course, the greatest difficulty in providing for herself and her relatively larger number of children. In any case, it is strikingly apparent that, regardless of how much education she does or doesn't have, the solomother need not bother applying for the position of SAHM: she is of necessity the sole provider for herself and her children.

BRINGING WOMEN BACK INTO THE SPIRITUAL SIDE OF WORK

As grave a matter as it is, reliance on economic privilege is not the deadliest flaw in the SAHM lifestyle. Instead, its most glaring defect is that it ignores genuinely traditional family values. The SAHM disregards the fact that for thousands of years, most women in most parts of the world engaged actively in productive labor. Andrew Sullivan reminds us that an authentic conservative honors tradition and agonizes over whether to keep it as is, or set it aside, or update it some manner.[41] I've suggested that a progressive approach to families seeks to blend conservative with liberal ideals. In the case of gender, conservative ideals pivot around the spiritual or intrinsic faces of work—problem solving, independence, respect, autonomy, and service. Those are among the most priceless elements of what it means to be fully human, and a conservative might well argue that we should reconnect women to those essential dimensions. The conservative might feel those dimensions are representative of something old that is well worth updating. She or he might agree that we should repair the bond between women and productive labor that existed for millennia prior to the 19th century—a bond severed by the industrial age.

Liberal contributions to this progressive approach begin with the insistence that, in the interests of social justice, repairing that bond must absorb girls and women at all social class levels, and from all racial and ethnic groups. The policy goal of girls and women at all class levels embracing the spiritual dimensions of work is no longer optional for reasons I discuss below. This is part of what I mean by something new. A second liberal contribution to this progressive approach pivots around boys and men—again at all social class levels. The Womanhood Cult placed severe and unwarranted limitations not only on women but on men as well. Despite the fact that children can offer an abundance of spiritual and intrinsic satisfactions, the cult denied men ready access to those rewards. It is thus essential that, in the interests of their own well-being, men should now have the same access as women to those spiritual pleasures. This too represents something new.

A NEW WORLD OF WORK

While crafting our progressive approach we should remind ourselves that there was a good fit between the agricultural age and its prevailing model of gender roles. And, despite the heavy price paid by women and men alike, there was a reasonable fit between the industrial age and its prevailing model of gender roles. Today, we are passing out of the industrial age and into the *post*-industrial era known also as the "information age." And sure enough it's déjà vu all over again. Growing numbers of persons on both sides of the Atlantic are struggling to craft the kinds of gender roles that will fit with or adapt to a rapidly changing economic environment. We can barely make out the dim outlines of what's happening. We get the sense, however, that although the information age is breathtakingly new it offers, paradoxically, the opportunity to restore something very old.

The chief symbol of the agricultural age was the mule-drawn plow. The chief symbol of the industrial period was the mechanical engine (steam or petrol). There is, however, no single icon or artifact—not even the computer—that evokes fully what the information age is all about. Peter Drucker, a distinguished information age guru, argues that it's not about any specific artifact in and of itself.[42] Instead, the information age is about the capacity of ever-evolving electronic technology of every sort to expand and unleash the potential of the human mind in ways not yet imagined. It's about a seemingly limitless technology in the service of the human mind. At its core, the information age is about a *mindtechnology partnership* never before experienced. It appears to me that this alliance is indeed a fitting symbol for the information age.

To be sure, in their day both the plow and the engine served the human mind. But the prime question put to those older technologies was readily understood and answered: "What can they do?" By contrast, the prime question underlying the myriad of 21st-century electronic technologies is mind-boggling: "What *can't* they do?" Though they are mind-boggling, they are not mind-paralyzing. Rather than stymie the human mind, the new technologies are in synch with and stimulate its very essence—the mind's capabilities to engage in rigorous and creative thinking that results in effective problem solving. Getting better at the (often daunting) pursuit of overcoming formidable challenges is the first and most basic of work's several spiritual satisfactions described above.

Though spiritual rewards marked a great deal of work for both genders throughout the agricultural age, intrinsic satisfactions during the industrial age were limited for the most part to relatively small numbers of white men who worked in UMC professional and managerial occupations—the top of the class ladder. The bottom of the class ladder consisted (and still does) largely of unskilled laborers known today mostly as service workers. For men and women in that situation work is anything but challenging, or creative, or innately satisfying. Despite the fact their wages are meager, they are sometimes able to attain at least some self-sufficiency and gain a bit of respect by pooling the incomes of several workers (some linked by blood and some not) and by sharing one dwelling. Many service workers are women (often solo-mothers) and/or members of minority groups, and make up a growing segment of today's labor force.

During the industrial age, the middle-middle-class, and also the lower-middle/working-class were sandwiched in between the top and the bottom layers of the class ladder. It was made up largely of both skilled workers (e.g., tool and die maker) and semiskilled (factory) workers. Skilled workers were able to exercise a limited degree of problem-solving initiative, though by no means as much as the managers above them. Because their wages were high, skilled workers enjoyed a marked degree of self-sufficiency and respect. On the other hand, semiskilled workers were paid less, had fewer problem-solving opportunities, and enjoyed less self-sufficiency and respect. Unfortunately, today's economists deliver the bleak news that the information age, together with the global marketplace, is gradually rendering many of those types of industrial age jobs (skilled and semiskilled alike) increasingly obsolete.[43]

By contrast, the top layer of UMC jobs is expanding steadily. For some time those jobs have been known as problem-solving jobs. Whatever the specific job title (coach, manager, dentist, engineer, nurse, teacher, or entrepreneur) what the jobholder in fact does is to think carefully about, and become as creative as possible in, solving problems. Accordingly, the typical worker in the top layer has both a specific and a broad, all-purpose identity.[44] He or she might, for example, reason that "who I am is a nurse or a coach—that is my specific identity." At the same time, the nurse or coach might also be developing an underlying and much more comprehensive identity—"who I am is a problem-solver—that is my identity."

One vital reason it's essential to cultivate that broader identity is the harsh reality that in the information age the type of job security that marked the industrial age is no more. The economic downturn of 2008/2009 was a reminder (as if one were needed) that no one—*including those within the UMC layer*—can be certain that one will not lose one's job for reasons largely beyond one's control. No job is fully protected from going elsewhere or simply going extinct. Accordingly, the future of work in the information age cannot be connected with any particular set of occupations—no matter how attractive they might appear at present. Instead, the future of work belongs to the problem solver—a person who possesses comprehensive and portable skills that permit transition from one specific job to another.

As the world evolves from an industrial to a postindustrial economy, the pool of occupations and entrepreneurial opportunities requiring the identity of problem solver is steadily expanding throughout North America, Europe, Japan, and emerging economies such as China and India. Those and related reasons prompt information age gurus to argue that work is undergoing a fundamental makeover that is, in many respects, as significant as the earlier revolution that gave us the industrial age. And if that is so, *then the future of gender implies that girls and women, and boys and men from all social classes and all racial/ethnic groups, must have the opportunity to participate fully in the abundance that the information age promises.* Such abundance is not, however, simply material. Its abundance is equally intrinsic, intangible, and spiritual.

If we'd been living during the early 1800s in either North America or Britain, we'd have surely been conscious of the sea change erupting around us, yet be unable to grasp fully all of its momentous implications. We'd perhaps be aware that a way of life that had flourished for centuries was yielding to quite a different way of life. We'd sense that the best interests of ourselves, our children, and indeed of our nation required us to play some role in that emerging industrial age drama. And many men did in fact play a direct and active role. Middle-class women on the other hand played a much more indirect and supportive role in that drama—the "hand that rocks the cradle rules the world" scenario.

A WOMAN'S OBLIGATIONS TO HERSELF IN THE NEW WORLD OF WORK

We've now launched ourselves into yet another sea change, and the question is this: Can a 21st-century woman afford to play the type of supportive role played by her grandmother and perhaps her mother? Can she afford *not* to play an active role in this new drama? I use *afford* in both its spiritual and material senses. My view is that she (as much as he) is in fact obliged to play an active role. I believe that she has compelling obligations to herself, her child (if any), her partner (if any), and her society to do so. Playing an active role implies that the information age woman adopts a stance toward work not unlike that of the agricultural age woman. Among women then and now, work was/is *not* an option. It was/is rather a responsibility or duty to develop her humanity and, just as essential, an opportunity to contribute.

The contemporary woman need not be a believer to feel the compelling logic of Jesus' words: "You should love your neighbor *as yourself.*" For some 150 years women were encouraged to disregard the equation that Jesus made between loving one's self and one's neighbor. They were taught instead to believe that "my child is the neighbor that I love *more* than myself."[45] For those women, being a mother was something far more profound than merely playing a role such as an actor might do in a play. Being a mother was rather "who I am, it is my *identity*— it lies at the core of my being." A contemporary gender model does not ask a woman to relinquish that identity. More precisely, she is being asked to consider the idea that the core of her being is able to incorporate more than one identity:

"I am both a mother *and* a problem solver: I love my child as much as (but not more than) I love myself."

In effect, productive or paid work in the information age is one crucial means of expressing her love for herself—a way of conveying one core identity of her being. Seen in this light, the notion that there is a built-in conflict between work supplying spiritual rewards and children becomes rather moot. Children do indeed offer a high degree of intrinsic or spiritual rewards. But mind-tech work likewise offers a high degree of intrinsic or spiritual rewards. Hence, the actual lifestyle choice is not materialism versus children. The infinitely more complex and typically agonizing choice pivots, more accurately, around competing sets of equally powerful spiritual satisfactions.

The midlife, mid-level manager I cited earlier told me, "I *love* what I do." (She is, incidentally, a married mother of school-age children. She had been a solo-mother for several years.) "And what do you do?" I asked. As she described the specific details of her daily round of activities I asked if, in effect, she and her team of colleagues spend their day together solving problems. "Yes," was her instant response. It is clear that loving what she does is one vital means of expressing her love for herself. She is reaping the rewards that spring from engaging in the processes of rigorous and creative thinking, and also from their outcome—effective problem solving. And from that flow ample material rewards giving rise to her sense of independence, respect, and autonomy.

If mind-tech occupations such as hers represent the future of work in the new century then we must, at the very least, entertain grave doubts about women's 19th- and 20th-century option *not* to work. In fact, one could say that, among many women below the upper-middle-class, the phasing out of their option began some time ago. Today, their option not to work exists chiefly in name only. For solo-mothers, the option does not exist at all. In effect, we must wonder if women's 150-year-old option may be giving way to the woman's obligation to carve out her distinctive identity as problem solver. We must ask if the contemporary woman from every social class, and every racial/ethnic group, does not owe it to herself to develop her talents and abilities as much as she possibly can, and thus to harvest the intrinsic abundance supplied via her mind-tech alliance.

Alongside the woman's obligation to cultivate her identity as problem solver is her obligation to cultivate still another identity: "I am an economically self-sufficient person." During the agricultural age, extended families sought material resources so they could be economically independent from other extended families—their larger community. Self-sufficiency was the surest means to get control over their destiny, thereby building their self-respect and gaining the good opinion of others. Next, during the industrial age, the goal of self-sufficiency remained constant but the players shifted. Nuclear families sought economic independence from kin and non-kin alike so they could be free from their unwanted control. As the designated provider, the husband was expected to earn enough money to enable his family to be self-sufficient and thus free from influence by kin and other outsiders.

As we evolve now into the information age, the goal of independence remains constant, but the players shift once again. Today, it is the woman's turn to seek economic self-sufficiency so that she can be free from the ultimate authority and control of her partner (husband, cohabiter). At the core of his being, the 20th-century man sought an occupation that might, among other things, permit him to be economically independent: He wanted to be able to feel that "because I am self-sufficient I am—at least to some degree—in charge of my own destiny." Excluding women from paid labor meant that men monopolized direct access to money and the sense of control over one's destiny that money fosters. And, owing to their self-sufficiency, men enjoyed unique entrée into the world of respect—from others and for themselves.

Though it may seem cheerless and perhaps unloving to suggest that a woman should view herself as economically self-sufficient vis-à-vis the man she loves, consider what we just said. Her partner (husband, cohabiter) almost surely views himself as being economically independent vis-à-vis the woman he loves. Claiming independence for herself would clearly make her no less loving than he. Cultivating self-sufficiency is a never-ending process that begins in boyhood or girlhood and extends throughout one's lifetime—regardless of whether one is currently partnered or not. For a boy or man, being partnered has always been entirely irrelevant to self-sufficiency—this is who he is, period! It is both indispensable and indisputable that self-sufficiency should now take root just as solidly among girls and women. Up through the 1950s, the typical woman's definition of a good match was marrying a man who would support her till death. Today, no relationship (legal or otherwise) can guarantee that level of certainty. Hence, quite apart from the spiritual satisfactions that flow from self-sufficiency is the built-in uncertainty of today's relationships in general—to say nothing of the lasting economic uncertainties stemming from the post-2008/2009 economy.

The woman's next obligation to herself is to cultivate her identity as an autonomous person. Foundational to that identity is the identity of problem solver and of being self-sufficient. An autonomous woman perceives that whatever her talents and abilities, they're being utilized and developed to the fullest extent possible: she's pursuing the kinds of mind-tech occupations that draw on and hone the full range of her abilities. Accordingly, she sees herself as being in charge or in control of that vital dimension of her life. She has the sense that,

"I'm not hindered from developing into all that I can possibly be—I am instead a growing human being."

If supporting herself and any dependents is the marker of a self-sufficient woman, is there any marker that might help us identify an autonomous woman? Until the 1970s, both state laws and tradition required a woman to adopt her husband's name at marriage. But during that decade, laws mandating the bride to relinquish her surname were gradually set aside. Despite their freedom to do otherwise, research showed that the majority of brides still took their husband's name.[46] Even so, throughout the 1980s there were increases in the percentage of brides who retained their surnames. More recently, however, that percentage has declined.

My experience during the 1970s and 1980s was that many of the women students in my college classes reported that they would *not* give up their surname at marriage. But today, most of the women and men in my classes say, "It's no big deal—who cares one way or the other? It's simply a matter of personal choice." In response, I suggest that if it were based merely on random choice, then we might expect that at least 50 percent of brides would keep their surname. I also suggest that one reason the tradition of taking the male's name persists is because many Americans believe that family unity is embodied by having one surname, and custom dictates it should be the husband's.

Recent research also reveals that women who marry later in life are more likely to retain their surname.[47] Many of those women had graduated from college, and had spent several years getting established in a career or profession where they were known by their own surname. Giving up the name to which their reputation was linked would have been, they reasoned, a setback to their career.

Not everyone would agree that retaining her surname is a useful marker by which to identify an autonomous woman. Some might argue that it's possible for her to be self-sufficient, and to cultivate her full array of talents, and still take on the man's name. It seems to me, however, that unless and until we start talking seriously about a man being just as likely as a woman to assume the spouse's name, the unspoken issue remains a big deal. At the very least, prior to the wedding she might raise the issue with him as a point for discussion. If it turns out they both feel it makes no difference whether or not she takes his name, or whether he takes hers, or whether they invent a new name they both use, then so be it. Their consensus has *not* reduced her sense that she is charge of her own life. To the contrary, their discussion is likely to have reinforced her sense of control.

But if, on the other hand, their conversation reveals that she does want to retain her family name but he believes she should take his, then serious negotiations are called for along the lines I describe below. If she feels strongly that retaining her name is a marker of her autonomy, then he will have to come up with some sort of compromise that they both can live with. The worst possible outcome would be one in which she reluctantly agrees to take his name, yet resents doing so, and thus feels that her sense of control is being undermined. She now feels less in charge of her life—less autonomous—than she did prior to their discussions.

Finally, let's consider one more identity that the 21st-century woman would be obliged to cultivate—the identity of contributor. One reason why today's woman should consider relinquishing her 20th-century option not to engage in paid labor turns on her obligation to serve persons beyond her private household. Recall that such service is often described as one's contributions to the *public* household. Margaret Mead believed that many 20th-century women were cheated out of the spiritual wealth that was their rightful due: not only were they denied a sense of autonomy, they were kept from making important contributions to society. As a result, children, men, and women around the globe were the poorer for it. Everyone was deprived of the contributions that many women were never able to make. Owing to 19th- and 20th-century models of gender, the public household was shorn of the full range of benefits that might have accrued to it via the women's skills, talents, and problem-solving capabilities. And women themselves lost out on the spiritual satisfactions of service to others.

Every schoolchild knows the inspiring story of Marie Curie—the first woman to receive the Nobel Prize in physics. That happened in 1903 and her husband Pierre was the co-recipient. He died accidentally soon thereafter and Marie was required to bring up their two young daughters by herself. Notwithstanding, in 1911 that same solo-mother was the sole recipient of her second Nobel Prize—this time in chemistry. Furthermore, not only did Marie contribute to the public household via her own research, her daughter Irene did the same thing. She was co-recipient with her husband (Frederick) of the 1935 Nobel Prize in chemistry.

Prior to the 1960s most citizens reckoned that Marie and Irene were the exceptions that proved the rule. Most believed that women typically possessed neither the native intelligence nor the skills necessary to compete with white men when it comes to serving the greater good. Mead argued to the contrary that in fact women do possess the requisite equipment—they simply require the chances to show it. Since that time opportunities for middle-class women have expanded greatly and they've proven Mead and others correct. But much more needs to be done by expanding the opportunities for less advantaged girls and women to contribute to society via their productive labor. A contributor feels deeply the duty to serve people beyond oneself and one's family. A contributor wants to make a difference in the lives of others: "I want to make the public household better." Hence, this too becomes added to the core of the woman's being: "I am a problem solver, self-sufficient, autonomous, and a *contributor*."

The ideal of serving others via one's productive labor was readily understood when almost everyone was engaged either in producing food that kept citizens alive or worked at jobs that enhanced food production. But once the transition was made into the industrial world the distances between work and serving the public household seemed to get wider all the time. The dots were especially hard to connect within business and commerce where the goal was to outwit one's competitor, and not to think of him as a neighbor that one was obliged to love and serve. In some cases, however, the links between work and service were more apparent. Examples included research, art, medicine, nursing, social work, clergy, firefighting, education, and others.

And today, as the world of work grows increasingly shaped by the mind-tech alliance, how does a woman (or man) express her (or his) identity as a contributor? (Needless to say, it is just as essential for men as it is for women to grow that very same identity.) While doing a mind-tech occupation, how does she (or he) make a difference in the lives of others—how does she (or he) help make life better? How do they get to enjoy the spiritual satisfactions that flow from serving others? Within the new century, youth will undoubtedly start experimenting with innovative ways to discharge their duty to serve the public household. One example of a previously nonexistent option is called *conservation professional* and is described in *Saving the Earth as a Career*.[48] Another example is men who, according to Ruth Simpson, do "gender differently" by entering "caring occupations."[49]

But regardless of the job title, the point is that every person's identity as contributor compels her or him to try to serve others in some manner. A man or a woman alike would be uncomfortable in a job situation that does not help cultivate problem-solving capabilities. She or he would be equally unnerved if their work was not enabling them to be self-sufficient, earn respect, and be autonomous. Similarly, it would be just as distressing to be in a job situation where she or he is unable to make some sort of difference.

MEN AND WOMEN AS PROBLEM-SOLVERS TOGETHER

Deep-seated social changes almost always take lots of time. But temporary swings in society—even if quite dramatic—can appear and disappear rather quickly. During World War II, for instance, millions of women (including many mothers) streamed almost overnight into defense plants (operating 24/7) doing

well-paid manual labor that was physically demanding, dirty, and often dangerous. But by 1945 the war was winding down and Rosie the Riveter was speedily
pushed out of the factories to make room for returning male veterans eager to
claim her job.[50]

The main reason it was so simple to eject Rosie was that the radical gender
roles invented a hundred years earlier had, by the mid-20th century, become
deeply entrenched in American society. Since the 1960s, trying to discard those
entrenched roles has required a great deal of energy and effort. One reason the
task been so difficult is christianist resistance to change. Another is that most,
though not all, of the energy aimed at getting past those entrenched roles has
been generated by women. But there are (mixed) signals that increasing numbers of men might also be getting serious about directing their energies toward
that same end.

A 2007 national conference of social science researchers concluded that recent studies in the United States and Europe provide evidence for what they
called a male helping-out pattern. The experts found that a certain degree of con-
vergence now exists between the genders regarding their attitudes about work
and children.[51] Nonetheless, despite what men *say* about fatherhood, the researchers also reported that most mothers continue to operate as the senior or
chief parent. She is the one who in the final analysis is ultimately responsible for
the child. Most women aim to cultivate the *identity* (this is who I am) of mother.
Most men, on the other hand, are content to play the *role* (these are simply the
things I do) of father. Most men continue to operate as the junior or assistant
parent, namely, the one who merely helps out the chief or head parent.

The researchers seemed dismayed by their findings that most mothers continue to be more involved than most fathers in the everyday lives of their children.
Many men, they say, remain stuck in the groove of simply playing a role rather
than cultivating the more profound identity of father. As one of the researchers
put it, "There is a limit to how much women's employment can continue to increase unless . . . men take up the slack."[52] Steiner offers a vivid contrast between
the *role* of father and the *identity* of mother:

> When kids come, [husbands'] lives don't change as much [as wives']. When my
> husband goes on a business trip, he just packs his suitcase. When I go away, I
> have to write a three-page memo for the nanny. I have to find three moms to
> pick up my kids from school. I have to tell the school to call my husband in case
> of an emergency. And I have to tell my husband to keep his cell phone on.[53]

Despite that grim scenario, there are hints of gradual evolutionary change.
Judith Warner interviewed mothers while preparing her 2005 book about to-

day's gender shifts. But when she asked her editors if she might also interview fathers she was told that no one would buy that book.[54] Hence, she excluded men from her study. But following the book's publication she says that "many men . . . reproached me for not having included fathers in it." The essence of their complaints is summed up by one father who told her: "*Don't shut us down with stereotypes. Some of us are living the same life as you—and we are capable of talking about it.*"[55] And as they reprimanded her, she came across a raft of new books about men struggling to get beyond the role of father and evolve into the deeper level of identity. She called it "Dad-Lit."

The message Warner gleaned from Dad-Lit is that "fatherhood wasn't at all a journey into some dark continent of maleness. Instead, time and again, I found myself." She adds that "What I wasn't prepared for . . . was the depth of the emotional connection I felt with these men. I wasn't prepared to find myself crying." She believes that Dad-Lit reveals something that up to now has been relatively rare: some men are in fact battling very hard to get beyond the mere *role* of father and to cultivate instead the much more profound *identity* of father.

In practical terms, those men are responding to Steiner's complaint that when children come the father's life does not change as much as the mother's life. Warner suggests that in some families, the father's life is in fact changing as much as the mother's life: "We are having the same life as you," some men told Warner. The Dad-Lit authors, she reports, "all rejected traditional fatherhood to become, in a certain sense, 'moms.'"

Although late 20th-century advocates encouraged men to participate as fully as women in the life of children, no one ever seriously confronted their option *not* to do so. Even today, MomsRising "says they will include the fathers later" in their efforts to help alleviate the travails of today's working mothers.[56] The mantra that women's and men's issues should be addressed in sequence (women first, men second) has been on the table since the 1960s. But as we evolve into the 21st-century information age, a contemporary gender model suggests that just as women are losing the option *not* to cultivate the identity of problem-solver in the workplace, men are at the same time losing the option *not* to cultivate the identity of father in the homeplace. Their 19th-century option is gradually being phased out.

Cultivating his father-identity begins for a man by facing several questions.[57] One, is he willing to commit himself to participate as actively as the mother in the everyday life of his child? Two, is he prepared to commit himself to ongoing problem solving with his partner regarding the specific details of his active participation? Three, does he understand that effective problem solving requires his commitment to the principle that *everything is negotiable except the principle that everything is negotiable*? In effect, all the details of his active participation both in the life of his child as well as in his job are now open for discussion and problem solving except the general rule that everything is now on the table. The man is more likely to respond yes to all three questions if he and she alike bury any remaining residue of the true womanhood cult. It was as unfair to him as it was to her—it discriminated against him no less than her. By relegating him to pursuit of the dollar, the cult rendered him a second-class citizen within the world of children. In order to enter fully into that world, he is now being asked to learn to love his neighbors—his partner and his child—as much as he loves himself.

Loving his partner starts by appreciating the subtle shifts already in play. For instance, up to now the case for the man being the less active parent than the woman was often couched in financial terms. Because he typically had greater earning power than she, it made economic sense for him merely to be the supportive parent and simply help out with their children. By default, he became the junior-parent to her as the senior-parent. But that old-fashioned idea has finally run out of steam. First, we now know that prior to motherhood many of today's younger women earn as much as or even more money than many younger men. Thus, the old economic sense argument no longer makes any sense at all.

An additional twist on that worn-out financial argument was demonstrated in very harsh terms during the 2008/2009 economic downturn: U.S. government data showed that as the recession worsened men became more likely than women to lose their jobs. Furthermore, among men and women who lost their jobs, women were more likely than men to find another job sooner—men were more likely to stay unemployed longer. In short, the recession had a greater negative impact on males than it did on women workers. Surprisingly, that negative impact appeared at all educational levels: "It has simply been harder for men to hold onto their jobs."[58]

An even more compelling reason to argue that the old-fashioned financial argument is indefensible is that it ignores entirely the spiritual features of work. Younger men in particular seem to be absorbing the reality that today's women are very serious about cultivating the several identities of problem solver, self-sufficient person, autonomous person, and contributor. Those men appear to sense that today's women are eager to regain what the womanhood cult stole from their foremothers.

Taking the spiritual faces of work into account means that the contemporary man must stretch himself into the core of his partner's being in order to discover and comprehend those several identities—identities that no doubt he himself also possesses. Without question, he values his several identities immensely— they mark who he is. Those identities are the signs of his love for himself. It follows that loving his partner requires him to value and encourage those very same identities in her as much as he does in himself. And that implies that he is prepared to be as active a parent as she so that she can be as active as he within the emerging world of mind-tech work, and thus cultivate those several identities.

Loving his other neighbor—his child—begins with yet another voyage into the core of his partner's being. And this time he discovers within her the identity of parent as expressed by the word *mother*. As he does so, she responds by entering into the core of his being. She demonstrates that she loves him (her neighbor) as much as herself by exploring with him the identity of parent as expressed by the word *father*. The major issue she helps him comprehend is that just as the *identity* of mother is far more powerful than the *role* of mother, the *identity* of father is likewise far more powerful than the *role* of father.

In effect, a contemporary gender model asks the man to dig far beneath the surface level of role in order to adopt and cultivate something much stronger and weightier. He's being asked to add an additional identity to the core of his being—the identity of father. Importantly, he does so in order to express his love for his partner as well as his child. What is more, by cultivating this identity he simultaneously expresses his love for himself. The identity of father, he slowly discovers, is indeed spiritually satisfying. It is as satisfying to him as the identity of mother is to women.

Hence, just as she determines that she cannot afford to miss the action—lose out on what's happening within the information age world of work—he makes up his mind that he cannot afford to miss out on what's happening within the multifaceted world of children. He is no longer content playing the role of supportive or junior parent. This contemporary model of gender rests on a set of firm commitments and expectations: each partner is committed actively to the new world of work. Each partner is likewise committed to participate actively in the everyday life of their child. Similarly, each partner expects the other partner to be committed actively to the new world of work. Moreover, each partner also expects the other partner to be committed to participate actively in the everyday life of their child.

But how feasible is such a model? Is it so rigid and inflexible that it allows no wiggle room for creative tweaking? The answer is, of course, that imagination and fine-tuning permeate the model's DNA. Jazz is a fitting analogy. The musicians operate within a set of clear guidelines and shared objectives. Yet within those parameters they're expected to innovate, or improvise, as creatively and yet as cooperatively as possible. Among couples, the hard work of joint problem solving requires improvisation. The painstaking and often lateral thinking of the mind-tech world are transported into, and become an absolutely essential feature of, this emerging gender world.

Within this new world, couples have the flexibility to negotiate whatever specific arrangements are necessary in order to fulfill their personal goals as well as the expectations that one's partner holds for her or him. Their situation is analogous, say, to nations making a solemn covenant that by the year X they shall reduce CO_2 emissions by so much. Once firmly in place, their shared commitment shapes the nature of their dialogue—it influences which specific proposals they invent, follow, set aside, or modify. Their give and take may on occasion get as heated as the atmosphere they're trying to cool. Their negotiations require each party to be entirely honest as to what it wants, and also completely candid in its assessments of the self-interest of all parties. No party gets all it wants, and each must make certain sacrifices. Hopefully, at some point they can agree on how to proceed in a manner that both partners can live with. We also hope that their negotiations have been civil and satisfying enough so that the door is left open for future bouts of problem solving.

Such complex and intricate processes apply just as much to couples struggling with their shared commitments to work and children as they do to nations grappling with climate change. One major difference is that nations send highly skilled and experienced negotiators to the table. Another is that their negotiators operate as part of a team, never as a solo act. But almost always the woman must deal on her own with her man. Moreover, until quite recently there's been no history or tradition of women asserting themselves vis-à-vis their man. They've not had a great deal of experience at standing up for themselves in ways that are honest, wise, and effective at achieving what they want.

To be sure, women have, for some time, been struggling to create precisely that sort of tradition. Social science research has for several decades shown that employed wives possess greater authority and influence than nonemployed wives vis-à-vis their husbands.[59] The reason is not mysterious. We saw earlier that money is a route to independence and control of one's destiny. It follows that the wife or partner with money is, through trial and error, more likely to figure out how to negotiate more effectively with her spouse or partner than is the woman without money.

Keep in mind that this problem-solving tradition surfaced within the context of the 20th-century gender model in which women retained their option not to work, and men retained theirs not to cultivate the father-identity. But within the aegis of a 21st-century model the flexibility that both options offered has, ideally, been removed. The upshot, however, is not inevitably a stalemate. There may in fact be occasions when one partner of either gender becomes less active than the other in either work or parenting. Although reducing one's activity in either sphere may at times seem feasible, great care must be taken that their long-term commitments to active participation in both work and parenting are not seriously compromised. Within the aegis of the 20th-century model most women were at greater risk than most men of making the sorts of concessions that undermined their access to the material and spiritual satisfactions offered by the world of work. In any case, couples committed to a contemporary model of gender face negotiations that are much more complex and arduous than anything confronting couples in the last century. Given those realities it is clear that the ideal of women's assertiveness that has, up to this time, been more or less implicit and incidental must now be made much more explicit and pivotal.

Specifically, the identity of being an autonomous person ought to be enlarged to include assertiveness as a prerequisite for engaging in effective negotiation and problem solving with her partner. Within the new world of work, she surely views herself as an assertive person who is skilled at careful and creative thinking and effective problem solving. She is well advised to carry that identity and those skills with her into her relationship with any man in her life—whether cohabiter or husband. The protagonist of Tom Wolfe's 2004 novel *I am Charlotte Simmons* is a freshman college student enormously proud of the fact that she is the embodiment of the 21st-century autonomous woman. In practically all her dealings with men, she comes across as a self-assured but fair negotiator. In one regrettable case, however, a popular and powerful frat boy launches an assault that staggers her and forces her into the compliant college girl role. She suffers accordingly but gradually recovers, more determined than ever to be what she truly is—a strong and autonomous woman.

Andrew Sullivan tells us that conservatives tend to be suspicious of any government because of its monopoly of power. More broadly, all of us do well to follow our founders' example and be wary of any entity or person that possesses any sort of hold on power. American history and traditions are marked by the reality that men hold a great deal more power than women: Abigail Adams said out loud that men controlled women but not the other way around. Those traditions are, of course, starting to fray around the edges—especially among better-educated couples. Still, we have a great distance to go before the majority of women within all social classes perceive themselves in the same ways as Charlotte Simmons. It seems reasonable to expect that as more women morph into becoming mind-tech workers, most will gain the experience, confidence, and assertiveness necessary to negotiate effectively and fairly the commitments they share with their partner—their mutual obligations to be active within the worlds of both work and parenting.

Power and physical force often go together, and this has been one major roadblock to establishing a new tradition of effective problem solving between women and men. Because the woman is typically alone while trying to be assertive with her (physically more powerful) partner, the customary public restraints on his anger, frustration, and violence are absent. Oddly enough, our media and politicians sensationalize women being attacked by a stranger, but give much less notice to an assault by her partner. That is totally bizarre because women are many times more likely to be assaulted or killed by the men they love (or loved) than by a stranger.[60] Needless to say, coercion and violence undermine creative improvisation; hence, force has no place whatever within the aegis of a contemporary gender model.

GENDER IDENTITIES AND ECONOMIC DISADVANTAGE

Lasting social change almost always starts among more advantaged persons. Here and in chapter 1 we saw that in the 19th century the husband-provider marriage was launched among the middle classes. Chapter 2 showed that the upper and middle classes were the first to initiate widespread use of effective contraceptives to limit family size, thus adding to their economic advantage. The same sort of thing is happening today. As the numbers of mind-tech jobs expand, they tend be filled mostly by women and men who come from advantaged backgrounds to begin with. At the same time those persons are also the ones most likely to experiment with innovative ways to craft a partnership (marriage, cohabitation) based on a model of gender identities that make sense for the 21st-century information age. They're trying very hard to forge some sort of match or fit between the new world of work and the new world of gender.

Everyone agrees that a major public policy issue facing the United States (and other Western nations) today is how to enable less advantaged women and men to participate in the new world of work. That issue takes on particular urgency in light of the fact that many skilled and semiskilled jobs are either vanishing or being severely scaled back. And, though unskilled service jobs are expanding, they supply little in the way of material benefits or spiritual satisfactions. It goes without saying that policy initiatives to narrow the widening economic gap between the well-off and the less well-off must proceed on several fronts, one of which is serious attention to the public schools as described in Chapter 6. American children and youth—including the less advantaged—must have the types of educational opportunities that cultivate the problem-solving skills requisite for the mind-tech jobs of the new century.[61]

More controversial is the notion that just as less advantaged persons should prepare themselves for work whose essence is problem solving, they should likewise be urged to prepare themselves for partnerships that at their core also demand problem solving. There is very little fit or match between the husband-provider marriage—or even the typical two-earner marriage—and the postindustrial era. Hence, continued reliance on either of those types of partnerships is fraught with numerous perils—especially for less advantaged persons. There is simply too much at stake—too great a danger of men and women alike losing out when it comes to both material and spiritual rewards. Accordingly, as I see it, policy initiatives should encourage youth and adults at all social class levels to embrace the challenge of forging some sort of innovative match between the new world of work and the new world of gender.

> What would Jesus do? Tom Davis, president of Children's HopeChest, says the Bible makes it clear: He'd feed the hungry, clothe the naked, and tell us to do the same.[62]

Davis is among those younger evangelicals described throughout the book as wanting to escape the christianist straightjacket by joining with liberals to feed the hungry and clothe the naked. While evangelicals have no problem helping economically disadvantaged persons after the fact, they tend to concentrate much less on how to address the issue of disadvantage *before the fact*. As far as I can tell, empowering less advantaged youth and adults to achieve economic self-sufficiency has never been one of their foremost policy goals. Specifically, it is not at all certain that most evangelicals would react positively to a contemporary model of gender—even though it would likely contribute to the material and spiritual well-being of less advantaged persons.

Based on her recent study at Patrick Henry College (PHC), Hanna Rosin makes it quite clear that even educated evangelicals are of two minds on the subject of gender. On one side, they want to escape the oppressive, harsh, patriarchal images of marriage that prevailed in the United States pre-1960s:

> [Evangelicals] tried to rewrite the roles a little bit, so that men's roles became more feminized. . . . Men were supposed to be more expressive and value friendship. . . . Men were supposed to be a different kind of husband and take their wife out—not the distant patriarch of the 1950s.[63]

Despite their desire for equity, Rosin notes that evangelicals still hold fast to "traditional male-female roles; men are supposed to do one thing, and women are supposed to do another thing." She adds that the Patrick Henry College students she interviewed "are deeply conflicted about women's roles, but still, they really do understand that a woman's role is to raise her children. No matter how ambitious she's been, how high she's risen in the White House, eventually she's going to raise her children." Rosin says that before marriage, evangelical couples "create what looks on paper to be a perfectly realized equal marriage." Nevertheless, after their wedding "the [actual] result is going to be the same" as it was pre-1960s: "The woman is going to quit whatever job she has, and she is going to raise their children." Needless to say, evangelicals have the right to preserve for themselves their ideal (husband-provider) marriage—despite its spiritual (and material) costs to men and women alike.

However, in light of their recent statements about alleviating the material needs of less advantaged citizens, it is fair to pose several questions. For instance, would evangelicals support a 21st-century model of gender if it can be shown to enhance the economic self-sufficiency of less advantaged Americans? Would they be willing to set aside their fervent endorsement of the husband-provider marriage? Most of all, would evangelicals support an image of womanhood along the lines of the *Charlotte Simmons* character? Recall that Charlotte (who grew up in a rural, working-class home in the mountains of North Carolina) was strong, assertive, and autonomous. And, would they endorse an image of manhood along the lines of the men described by Judith Warner—men struggling to craft the identity of father? Psychologist Stephen Ducat says that evangelical men are terrified by what he calls the "wimp factor."[64] They fear that if they're not forceful, and/or if they appear too nurturing, they'll be thought of as weak and not strong—they'll be seen as a wimp. Hence, could evangelicals ever get past such irrational fears and instead accept a model of manhood that at its core embraces nurturance, flexibility, and cooperation?

Finally, could evangelicals ever come to terms with the reality that the normal family of the mid-20th century is being replaced inescapably with new and very different kinds of families? Or, even if they could not bring themselves to acknowledge one of history's unstoppable trends, would they be willing at least to sit on their hands? Given that the emerging changes in gender identities and behaviors are likely to benefit less advantaged women and men, might they refrain from mounting political opposition against them?

Some younger evangelicals might perhaps adopt that passive political stance. Others, however, might succumb to the christianist mindset and advocate legislation that shores up the husband-provider family while opposing legislation aimed at crafting contemporary families. One such christianist is Allan Carlson (president of the Howard Center for Family, Religion and Society in Rockford, Illinois). In 2006, he wrote that "at the level of net incomes, the one-earner family today is worse off than it was 30 years ago, when the G.O.P. began to claim the pro-family banner."[65] He grumbles that advocates for the husband-provider household

> *have little to show from the years of the Republican alliance. Indeed, the G.O.P. has done absolutely nothing to curb the egalitarian frenzy and the gender-role engineering set off by Title VII of the Civil Rights Act and Title IX of the Education Amendments of 1972 and enshrined at the Pentagon. Equity feminism still rules these roosts.*

It seems to me that Carlson expresses the deepest sentiments—the bedrock feelings—of many evangelicals and virtually all christianists. They yearn for the days of the husband-provider household with the father assuming his rightful place as the head of the family. They crave that tradition even though many evangelical and christianist families themselves cannot afford the luxury of the man as sole earner. Hence, they would dearly love to see the sorts of legislation Carlson proposes—federal and state programs that would make it more affordable for mothers to stay home with their children.

Nonetheless, given that evangelicals are, as Rosin observes, of two minds about gender, it is possible that ultimately the better angels of their nature shall one day prevail. I take them at their word when they express their anxieties over the plight of citizens who are economically less well off. Hence, it may be that given enough time, at least some younger evangelicals will eventually join with most other citizens to explore and implement a contemporary gender model among both disadvantaged and advantaged persons alike.

NOTES

1. Gitlin 1993.
2. Lindsey 2007.
3. Scanzoni 1973.
4. Gerth and Mills 1958:267ff.
5. Dillon 2008.
6. Rosin 2007; Pew Research Center October 11, 2007, "Evangelicals and the Public Square," www.pewforum.org.
7. Martin 1996:231.
8. Miles 1988; Wall 1990; Strasser 1982; Mintz and Kellogg 1988; Coontz 2005; Fairchilds 2007; Sharpe 1998.
9. Proverbs 31:10ff, KJV.
10. Coontz 2005:6.
11. Miles 1988:140 italics added.
12. Thomas 1981:xiii.

13. Alston 1995; Sharpe 1998; Osterud 1991.

14. Wood 1992.

15. James 2006

16. Parsons 1965.

17. Sharpe 1998; Osterud 1991; Horrell and Humphries 1998.

18. Mohler 2000.

19. See http://chattahbox.com/us/2009/07/20/jimmy-carter-leaves-southern-baptist-church-for-repugnant-sexism/.

20. Erzen 2000.

21. Manu Raju, John Bresnahan, Alexander Burns, 2009. *Politico,* June 16, 2008, viewed online at politico.com.

22. Lindsey 2007.

23. See Scanzoni 1972 for a review of these advocates.

24. Mead 1967:875.

25. Cites are from Welter 1978:325–26.

26. Pew Research Center, July 12, 2007, "Fewer Mothers Prefer Full-time Work—from 1997 to 2007," http://pewresearch.org/pubs/536/working-women.

27. Jesella 2007. See also Correll et al., 2007.

28. Leonhardt 2006.

29. Roberts with Maldonado 2007b.

30. Jesella 2007; Blades and Rowe-Finkbeiner, 2006.

31. Hirshman 2006.

32. See mommysavers.com/stay-at-home-moms.

33. Warner 2007. She writes: "Neal Pollack's *Alternadad* has already gotten considerable press, though more as a hipster manifesto than as a dad memoir, which is perhaps too bad. The next month or so brings two more father confessionals: Philip Lerman's *Dadditude: How a Real Man Became a Real Dad* and Cameron Stracher's *Dinner with Dad: How I Found My Way Back to the Family Table.* (And then, aiming at making sense of it all, there's psychoanalyst Michael J. Diamond's *My Father before Me: How Fathers and Sons Influence Each Other Throughout Their Lives.*)"

34. Graff 2007.

35. Goldin 2006.

36. Warner 2009. And see Greenhouse 2009.

37. Hirshman 2005, 2006.

38. Steiner 2006.

39. Bennetts 2007.

40. Hertz 2006.

41. Sullivan 2006.

42. Peter Drucker, "Beyond the Information Revolution," in *The Atlantic Online,* published October 1999, http://www.theatlantic.com/issues/99oct/9910drucker.htm.

43. Kenworthy 2008; Herbert 2008.

44. Burke and Stets 2009.

45. Horrell and Humphries 1998.

46. Goldin and Shim 2004.

47. Johnson and Scheuble 1995.

48. Hunter et al., 2007.

49. Simpson 2009.

50. Andersen 1981.

51. Cohen, Patricia 2007.

52. Cohen, Patricia 2007.

53. Steiner, as cited in "Covering the Mommy Wars," *Business Week*, March 13, 2006, p. 92. Her book is cited in my bibliography.

54. Cited from Warner 2007.

55. Warner 2007, italics in original.

56. Jesella 2007.

57. Deutsch 1999; Dermott 2008.

58. Norris 2009.

59. Scanzoni 2000.

60. Gelles 1977; Scanzoni 2000.

61. Blank 1997; Sizer 2005; Scanzoni 2005.

62. http://www.beliefnet.com/gallery/HowtoDoWhattheBibleSays.html, July 17, 2008.

63. This and the quotations that follow are comments Rosin made at a forum sponsored by the Pew Research Center on October 11, 2007, "Evangelicals and the Public Square," www.pewforum.org. Her book is cited in my references. See also Scanzoni (1979)—a book addressed primarily to evangelicals.

64. Ducat 2004.

65. Taken from *The Weekly Standard* (March 27, 2006) and reported by the *New York Times* (March 26, 2006).

Human Sexuality: From Taboo to Celebration

Bless me, father, for I have sinned.

Those are the final words of the closing scene from *Circle of Friends,* a delightful 1995 Irish film. No characters appear in the scene. The voice of Benny (Minnie Driver), the film's protagonist, is heard on the soundtrack. We're standing several hundred yards away from an isolated country cottage illuminated in brilliant sunlight. The prior scene showed Benny leading her boyfriend hand-in-hand into the cottage, and we know at once her words are not those of a grieving penitent. She's not petitioning a celibate priest within the dreary confines of a confessional booth. Her words are instead a tongue-in-cheek cry of sheer joy. Playful and witty, Benny is spoofing an ancient church shibboleth. She's in ecstasy because she's finally demystified the taboo that for so many years imprisoned her sexuality and thus herself.

The film is set in and around Dublin of the late 1950s and captures the anguish that Benny and her equally devout Roman Catholic friends experience as each one navigates a series of perilous transitions: First is their transition from high school to college. Second is their passage from the working class into the middle class. Finally, they're caught up in the evolution of sexuality described in chapter 2. In both Europe and North America, sex in the 1950s was on the way toward disentangling itself from the shadowy underworld of the furtive and the clandestine. Bennie and her friends are becoming convinced that by repressing their sexuality the church has in fact been stifling their humanity. But they don't quite know what to do about it. One by one, the women violate church dogma by having sexual intercourse. Though they're committing a heinous sin they keep on doing *it* anyhow while feeling terribly guilty. All that is, except Benny, who feels no guilt at all. But she doesn't do *it* until she's had an epiphany: She comprehends that for her and her boyfriend of several years, intercourse is no sin at all. It is rather a cause for exultation.

While watching the film, I felt keenly the women's angst. I was in Bible college around the same time as the film, and "Which is the worst sin of all?" was a recurring question for our late night bull sessions. After a long period of heated deliberation, it usually came down to this: "Is taking human life a greater evil than fornication, adultery, and homosexuality, or are sexual sins more reprehensible than killing?" The Bible talks about both sex and killing and we were hardpressed to argue which was the greater abomination. Most of us reasoned that sexual sins are probably the greater menace because the Christian churches have never officially sanctioned either fornication or adultery for any reason whatsoever. Sexual sins, we thought, must somehow be more degrading and monstrous. It seemed reasonable to assume that within the vast catalog of sins, those tagged "sexual" are indeed the vilest. Growing up in evangelicalism imbues one with an overwhelming sense of repugnance, loathing, and revulsion for sexual sins— negative feelings far more intense than for any of the other seven deadly sins.[1] Deep in his gut each of us was gripped by the intense conviction that sexual transgressions are truly an unspeakable abomination, and we were utterly terrified by them.[2]

In contrast to the iron law of "no official exceptions for sex," the Roman Catholic Church taught that God sanctioned the killing of Muslims during the Crusades, and also the killing of heretical Catholics and of Jews during the Inquisition. Protestants and Catholics alike killed one another in the name of God during their holy wars. Europeans also invoked God's name to permit the destruction of Africans and the extermination of Native Americans. Today, most (not all) evangelicals endorse killings in war and by state execution—to say nothing of those christianists who either approve or do not condemn the killing of abortion providers.[3] During a recent class discussion a student captured the grim irony by asking, "Why do many Christians believe that a soldier sleeping with a prostitute commits a gross sin, but when he leaves her bed the next morning to kill people, he's guiltless?"

When today's christianists cry out that our culture has stumbled into a "moral cesspool," they refer not to drive-by shootings of children at play or to state executions of innocent persons but to Americans' violations of sexual taboos. Their revulsion over sexual sins leads them to conclude that "America is no longer good. Unrighteousness, evil, corruption, perversion [permeate the United States]. If we do not put an end to it now . . . then God will and should judge America."[4] Those comments were made at a 2006 christianist conference in which, among other things, homosexual behaviors were the chief target of their bile. Although the conference speakers expressed genuine disgust for heterosexual violations, homosexuals made them feel specially enraged and furious—bordering on the apoplectic. "Love the sinner, but hate the sin," the preachers told us. And the hatred was and is never more fanatical than when the sin is sexual—hetero or homo. I said earlier that christianists are driven by a gene for theocracy—the view that government must act on behalf of the devout to impose the will of the divine on the doubters. And nowhere is their fervor to coerce doubters any more obvious than it is with regard to sexuality. Indeed, some have argued that at its core the religious right (RR) is all about controlling people's sexuality.[5] Delete sex from the picture and RR goes limp and flaccid.

WHEN IS SEX RIGHT OR WRONG?

Chapter 2 closed with christianists from the 1960s and 1970s mounting a counterrevolution against the long-term evolution of sexuality—and they're still at it. Their successful battle against the Equal Rights Amendment (ERA) was a major front in the christianist war. Among other evils ERA would, they implied, have marked the triumph of sexual license over sexual restraint. They feared that "the traditional Christian teaching that sex should be kept for [heterosexual] marriage" would be forever consigned to the dumpster of history.[6] In its place a new teaching, value, or belief would reign supreme, namely, that there are no sexual boundaries or restraints—*if it feels good do it.*

Needless to say, ERA was *never* about sexual license. It was instead an umbrella that covered several themes—one of which was the value of and belief in sexual responsibility. Recall that in the early 1960s public opinion polls showed that "most parents were in favor of school-based programs to help prepare their children for *responsible* sexual behavior in the changing social climate."[7] Recall too that Margaret Mead asserted that liberals failed to build responsibility into the sexual freedoms they were advocating.[8] Freedom, innovation, and change are liberal ideals and Mead endorsed them strongly. But she added that responsibility, self-discipline, and social order (conservative ideals) should be combined with them to help craft what I'm calling a *progressive* approach to sexuality.

The christianist approach is very different indeed. The religious right believes that the morality of sex stems from something existing outside of human beings, namely, the social situation of marriage: sex bounded by that sacred setting is right or moral; sex beyond it is wrong or immoral—*taboo.* However, researchers recently studied the sexual views and behaviors of persons in their twenties. They concluded that the hope of some 1960s adults, namely, that youth should learn to do sex in a responsible manner, seems finally to be taking hold. Among today's younger and more advantaged adults, a perspective on sexuality appears to be emerging that contrasts sharply with the christianist view.[9] The evolving view is that the morality of sex springs not from the imprimatur of marriage, but from what the sexual partners themselves do and don't do: sexual morality arises, in short, out of the partners' own behaviors. If they are doing sex in a responsible manner, they are being moral or right—*whether or not they may be married.* Responsibility, or accountability, involves loving one's neighbor (paying close attention to what's best for one's sexual partner) as well as loving (or paying attention to) oneself. But to be *ir*responsible in any way at all means that one or both partners are being immoral or wrong—*whether or not they may be married.* Seen in that light, one might say that the morality of sex rests in part on a conservative ideal—the level of responsibility exercised by the partners.

For over a half century, social scientists have used certain words when asking citizens about sexual morality—words compatible with the christianist view that the social situation shapes what is right or wrong. As recently as 2007 the Pew Center asked Americans whether a man and woman having sex before marriage is "*wrong* always, almost always *wrong,* sometimes *wrong,* or not at all *wrong.*" Pew reports that

> *Fewer than four-in-ten American adults (38%) now say that sexual relations between a man and woman before marriage is always or almost always wrong compared with nearly six in ten (59%) who say that it is only sometimes or never wrong.*[10]

It is plain enough why mid-20th-century researchers used the term *wrong* instead of *right* to describe nonmarried sex. When researchers started looking into Americans' sexual lives, most viewed sex outside of marriage as taboo—something *wrong*—dirty, unclean, sullied, and defiled. In effect, the researcher was silently telling the respondent "Just as we know the world is round we know that nonmarital sex is *immoral* or wrong. However, might there perhaps be certain occasions when nonmarital sex is perhaps not *quite* so tainted?" The researcher and respondent shared the same premise: nonmarital sex is taboo, but there may be instances (such as engagement) when it might be okay to do *it* anyhow. Underlying their shared premise was the belief that marriage is the only detergent strong enough to decontaminate sex and make it entirely pure and moral.

Recently, however, I came across a study from the U.S. Centers for Disease Control (CDC) that used the word *right* when asking about nonmarried sex—the first time I'd ever seen that.[11] In 2002, CDC asked U.S. teens (aged 15–19), "Is it all right for unmarried 18-year-olds to have sexual relations if they have strong affection for each other?" Almost two-thirds of the teens agreed or strongly agreed that it is all right, or moral. Interestingly enough, when the teens were asked about "16-year-olds" only about one-third said that sex is all right, or moral. Finally, when asked whether "Any sexual act between two consenting adults is all right" almost three-quarters agreed or strongly agreed that such actions are right or moral.

What this study suggests is that 21st-century researchers and many youths may now operate from a different ideal than the traditional ideal of sex as taboo. Today's researcher is compelled to ask a different set of questions about the sexual activities of all persons—married and unmarried alike. Operating from a progressive point of view, today's researchers are silently saying to citizens: "More and more North Americans and Europeans are developing a vision of sex comparable to Benny's—inherently good, clean and pure, beautiful and healthy. They believe that because sexual pleasure is a gift—whether from God or from nature—it should be enjoyed and celebrated. However, like any good gift (food, for example) sex must be celebrated *responsibly*. All of us are quite aware that what is inherently good is not always good for us. The questions we ask assume that sexual morality is built on a foundation of responsibility and self-discipline. Responsibility requires loving one's neighbor (accountability) as well as loving oneself (integrity). Accordingly, how and when are persons—regardless of marital status—doing sex in a responsible and thus a *moral* manner?"

It seems to me that the teens' responses to the questions in the CDC study, first, about the partners' consent and, second, about the partners' ages revealed that they grasp the reality that accountability is indeed a core element in assessing whether sex is right or not. They comprehend, for instance, that nonconsensual sex is irresponsible and thus could never under any circumstances—including marriage—be right or moral. Alongside coercion, U.S. teens sense that age is another important factor in measuring responsibility: The chances are greater that sex among 16-year-olds would be less responsible (and thus less likely to be right) than it is among 18-year-olds for any number of reasons. One of the most obvious is that a naïve 16-year-old girl is more likely than an older girl to succumb to a boy's insistent persuasion to have sex although she doesn't want to, and/or apart from effective contraception.

It thus follows that sex among 13-year-olds is likely to be less responsible (and thus less likely to be right or moral) than sex among older teens. Recently, several observers have argued that younger teen and preteen girls are being sexualized by advertisers, fashion designers, and the legitimate media, to say nothing of internet porn and the lyrics of some rap music. Motivated by greed, those venues ignore entirely the issues of responsibility and the greater good. They are repeating the same error—equating license with liberty—made by some 1960s youth. A number of psychologists and counselors are responding to this growing challenge by urging parents and other adult figures to connect deeply with preteens and younger teens about sex.[12] Their goal is to figure out what the delicate balance of sexual freedom with personal responsibility might look like for those very young persons. Such conversations would, it seems to me, revolve around what below is called "sexual smarts." Not incidentally, studies suggest that those sorts of daunting conversations are managed more effectively by upper-middle-class parents than by parents who are less advantaged.[13]

In any case, it would have been most enlightening had CDC also asked teens when sex among married couples is "all right." Would more than 90 percent have said it is always all right? Probably so, because few Americans of any age appear to question the tradition that marital sex equals moral sex. But suppose the teens had been asked if sex is all right when the wife does not consent and is thus being coerced. My hunch is that a sizeable chunk would then say the couple's sex is *not* all right—it is not responsible and thus immoral. It seems to me in short that among younger North Americans and Europeans the ideal of responsibility may gradually be replacing the fact of marriage as the key element in assessing the morality of sexuality: One's status (marriage) is far less significant than whether or not one's sexual behavior demonstrates both integrity and accountability.[14]

That said, most citizens of whatever religious or political stripe would not think to quibble with the Bible's assertion that the "marriage bed is undefiled."[15] Unless asked a direct question about, say, coercion of the wife by the husband, most would probably assume that by definition marital sex is moral sex. Until so many people started doing it, the now quaint expression "living in sin" was widely used to describe cohabitation.[16] Citizens believed that, by its very definition, marriage *cannot* be living in sin. Nonetheless, the impregnable wall surrounding the morality of marital sex was finally breached in the 1970s and 1980s as researchers began to tell us about something previously shrouded in darkness: They called it "marital rape."

A "LICENSE TO RAPE"

Their evidence showed that a "number of women are forced into having sexual relations with their husbands through intimidation or physical force. . . . Sexual intercourse was forced on a wife after her husband beat her."[17] At that time state laws did not entertain the outlandish idea that there could even be such a thing as *marital* rape. The result was that until recently the married man had, as researchers put it, a "license to rape."[18] Today, almost all 50 states have grudgingly come round to making rape a crime in the contexts of marriage, cohabitation, or dating. However, most states impose far harsher penalties on rape by strangers than they do on rape by husbands or partners. States also demand a much higher standard of proof of rape from a wife or a partner than they do from a woman who did not know her assailant.

Sex as a man's right and a woman's duty has always been part of the Judeo-Christian tradition and the Western culture it helped to shape. The fact that a woman has married and/or moved in with a man was considered to be legal proof enough of her blanket consent to sex. Researchers believe that the actual frequencies of marital and cohabiting rape are vastly underreported, as is the physical abuse of wives and partners.[19] The reason is plain enough. The wife or partner fears that if she talks to outsiders about her rape and/or physical abuse, her husband or partner would assault her more ferociously than ever.

It appears, in short, that marriage covers up a substantial amount of irresponsible and thus immoral sex. The immorality stems not simply from the sheer injustice of a husband sexually coercing his wife. The wickedness is compounded by any pregnancy that might be caused by her husband's rape—a pregnancy she neither planned nor wanted. Christianists are fond of reminding adolescents that contraception can be dicey. That is no less true for married couples, especially if the wife is not on the pill and the husband refuses to wear a condom and/or the wife does not have time to prepare, say, her diaphragm. When prochoice and antichoice advocates debate whether pregnancy from rape is a sufficient cause for abortion they typically mean *stranger* rape. On the other hand, an antichoice woman who is christianist or evangelical is hardly likely to tell her friends or family that her (unwanted) pregnancy stems from her husband raping her. In any case, it seems safe to conclude that the immorality of marital rape may all too often be compounded by an unwanted pregnancy resulting in an unplanned child or an abortion.

Furthermore, the formula that marital sex equals moral sex requires, at a minimum, that the spouses only ever have sex with one another. But throughout history the reality is that in all cultures the rule of monogamy was imposed far more stringently on the wife than on the husband.[20] Chapter 5 explains why and how the sexual double standard was built into the Judeo-Christian tradition from its very inception. The Old Testament laws touted so fondly by RR imposed far harsher penalties on women's sexual sins than on men's. The adulterous woman was, for example, typically tortured to death by stoning. The adulterous man, on the other hand was, for the most part, simply required to pay a fine to the aggrieved husband or father. One of the best known incidents in Jesus' ministry occurred when religious leaders confronted him dragging a woman they "discovered" *in flagrante delicto*—in the very act of adultery.[21] The leaders reminded Jesus that God's law requires she be stoned to death. Nothing was said, however, about her fellow-adulterer whom they'd allowed to slink home to his wife. The leaders' turn to creep away came when Jesus invited the one "without sin to cast the first stone."

The Bible stories of devout men such as Abraham, Isaac, Jacob, and David are also well known. Less well known are the fascinating stories (though fewer in number) about courageous women of note such as Deborah, Ruth, and Esther. Although each of the cited male figures openly practiced the double standard, King David did it with a vengeance.[22] (Still, his son Solomon exceeded him with 300 wives and a harem of 700 mistresses.) In a most sordid incident, David slept with the wife of one his generals and she got pregnant.[23] In an effort to trick the general into thinking he was the father, David tried to maneuver him into sleeping with her. But he would not, and so David conspired to have the general killed in battle. Nonetheless, St. Paul called David a "man after God's own heart," and the preachers urge us to model our lives after him.[24] Had an Old Testament woman of note slept with as many men as David did with women, it's hard to imagine St. Paul sweeping her transgressions under the rug quite so handily.

Formally, of course, the Christian tradition expected both wife and husband to be monogamous. But informally, traditional cultural values allowed the husband tacit permission to release his "natural, pent-up male urges" with other women including prostitutes.[25] As long as he did so in a discreet manner (causing no undue embarrassment to his family) people looked the other way. Kinsey and other 20th-century researchers used numbers to establish what everyone had known for centuries about the good old days when people were sexually pure. The reality is that during those idyllic times, the vast majority of single men (but far fewer single women) reported they'd had sex before marriage—typically with prostitutes.[26] Moreover, a substantial number of husbands (but far fewer wives) reported they'd had extramarital sex—typically but not always with prostitutes.

Whether or not the wife knew about her husband's sexual escapades—discreet or otherwise—was beside the point. She had no choice but to accept her lot in life as God's will for her—though she should pray for him to repent and change his ways. If not religious, she was told simply to accept life as it is—that's the way men are. Surely, bullying the wife to submit to such gross injustice in the name of God or social custom is blatantly immoral. And, as if that injustice is not sleazy enough in and of itself, his consorts were all too often the source of STDs (typically syphilis and/or gonorrhea, and more recently HIV) that he might in turn pass on to his wife either during rape or consensual sex.

CURRENT HAPPENINGS IN ADOLESCENT SEXUALITY

Chapter 2 showed how the liberal push for sex education in grades kindergarten through 12 during the 1960s helped crystallize what eventually became RR. The liberal policy regarding adolescent sexuality was based on the notion of risk reduction. Adolescents were advised *not* to have intercourse—it was unwise, they were warned, for any number of reasons: "However, if you do have sex you must be prepared. You must protect yourself!" However, liberals seldom raised the underlying issue of the morality of sex.[27] There was little or no attempt to get adolescents to ponder when their intercourse might be either right or wrong. The tacit assumption that nonmarital sex is immoral was seldom examined critically. Instead, liberals adopted a practical strategy. They assumed that because many adolescents would experiment with sex no matter what they were told, common sense required that every effort should be made to avoid pregnancy and/or sexually transmitted diseases (STDs).

During the 1960s, christianists started consigning the liberals' risk-reduction programs to oblivion.[28] After gutting the liberals' programs, RR shoved abstinence-only (AO) programs into the resulting vacuum.[29] Bear in mind that christianists took great care not to sell AO policy to the public on biblical grounds. Instead, abstinence was palmed off as a sure-fire means to guarantee both adolescent health (protection against STDs) and their well-being (freedom from pregnancy). One of several reasons for RR's success was and is that it capitalizes on the ambivalence of adult Americans toward the morality of nonmarital sex. For example, a 2005 Pew Survey of adult Americans showed that "78% favor allowing public schools to provide students with birth control information."[30] However, "nearly as many (76%) believe schools should teach teenagers to abstain from sex until marriage."

On one side, the survey tapped into the traditional taboo that sex is *wrong* until and unless one is married. But at the same time, it tapped into the 20th-century liberal policy of risk reduction, wherein non-marital sex is *not* okay, but if you do it anyhow, you should be protected." Little wonder then that christianists had no difficulty skewering liberal policy on moral grounds. If something is wrong, it is wrong, affirms RR. Why not assert that, like drunk driving, nonmarital sex should never happen? Why not declare risk reduction to be bankrupt public policy with no moral basis whatever, whereas abstinence is an obviously moral public policy? Furthermore, added RR, abstinence has enormous practical benefits as well: it keeps adolescents healthy and free from pregnancies.

In 1986, researcher Peter Scales concluded that among the liberal risk-reduction programs existing at that time few "are successful in reaching their goals, and that the most effective [programs] are often resisted because of the moral-political implications."[31] Twenty years later, researcher Kristin Luker arrived at similar conclusions about the futility of risk-reduction programs:

> *One way of reading the finding that sex education doesn't encourage teenagers to have more sex or to have it sooner is that sex education doesn't affect teenage sexual behavior much at all, for better or for worse. In fact, it is surprisingly difficult to show that sex education programs do in fact increase teenagers' willingness to protect themselves from pregnancy and/or disease.*[32]

Next, scrutinizing the other side, Luker concluded that "Evaluation of abstinence-only courses to date shows little clear evidence that they affect teen sexual behavior. . . . No evaluation so far shows that students have changed their *behavior* in any significant ways."[33] Though well aware of that common-sense conclusion, the U.S. Congress (under George W. Bush) nonetheless caved to christianist demands to spend some $176 million annually on AO programs.

To cover its folly, Congress also mandated a very sophisticated evaluation of AO programs that eventually discovered—much to RR's chagrin—the same things as Luker: "Students who participated in sexual abstinence programs were just as likely to have sex a few years later as those who did not. . . . Also [they] reported having similar numbers of sexual partners as those who did not attend the classes, and they first had sex at about the same age . . . 14 years and nine months."[34] A separate and equally sophisticated study aimed at discovering if AO programs helped to prevent HIV/AIDS. They do not. AO programs neither increased nor decreased risky sexual behavior: "None of the abstinence-only programs made any significant difference in preventing pregnancy, reducing unprotected sex, or delaying sexual initiation."[35]

Meanwhile, as christianists and liberals fight over their respective—and equally flawed—strategies, something else is going on underneath the radar. It seems to me that some adolescents and older youth (particularly those in the upper middle class) are quietly forging yet a third approach to sexuality that is neither liberal nor christianist. It is rather a progressive position that blends emerging freedoms with the conservative ideal of responsibility.[36] We saw hints of their third way strategy earlier when we learned that today's teens and youth apparently believe that sex is right or moral if it is done in a *responsible* manner. They seem to be fashioning a progressive position that turns out to be quite similar to what their European peers have been devising for some time.[37] Their emerging approach to sexuality—which is still very much a work in progress— can also be inferred, in part, from several recent and interrelated trends in U.S. adolescent sexual behaviors.

TEENS HAVING SEX: A PLATEAU

One trend has to do the percentage of teens who report they've ever had sexual (vaginal) intercourse. Between the late 1960s and the late 1980s the rate for girls doubled—"from roughly 17 percent to 40 percent of all 17 year olds."[38] And, between 1979 and 1988, the numbers of boys who reported intercourse "jumped from two-thirds to three-quarters." But since that time, says Luker, the rates of intercourse for 17-year-old girls (40%) and boys (75%) have flattened out and stayed pretty much the same. Recent national studies suggest that the percentages of adolescents actually having intercourse may perhaps be dropping slightly—especially among younger aged teens.[39]

TEENS USING CONTRACEPTIVES: AN UPWARD SLOPE

A second and highly significant trend has to do with increases in contraceptive use over time. The percentage of sexually active boys who report using condoms while having intercourse rose from around 50% to around 70% over the past 20 years.[40] Likewise, the percentage of girls who report their sexual partners used condoms also rose from 50 to 70 percent. A more recent study of U.S. teens reports "dramatic improvements in contraceptive use between 1995 and 2002."[41] Not only are growing numbers of teens using either condoms or the pill, more of them are using some combination of methods. The most typical combination is using the pill or other hormonal methods (to reduce the risk of pregnancy) as well as using the condom—to reduce the risk of STDs as well as pregnancy.

Some experts highlight the recent studies showing that some boys and young men are now willing to use condoms. Perhaps, say the experts, some males may be evolving away from the stereotypical image of the reckless male as voracious sexual predator.[42] It may be that some males are increasingly aware that a pregnancy and/or STD may in fact spin their own and/or their partner's life totally out of control. In short, while the percentages of sexually active teens have leveled off, those who are sexually active appear to demonstrate a greater degree of cleverness and expertise than did earlier sexually active adolescents. Compared with yesterday's sexually active teens, many of today's active teens seem much more astute at carefully managing the risks of sexual activity.

TEENS HAVING BABIES: A DOWNWARD SLOPE (UNTIL RECENTLY)

If higher percentages of sexually active adolescents are using contraceptives—and using them more astutely than yesterday's active teens—it follows that U.S. teen pregnancy and birth rates should be dropping, and that's precisely what happened, at least until 2006. Between 1991 and 2005, the percentage of females ages 15–19 who'd ever gotten pregnant declined 27 percent.[43] Likewise, the actual birth rate for females ages 15–19 dropped 33 percent. Christianists claim (falsely) that the explanation for these two declines lies with its abstinence programs. But we just learned that there is no connection at all between AO programs and the teens' actual sexual behaviors.

In sharp contrast to RR's phony claims, a recent, carefully done study demonstrated that more than any other single factor, teens' increased and clever use of contraception is responsible for their lower pregnancy and birth rates. However, that same study reminds us that the United States still has "the highest rate of adolescent pregnancy of any of the world's developed nations."[44] And it's worth noting that none of those other nations has anything even remotely akin to AO programs. Indeed, European officials seem amused by the silliness of AO. Researchers report that the chief reason sexually active youth in other developed nations have lower pregnancy and birth rates than U.S. teens is because more of them use contraception and use it more effectively.[45] Nonetheless, it appears that at least some U.S. teens are gradually catching up on both counts.

However, on a somber note, in both 2006 and 2007, the U.S. teen birth rate turned upward—"a rise of 2 percent in 2006 and 1 percent in 2007."[46] Researchers are not yet certain why that reversal occurred, and whether or not the upward trend will continue.[47] At the very least, it seems clear that the need for public policy blending sexual choices with personal accountability, and requiring the effective use of contraceptives, is as great as it has ever been. Such a policy would pivot around the notion of sexual smarts.

CULTIVATING SEXUAL SMARTS

Looking back over the past two decades, it appears that some U.S. teens and youth seem to be gradually embracing the view of sexuality held by their European peers: Namely, regardless of its context (in or out of marriage), sexuality is a good thing—a gift to be celebrated, but in a *responsible* manner. Moreover, responsibility imposes a number of firm obligations: among the most vital is the cultivation of sexual wisdom or *smarts*. Until recently, it was common to say that a youth becomes a woman or man when she or he *loses* something—namely, virginity. But in the new century we might say instead that a younger person is on the way to becoming sexually responsible to the degree that he or she *gains* something—namely, sexual smarts. *Fundamental to sexual smarts is the insight that while sex is great, some things are even greater.* Perhaps the most significant of these is what chapter 3 called autonomy—the necessity of taking charge of one's life to the fullest extent possible. Taking control definitely includes one's sexual life. To be in charge of all aspects of one's life is another way of saying that one loves oneself. Moreover, to love one's neighbor as much as oneself is to do all one can to ensure that the neighbor too enjoys autonomy.

The first step in cultivating sexual smarts is to recognize that although one may be free to have intercourse, having sex at this time and/or with this person may *not* be a wise or prudent thing to do—it may not be in my own best interest. And the younger one is the brighter that caution light becomes: *Intercourse could (at any age) harm me because, among other things, it could undermine my quest for autonomy.* Recall from chapter 3 that autonomy springs from economic independence, and it is obvious that an unplanned child makes self-sufficiency that much harder—especially for a younger woman, and doubly so if she's economically less advantaged to begin with. An unintended pregnancy suddenly forces her onto the horns of an agonizing dilemma: do I opt either for an unplanned birth or an (always unwanted) abortion? If she chooses the former route, and if the father fails to participate in the child's life, the challenges to her independence and thus her autonomy are compounded severely. And, even if he participates, an unplanned child poses a daunting challenge to his independence and autonomy, and doubly so if he is economically disadvantaged.

Furthermore, quite apart from pregnancy, assessing whether sex with this person is prudent or not must also take into account the potentially life-threatening risk of an HIV infection. That dreaded STD could definitely send one's life into freefall. Although other types of STDs may be less serious, their required treatment would do nothing to enhance one's economic independence and thus one's autonomy. Bluntly put, one must never knowingly expose one's partner or oneself to any type of STD. Given the risks of an STD and/or pregnancy, one must never allow oneself to be coerced into having unwanted and/or unprotected intercourse.

Importantly, one is *never* required to furnish a reason to say no. Reasons to say no may pivot around the potential threat to one's autonomy; or a person may be dubious about sex for any number of reasons. No matter the reasons or lack thereof, no is no. One should have intercourse *only* if she or he perceives it as being in the best interest of oneself *and* one's partner. Is this good for me *and* my partner? In short, do I really want to do this or not? Or am I doing this simply to appear cool? The extreme form of coercion is, of course, violence, and we just saw that marital violence is not uncommon. It turns out that violence is all too common among singles as well.[48] Violence or its threat is all too frequently used as a means for coercing girls and women into having sex.

The flip side of refusing to be coerced is, of course, that one must never compel another person to have intercourse of any type. That is not to say that seduction might not sometimes (though with great caution) have its place. It is rather to remind us that seduction is a dicey game—particularly so for adolescents—consisting of seeker and sought. If one senses that one is being sought, one must be entirely clear as to what outcomes one does and does not want. And if one is the seeker, one must take great pains to ensure that the participation of one's partner is nothing short of entirely voluntary.

Sexual smarts requires one more essential feature: She or he must include the identity of contraceptor within the repertoire of Who I Am. Whether adolescent or adult, and whether married or unmarried, a sexually smart person adds contraceptor to the list of indispensable 21st-century identities described in chapter 3. A contraceptor is someone who carefully practices what researchers call "contraceptive efficacy."[49] In plain English, "I am successful at making contraceptives work for me—I typically get them to do what I want them to do." Being a successful contraceptor starts (but cannot end) by grasping the technical aspects of the varied contraceptive methods: How does each one work? What does each one do? What does each *not* do? What are the upsides and downsides of each one? What are the considerable benefits of using multiple methods at a time? The contraceptor understands that although no single method (not even the pill or other hormonal methods) comes with a 100 percent guarantee, some methods are much less likely to fail than others. The contraceptor also comprehends that what researchers call a method's failure rate is linked with how difficult it is to use.

The failure rate of a method and the difficulty of its use have far more to do with the social rather than the technical aspects of contraception. The contraceptor realizes that preventing births and STDs is first and foremost a social action—not a mechanical act. Even going on the pill would make no sense for a woman apart from another (perhaps unknown) person in the picture. To be sure, the pill does not require the active cooperation of her partner, and that is obviously a huge advantage over the condom. But the pill does nothing for STDs. Hence, even if she's on the pill, a woman and her sexual partner are well advised to use condoms as well. To increase the chances of successfully preventing both pregnancy *and* STDs she and her male partner have no choice but to become skilled at the effective use of condoms.

The most memorable scene in the 2007 film *Knocked Up* shows Alison (Katherine Heigl) and Ben (Seth Rogen) locked in a passionate sexual embrace on their way towards actual union. At the height of their ardor Ben fumbles as he tries, unsuccessfully, to get a condom out of its wrapper. Alison moans "just do it" meaning he should hurry up and fit the condom onto his penis. But Ben misinterprets her moan to mean she doesn't need a condom. The camera then zooms in on the half-open package with condom intact floating in slow motion to the floor while the couple finally merges. Alison gets pregnant, and the film descends into a series of gags about two people who don't much like each other trying to cope with an unintended pregnancy.

When NPR's Terry Gross asked Rogen why the filmmakers decided that Alison (a high-powered career woman) would not have an abortion, he replied that it was *not* because they were antichoice.[50] He added that none of them doubted that in real life a woman like Alison would be likely to have an abortion. But he laughingly admitted that if they'd written in an abortion, their movie would be over before their gags began. Rogen's comic response stands in sharp contrast to a naïve, straightfaced christianist assessment that *Knocked Up* (along with certain other films) might signal a new trend towards "choosing Life at the Movies—2007 could be remembered as the year of Pro-Life Cinema."[51]

Rather than promoting an antichoice agenda, the film demonstrates how two lives can spin out of control when, overwhelmed by sexual passion, one or both partners allows their identity as Contraceptor to falter. The pivotal moral theme in all the films cited by the christianist reviewer is the perils of *ir*responsible sexual behavior—behavior that fails to incorporate effective contraception. As with anything else of grave importance, becoming a skilled and successful contraceptor is not something that happens by mere chance. It requires considerable time and thought prior to the person's first experience of intercourse—before D-Day. Furthermore, it demands careful cultivation ever after, as demonstrated through the woes endured even by sexually experienced persons such as Ben and Alison.

And that is one reason why advocates urge that adolescents postpone for as long as possible the age at which they have their "first intercourse."[52] Researchers reason that the older the girl or boy is the more likely it is that first of all, she or he has gotten conversant with the technical aspects of contraception. Second, the older an individual is, the more likely it is that the individual has anticipated its social aspects. In short, the older adolescent is more likely to have a greater sense that if and when the occasion arises, each partner will do all in their power to ensure that both partners successfully use condoms as well as hormonal methods. Each partner will, in effect, be well on the way toward cultivating the identity of contraceptor, and thus doing everything possible to avoid repeating Alison's and Ben's "screw-up."

SEXUAL SMARTS, AUTONOMY, AND ECONOMIC ADVANTAGE

For most persons, the essence of the pre-1960s sexual smarts was captured by the simple-minded ideal of virginity until marriage. What was perhaps the first evangelical sex manual ever published appeared in 1948.[53] It was grounded in the reality that its readers would accept abstinence as a given, period! Two current evangelical sex manuals (*Naked and Not Ashamed;* and *Real Sex—The Naked Truth about Chastity*) show them sticking to the ideal of virginity.[54] However, in sharp contrast to the 1948 manual, both current books devote most of their space trying to convince evangelical youth to abstain. The reason is that today's wavering evangelicals must be persuaded that if they do in fact toe the virginity line, the sensual pleasures they enjoy once they finally marry will be pumped up to unimaginable heights precisely because of their commitment to chastity.

But in today's world the reality is that sexual smarts has developed into something far more complex than taking a solemn vow to abstain until marriage. Recall from chapter 2 that in the 19th century both the acceptance and the actual practice of artificial contraceptives got started among married couples who were economically advantaged. Next, those ideas and practices spread gradually to married couples who were less well off. The common-sense argument that "limiting family size would contribute to their economic well-being" helped persuade the less well off to adopt those radically new ways.

That same sort of pragmatic approach toward sexuality is repeating itself among today's economically advantaged persons—only this time around they are *not* married.[55] Regnerus describes it as an "emerging sexual morality" which is "characteristic of the upper-middle-class."[56] He adds that it is "strategic" and "education-minded." As they approach sexual activity the chances are that advantaged adolescents and youth are motivated by a sense of urgency to prevent a happening (pregnancy, STD) that could easily spin life out of control.[57] And, because so much more is at stake for them, that sense of urgency is probably felt more keenly by advantaged girls and women than it is by advantaged boys and men.

In short, there tends to be a link between economic advantage and being an autonomous girl/woman who, whether unmarried or married, views herself as a contraceptor. Hence, her urgent quest for autonomy becomes a primary motivation for and a springboard towards responsible—and thus moral—sexual behavior. Keep in mind, however, that the likelihood of being an autonomous person flourishes within a context of being economically well off in the first place. Girls/women from advantaged backgrounds are strongly and explicitly encouraged by parents and other adult figures to cultivate autonomy. Not only do those adults encourage the goal of autonomy, they also provide the material wherewithal necessary to help make it happen. Attached to that package is the implicit message that they must add the identity of Contraceptor to the core of Who I Am.

On the other hand, the situation among girls and women from less advantaged backgrounds is far less promising. Compared to girls and women who are unmarried and advantaged, girls and women who are unmarried and *less advantaged* are less likely to use contraceptives, more likely to get pregnant, more likely to give birth to an unplanned child, more likely to fall victim to STDs, and more likely to obtain abortions.[58] Furthermore, a 2007 study reported significant increases among less advantaged teenage girls in rates of "human papillomavirus (HPV), chlamydia, genital herpes, and trichomoniasis, a common parasite."[59] HPV (which can be prevented by childhood vaccination) is associated with cervical cancer and other serious diseases. Moreover, recent increases in rates of HIV in the United States are concentrated among heterosexual black women and men (most of which are less advantaged) as well as gay and bisexual men of all races.[60] A 2009 CDC report summed up the gravity of the current situation by concluding that, "Noticeable disparities exist in the sexual and reproductive health of young persons in the United States."[61] The report made it clear that sexual and reproductive health is not an equal opportunity benefit—youth who are economically advantaged are a whole lot healthier than those who are not.

Chapter 3 noted that today's evangelicals are proud of their efforts to join with liberals who, for more than a century, have been serving the needs of less advantaged persons. But as far as I can tell, the efforts (though laudable) of most evangelicals are after-the-fact—feeding the hungry and clothing the naked. Though eager to give people fish, evangelicals seem less inclined to coach people on how to fish. Hence, it seems to me that evangelicals might also wish to take action before the fact by supporting public policies that cultivate fishing skills.

Specifically, would it not make sense for evangelicals to help devise policies that might encourage and empower less advantaged girls, boys, women, and men to pursue their quest for economic independence and thus autonomy? Chapter 6 describes one practical means in support of such a policy, namely, reorganizing K–12 so that it effectively prepares children and youth from all social classes for the emerging information age. Another pragmatic means might be for evangelicals to toss out vacuous AO programs and focus instead on strategies that encourage a progressive approach to human sexuality—one that cultivates the notion of sexual smarts including the identity of contraceptor.

It seems to me that if evangelicals are genuinely concerned about the long-term economic well-being of less advantaged persons, they must eventually come to grips with several vexing issues: Shall they, for example, continue to insist on their *sex as taboo* ideal? Obviously, they have every right to retain this ideal for themselves. But should they remain adamant that their ideal should also be integral to public policy? If some evangelicals are willing to be flexible on that matter, might they participate in crafting strategies for economic well-being that take into account the ways sexuality is actually viewed and practiced by increasing numbers of citizens in other Western nations? Might some evangelicals start to recognize the simple fact expressed by respondents in one study—"Sex is just a Normal Part of Life?"[62]

THE RELIGIOUS RIGHT'S WORLDWIDE WAR ON SEX AMONG LESS-ADVANTAGED PERSONS

The RR's influence on public policies that negatively impact the sexual and reproductive health of less advantaged citizens is not limited to the United States. Not content to sow hardship here, it also flexes its political muscle overseas. In 2006, christianists insisted that the George W. Bush government should cease funding contraceptives for poor Africans. Despite the fact that persons in the West are becoming increasingly aware that marriage does not necessarily add up to moral sex, christianists are attempting to export that fantasy to the poorest regions of the developing world.[63] Prior to 2005 the U.S. government had for some years provided Uganda with funds to assist in fighting its overwhelming AIDS epidemic. The money was linked with a program called Pepfar which "emphasizes a policy known as ABC, which stands for abstinence, be faithful and use condoms."[64]

Until 2005, Pepfar provided free condoms to all Ugandans regardless of age or marital status. However, under christianist pressure, U.S. funds for condoms were scaled back drastically, resulting in a condom shortage and higher prices. The great bulk of the Ugandan population is desperately poor and cannot afford to buy condoms at inflated prices. Some men resorted to using garbage bags as a condom substitute. One prominent critic charged that the reduction in U.S. funds for condoms is the result of a "'dangerous and profound shift in U.S. donor policy from comprehensive prevention, education and provision of condoms to focus on abstinence only.'"[65]

Ambassador Stephen Lewis, the UN's secretary general's special envoy for HIV/AIDS in Africa since 2001, and the former Canadian ambassador to the

UN, agreed: "There is no question that the condom crisis in Uganda is being driven and exacerbated by Pepfar and by the extreme policies that the administration in the U.S. is now pursuing."[66] Lewis added that "the emphasis on abstinence in the administration's program, even more than the issue of condom distribution, is a 'distortion of the preventive apparatus and is resulting in great damage and undoubtedly will cause significant numbers of infections which should never have occurred.'"

Lewis and other observers found that the Ugandans most vulnerable to an HIV infection are, first, poor married women and, second, poor adolescents. U.S./RR policy stated that the United States should *not* pay for married couples' condoms used to prevent HIV. Instead, U.S./RR policy insisted that married couples should be monogamous, thus eliminating their need for disease-prevention via condoms. But most Ugandan women do not have the educational and economic opportunities available to Western women. Self-sufficiency, much less autonomy, is not a live option for most Ugandan women. They have no choice but to marry (frequently in a polygynous situation) at a very young age and remain with husbands who are more committed to the double standard than to them. The upshot is that those wives suffer very high rates of HIV infection. Similarly, christianist-inspired U.S. policy insisted that unmarried persons should be abstinent, thereby further reducing any need for U.S. condom-funding. But many Ugandan adolescents are in fact sexually active, and they have even less money than adults to pay for condoms. The outcome in terms of their increased rates of HIV infections is obvious.

In March 2007, a reporter asked presidential hopeful John McCain if he supported the "distribution of taxpayer-subsidized condoms in Africa to fight the transmission of HIV."[67] His response was an embarrassing muddle of words resulting from McCain's fear of offending the christianist voters needed to get the GOP nomination. As he stumbled through his confused response, he seemed unable to commit himself either to the christianist position or to the progressive position favored by many Americans and by leaders in the worldwide fight against AIDS.

And while poor people throughout the developing world suffer because of U.S./RR policy, their emerging but small middle class and their even tinier wealthy class can afford not only condoms, but also highly effective hormonal contraceptive techniques. And, in the event of an unwanted pregnancy, they would be able to obtain an abortion, whether legal or not. Moreover, should they become HIV-infected they could afford the best life-enhancing treatments available in the West. Such access to contraception, abortion, and HIV treatment is typically unattainable for the masses of poor citizens anywhere in the developing world. Needless to say, if a poor pregnant woman (married or not) inquired about an abortion, Pepfar-funded clinics would quickly show her the door and insist she carry the fetus to term. In all too many cases, the upshot of that policy is to increase the mother's already sizeable and barely surviving brood of children. Further compounding their family's anguish is the awful chance that her newborn could have HIV.

RR's anticondom campaign springs of course from its belief that marriage alone makes sex right. Never mind that throughout the world today many married women are infected with HIV by their husbands: a CARE official observed that, "For a woman [throughout Africa], the greatest risk factor [for getting HIV] is getting married."[68] Plainly, an HIV-infected husband having unprotected sex with his wife is being immoral. A start might be made towards reducing the spread of HIV infections by asserting publicly that what makes sex moral or right is responsibility, *not* marriage. Human reason dictates the necessity of using condoms whenever and wherever there is risk of HIV—regardless of marital status.

But christianist leaders dismissed reason and continued to insist that U.S. dollars be contingent on both genders being sexually abstinent prior to marriage and faithful afterwards. Alas, many husbands in all cultures have practiced the double standard for millennia, and past efforts to appeal either to their sense of integrity or to being accountable for their actions have been ignored if not ridiculed. The fatal flaw in the christianist strategy against HIV is exposed for all to see: in both the developing world and in the West, marriage never has been and is not now a guarantee that husbands will not sexually exploit their wives. And that is doubly so if she is economically less advantaged.

Among the most outspoken critics of U.S./RR policies limiting the access of poor people to contraceptives overseas and at home is Nicholas Kristoff. First of all, he notes that, ironically enough, such policies actually increase the incidence of abortion:

> One of the Bush follies that has bewildered and antagonized our allies has been the vacuous refusal to support family planning through the United Nations Population Fund.
>
> The upshot of the failure to support contraception has been millions of unwanted pregnancies and abortions.[69]

And, in another place, he remarked about

> the paradox of a "pro-life" administration adopting a policy whose result will be tens of thousands of additional abortions each year—along with more women dying in childbirth.

> *We see it in the opposition to condoms to curb AIDS in Africa and in the in-*
> *sistence on abstinence-only sex education in American classrooms (one reason*
> *American teenage pregnancy rates are more than double those in Canada).*[70]

Kristoff was spot-on to connect RR's power in Africa with its political clout in the United States. By restricting the access of poor U.S. women to contraception, christianist policies punish disadvantaged women here just as they harm poor African women. A 2006 report suggests that because of RR's efforts to restrict the access of less advantaged Americans to contraceptives, there has been a corresponding increase in the incidence of U.S. abortion rates:

> *Contraception use has declined strikingly over the last decade, particularly among*
> *poor women, making them more likely to get pregnant unintentionally and to*
> *have abortions. . . . The decline appears to have slowed the reduction in the na-*
> *tional abortion rate that began in the mid-1980's . . . The researchers blamed*
> *reductions in federally and state-financed family planning programs for declining*
> *contraceptive use. They called for public and private insurance to cover contracep-*
> *tives, and for over-the-counter access to the so-called morning-after pill, which can*
> *prevent pregnancy if taken within 72 hours after sex.*[71]

In an effort to remove the burdens imposed by RR on poor women overseas (but not in the United States) the newly elected President Barak Obama, in January 2009,

> *repealed rules . . . that restricted federal money for international organizations*
> *that promote or provide abortions overseas, sweeping aside a pillar of the social*
> *policy architecture of George W. Bush's presidency. . . . "For the past eight years,*
> *they have undermined efforts to promote safe and effective voluntary family plan-*
> *ning in developing countries," Mr. Obama said of the restrictions. "For these rea-*
> *sons, it is right for us to rescind this policy and restore critical efforts to protect*
> *and empower women and promote global economic development."*[72]

POOR WOMEN TAKING CHARGE AND TAKING CARE

By connecting family planning (condom use and abortion) with the empowerment of women, Mr. Obama was echoing the views of progressive advocates worldwide:

> *Beatrice Were, a brave H.I.V.-positive activist in Uganda . . . [remarks] "I am*
> *often asked whether there will ever be a cure for H.I.V./AIDS, and my answer is*
> *that there is already a cure," she says. "It lies in the strength of women, families*

*and communities who support and empower each other to break the silence
around AIDS and take control of their sexual lives."*[73]

Were's ideas regarding a cure for HIV/AIDS are drawn from research carried out in Uganda in the late 1980s and early 1990s. Uganda's president at the time urged citizens to participate in a national conversation in which all facets of HIV/AIDS were openly discussed. An obvious point emerging from their conversations was that a couple testing HIV-negative at marriage could remain that way via monogamy. A second and more controversial point is that every wife must take charge of her sex life and aim to ensure that her husband should remain monogamous so that neither of them should ever test HIV-positive. If she has any suspicion at all that her husband might be wandering from her bed, she must insist on an HIV test and/or that they use condoms in addition to their other contraceptive(s). Complicating the issue further is the fact that either of them could have contracted HIV prior to their marriage. That would, of course, oblige condom use in order to protect the noninfected partner.

The third point was even more controversial—the woman's assertiveness vis-à-vis her man must be bolstered by strong social support.[74] The woman who aims to protect her interests and those of her children should *not* be forced to take action alone. Instead, her extended family and community should line up on her side and back up her efforts to protect her own and her children's well-being. For instance, the researchers reported that when a husband had extramarital sex the community did not shrug and say, "Well, that's the way men are." Instead the entire community subjected him to public shame and humiliation until he changed his ways. But if he persisted, the community empowered the woman to divorce her husband and helped her gain a level of economic independence and thus autonomy. The research revealed that the Ugandan communities that adopted this nontraditional approach to gender and family were thus able to reduce substantially the rates of HIV infection among women and newborns.

It is plain to see that their community-based agenda did not rely for success on the christianists' naïve nostrums. Their realistic agenda undermined RR's traditional take on gender roles in which the husband is the ultimate family authority. The community took a long, hard look (skeptical, not cynical) at both men and marriage. In their scenario, the woman must have the resources to actively protect her own interests. When push comes to shove she cannot afford to rely on the goodwill and honorable intentions of her husband. Their scenario required the availability of divorce and of community support in order to achieve her goal of economic autonomy. And, their scenario demanded tangible resources for marrieds and singles alike in the form of ongoing access to HIV testing, condoms, and abortions.

A study in rural South Africa offers a similar case study of the community coming down solidly on the side of the wife vis-à-vis her husband. This study sprang from the grim reality that when the wife insists that her husband should use condoms to prevent HIV, he all too frequently beats her up. He then rapes her and potentially exposes her and the fetus to HIV. To cope with unrestrained husband power, women in the community have arranged the option to borrow money in order "to start small businesses. Most women sold fruit, vegetables, clothes, or offered tailoring services. With economic and social independence, women were no longer obligated to remain in violent relationships."[75] As in Uganda, the rural South African wife is empowered by her extended family and community to act independently from her husband in order to control and protect her life and family.

UN Ambassador Lewis linked women's empowerment to the worldwide struggle against HIV-AIDS by arguing that:

> "Gender inequality is driving the [AIDS] pandemic, and we will never subdue the gruesome force of AIDS until the rights of women become paramount in the struggle. . . . The inequality of women makes them highly vulnerable to becoming infected through 'marital rape to rape as a war crime,'" Mr. Lewis said, adding that, while sexual violence occurs everywhere, in Africa, "The violence and the virus go together."[76]

In the West, advantaged women are able to achieve economic independence and autonomy via their own educational and occupational attainments. Those fortunate women are growing the sexual smarts necessary to avoid the injustice and humiliation of the sexual double standard and of marital or partner rape. They are less likely to fall victim to unwanted pregnancies, unplanned children, denial of access to abortion, and to STDs including HIV-AIDS. However, among less advantaged American women and for the masses of women in the developing world, an educational and economic lifeline resulting in control over each part of their lives—including the sexual—is hard to come by.

First, in the developing world, the woman's quest for autonomy frequently requires (among several other things) her extended family and community to get actively involved in her life and the life of her immediate family. Second, throughout North America, the challenge for all persons of goodwill—including evangelicals—is to figure out how to empower less advantaged girls and women, and boys and men, to take control of their lives—to become an autonomous

person. That of course requires economic self-sufficiency, which in turn demands access to relevant educational and economic opportunities. Autonomy
also requires the development of sexual smarts; and that, among other things,
calls for ready access both to the full range of contraceptives (including hormonal
methods) and to the option of abortion.

ABORTION, SEXUALITY, AND SOCIAL CLASS

Recently, a half-dozen freshmen and I were chatting informally following a class
in which we'd discussed social class, gender, and sexuality. Among them was
Jean (pseudonym), an academically gifted, articulate 18-year-old African American woman. She told us she was from a low-income family, and that her mother
and grandmother had each been a solo-parent. Jean clearly fit the description
of someone who'd grown up in disadvantaged circumstances. Accordingly, our
university took steps to help her cultivate her identity as an autonomous person: her academic talent, combined with the fact that neither parent had ever
earned a bachelor's degree, made her eligible for an opportunity scholarship.
That meant she didn't have to work or borrow money because our university
provided an award that fully covered all her expenses (tuition, books, housing,
meals) for four years.

Things were not so tidy, however, when it came to her sexual smarts. Jean
shocked us by revealing that she planned to give up her splendid and much-
coveted scholarship, and drop out of college at semester's close because "I'm
pregnant." She told us that her boyfriend is a traveling rock musician, and so
she's moving back to south Florida to be near his mother, who'd offered to help
care for their infant. Jean said she hoped to squeeze in classes at a community
college and one day, hopefully, earn her degree. When asked *why* she got pregnant she smiled wistfully and replied, "I don't know—it just happened!" And,
when asked about the abortion option, Jean replied "I'm a Christian and don't
believe in it."

My hunch is she meant *evangelical* Christian.[77] I also think that if asked, Jean
would endorse AO courses in high school, and she'd affirm that premarital sex
is *wrong*. If asked whether sex is wrong when the couple's in love, she'd hesitate,
but end up saying, "Probably." And I have no doubt that, if asked, Jean would
most emphatically disapprove of the notion of teens developing a sense of sexual smarts. She'd be put off by the idea of teens and youth becoming thoroughly
familiar with the varied methods of contraception, as well as becoming as com-
petent as possible in their effective use. Her evangelical background had successfully short-circuited the view that all persons—including the unmarried—
should grow the identity of contraceptor.

Jean is gambling with her autonomy, namely, the degree of control she'll have over her own life both now and over the long haul. She's playing a risky game of roulette hoping the ball will *not* land in the slot marked "repeat the life experiences of your grandmother and mother." Jean is also gambling with the socioeconomic and emotional well-being of her child. And, if it's a girl, what are the chances for a fourth generation of solo-mothers? Studies of adolescents such as Jean reinforce a theme of certain movies or novels—the girl gets attracted to an older guy who seems exciting and appealing.[78] Being a rock musician adds to his mystique. However, owing to her evangelical convictions, she neither goes on the pill nor does she routinely carry condoms. Nor, needless to say, is she in the habit of insisting that her boyfriend carry and use them effectively.

But during a moment of intense passion she acquiesces to her boyfriend's persistence and they have vaginal intercourse—"It just happened." It may have occurred apart from any condom use at all. Or, like Ben and Alison, their attempted condom use may have been clumsy and in the end futile. Researchers tell us that if a youth (such as Jean) believes that nonmarital sex is morally wrong, that youth is likely to feel immobilized if and when attempting to manage contraception effectively.[79] Indeed, a 2009 study reported that in America, the states that are the most "religious" are the same states with the highest levels of teen pregnancy.[80] Contraception can be a stern challenge even in the most congenial of circumstances. Carrying feelings of guilt, shame, and wrongdoing into the heat of youthful passion is likely to deter the use of any contraceptive at all. Or, if the couple tries to use a condom, their shame and guilt increase the chances that they'll fail to use it properly.

Jean got pregnant at the same time she was thriving both intellectually and personally. Her fabulous scholarship was enabling her to gain more control over her life than she'd ever dreamed possible. Not only that, she was gaining the sense that her prospects for one day becoming an autonomous adult were looking very good indeed. But no matter how she sliced it she realized that her pregnancy undermined her sense of control over her daily life. Furthermore, it set high hurdles in the path of her hoped-for future autonomy. Nevertheless, abortion was not an option to restore Jean's sense of control. So instead she gambles that having her child will simply defer her quest for autonomy—not derail or undermine it. She hopes that by squeezing in college courses she'll eventually regain at least some semblance of control over her life.

Compare Jean's dicey situation with that of Senator Barry Goldwater's family. His granddaughter, CC Goldwater, produced a 2006 film (*Mr. Conservative: Goldwater on Goldwater*) showing that Barry (the 1964 GOP presidential nominee) felt ill at ease with and objected strenuously to the growing christianist influence over the GOP. A journalist observed to CC that in the film Goldwater "emerges as a complex figure—a half-Jewish cowboy from Phoenix who believed the government should stay out of our hair. He thought gays should be allowed in the military and was also pro-choice."[81] In another place, Senator Goldwater remarked that

> *I'm frankly sick and tired of the political preachers across this country telling me as a citizen that if I want to be a moral person, I must believe in A, B, C, and D. Just who do they think they are? And from where do they presume to claim the right to dictate their moral beliefs to me?*[82]

CC told the journalist that, "My mom had an abortion in the mid-50's, before she had me. She was in college, and she wanted to finish and get a degree and not have a child then. Barry felt it was a woman's right to make that choice."

The reality is that long before abortion was decriminalized in the United States (California's Governor Ronald Reagan signed the first modern prochoice bill legalizing first-trimester abortion in 1967, followed at the national level by *Roe v. Wade* in 1973) families with economic resources had little trouble obtaining a safe abortion. The social and economic advantages enjoyed by CC's mother got her what she needed—even though it was entirely illegal. In turn, her abortion enabled CC's mother to maintain her sense of control over her current and future life. She was able to pursue the degree that benefited her and later on her children including CC.

Until the late 1960s, women and girls who were not fortunate enough to belong to an advantaged family such as the Goldwaters were denied access to a safe abortion. If Jean had lived back then and wanted an abortion her only option was to visit the "back-alley butcher."[83] Just as upper-middle-class and wealthy women have always had (and always will have irrespective of any laws) access to safe abortions, less advantaged women have forever faced the horrors of the unscrupulous crook whose chief concern is to extract money from a desperate woman with no thought at all for her emotional or physical well-being.

Occasionally, the less advantaged woman was fortunate enough to encounter a high-minded abortion provider such as depicted in the 2005 film *Vera Drake*. Set in 1950s Britain, Drake's limited knowledge and resources sometimes placed her girls (abortion clients, whom she served gratis) at risk of serious infection. In the film, one of them nearly dies and Drake is imprisoned. As an ironic counterpoint to the grim circumstances facing Drake and her girls, the film depicts a young woman (daughter of a wealthy matron whose house Drake cleans) obtaining a safe (though illegal and expensive) abortion from an obstetrician, recommended by a psychiatrist, who was in turn recommended by her family physician.

During recent class discussions of abortion, it hit me that today's youth have no clue as to what a back-alley butcher is, and have no feeling for the horrific images those words convey. Several decades of a prochoice climate benefiting less-advantaged women have erased that dark blot from our collective national memory. But obstetrician Waldo Fielding warns that those who forget history are doomed to repeat its mistakes. He cautions that if we fail to remember the backalley butcher era of U.S. history we may be unwitting accomplices of the christianist crusade to restore the butchers. Now in his mid-80s, Dr. Fielding worked from 1948–53 in two of New York City's large municipal hospitals whose mission was to serve the medical needs of less-advantaged citizens. He writes:

> *There I saw and treated almost every complication of illegal abortion that one could conjure, done either by the patient herself or by an abortionist—often unknowing, unskilled and probably uncaring. Yet the patient never told us who did the work, or where and under what conditions it was performed. She was in dire need of our help to complete the process or, as frequently was the case, to correct what damage might have been done. . . . The woman had put herself at total risk, and literally did not know whether she would live or die. . . . The familiar symbol of illegal abortion is the infamous "coat hanger"—which may be the symbol, but is in no way a myth. In my years in New York, several women arrived with a hanger still in place. Whoever put it in—perhaps the patient herself—found it trapped in the cervix and could not remove it. . . . Almost any implement you can imagine had been and was used to start an abortion—darning needles, crochet hooks, cut-glass salt shakers, soda bottles, sometimes intact, sometimes with the top broken off. . . . It is important to remember that* Roe v. Wade *did not mean that abortions could be performed. They have always been done, dating from ancient Greek days. What Roe said was that ending a pregnancy could be carried out by medical personnel, in a medically accepted setting, thus conferring on [disadvantaged] women, finally, the full rights of first-class citizens—and freeing their doctors to treat them as such.*[84]

The 2007 film *4 Months, 3 Weeks and 2 Days* is based on similarly frightening circumstances. Though living under a communist regime which severely punished abortion, a pregnant woman manages to locate a back-alley butcher who agrees (for a large sum of money) to perform what turns out to be an unsafe and horrendous abortion. And, as if that were not pain enough, at the last minute the butcher demands and gets sex from the friend who had accompanied, and was seeking to comfort, the desperate woman. The film was set in Romania during the late 1980s—just prior to the collapse of the regime, after which abortion was promptly decriminalized.

In 2005, the Public Broadcasting Service (PBS) presented a *Frontline* report called "The Last Abortion Clinic."[85] One segment reported that Mississippi anti-choice (mostly white) advocates have, over the course of several years, managed to close every abortion clinic in the state except the last one in Jackson. The reporter then visited the state's isolated, impoverished, and mostly black rural areas. Girls and women who live there have only limited access to effective and affordable contraceptive methods. And when they become pregnant (often because their partner or family member coerces them into sex and/or refuses to wear a condom) they either cannot afford to miss days from their minimum-wage job for the trip to Jackson, and/or they have no money for the trip, and/or they have no money for the overnight lodging necessary because Jackson is so far away.

Compounding the women's misery is the reality that even if there were a nearby clinic most of them have no money to pay for an abortion. Most rural black persons in Mississippi and the entire rural South are poor. Many never finish high school. And even if they do, their schools are low quality even by the flawed criteria of the No Child Left Behind Act.[86] And, among the women to whom the reporter spoke, all but the very youngest teens already had one or more small children. The stark reality is that upon the birth of their first/next child, they will become even poorer than they already are. And, through no fault of their own, their current and future children likewise face a life of severe economic disadvantage. In a rather bleak essay, Sharon Lerner asks, "[Is] Ole Miss our future? Having all but outlawed abortion, Mississippi has become a laboratory for anti-choice strategists."[87]

Following the 1973 U.S. Supreme Court *Roe v. Wade* decision, the federal Medicaid program routinely paid for the abortions of poor women. But in 1976, Congress passed the Hyde Amendment prohibiting any federal funding for abortion.[88] It was later modified to allow exceptions in cases of rape or incest, or when the mother's life is in danger. By 2004, some 17 states had taken up the slack left by the feds and paid for the abortions of poor women—but no Southern state is among them.[89] It seems to me that Hyde ranks among the most mean-spirited policies that christianists have ever managed to inflict on Americans. Its target is poor women in general and, because so many of them are poor, black women in particular.

Hyde is a vivid reminder (if any is needed) that christianists are *not* in the business of peddling equal-opportunity public policies. Citizens (white, black, Latina, Asian) who are economically well off are securely insulated from christianist violations of their freedom to practice sexuality in a responsible manner. Like double standards of any sort, RR's is morally squalid. Citizens here and abroad who are well off can and will ignore and/or wiggle out of any and all christianist rules and regulations. It is the less fortunate among us (the least of our sisters and brothers, to paraphrase Jesus[90]) who bear the brunt of the obsession of christianist leaders with political clout.

Christianists and evangelicals who endorse Hyde insist that "my tax money must not be used to support immoral behavior such as abortion." That is, however, a deeply flawed argument. Many citizens take issue with the morality of any number of government policies, yet pay their taxes. Some citizens, for instance, believe that both state-sponsored executions and killing soldiers and civilians in warfare (especially Iraq II, or Afghanistan), are exceptionally immoral government policies. Nonetheless, despite their moral qualms, their tax monies are used to support those activities. The fact that RR is able to subvert such a basic principle (shared taxes) of any democracy indicates the extent of its leaders' political muscle. The added fact that most of Hyde's victims are poor (whether black, white, Latina, or Asian) and thus powerless helps explain christianist success in keeping Hyde alive despite the efforts of critics to repeal it.

The most recent of RR's crusades to deny abortion to disadvantaged women occurred during the summer of 2009, and at this writing its eventual fate is uncertain. As part of the broader health care reform bill it is likely "that coverage of abortion will be mandated, unless Congress explicitly excludes abortion from the scope of federal authority to define 'essential benefits.'"[91] If christianists have their way, abortion would indeed be excluded. Advantaged women would not be penalized by that limitation. But poor women would in fact suffer. Randall Terry and his group *Operation Rescue* have a long history of mounting coercive attacks, including violence, against abortion providers and clinics.[92] Terry warned the *National Press Club* that if the bill does include abortion benefits, "such an evil policy will lead some people to absolutely refuse to pay their taxes. And I believe . . . that there are others who will be tempted to acts of violence. If the government of this country tramples the faith and values of its citizens, history will hold those in power responsible for the violent convulsions that follow."[93]

THE SOCIAL EVOLUTION OF VIEWS ON ABORTION

Christianists are fond of targeting the 1973 *Roe* decision as the start of America's descent into utter moral depravity. But as is so often the case, the facts do not fit the christianist spin: "In 1800 no jurisdiction in the US had enacted any statutes whatever on the subject of abortion; most forms of abortion were not illegal and those American women [midwives] who wished to practice abortion did so."[94] The United States was of course founded during that same period—the years prior to 1800. In effect, prochoice was among the family values followed both by our founders and everyday Americans. However, during the 19th and early

20thcenturies, the ground shifted steadily so that by the 1950s "virtually every jurisdiction in the US had laws upon its books that proscribed the practice sharply and declared most abortions to be criminal offenses."[95] The traditional American value of prochoice was gradually replaced by a new value called antichoice.

Despite the fact that by the mid-20th century most abortions were illegal, Americans were well aware that abortions occurred anyhow—but on a two-tier basis: infrequent and safe for women who could afford them; frequent and deadly for those who could not. That gross social injustice helped pushed California toward restoring pre-1800 American ideals. The social injustice of most abortion laws, the California bill setting it right, and the approval by the federal government in 1960 of the oral contraceptive pill were all part of the context surrounding a 1968 conference sponsored by the (evangelical) Christian Medical Society. Participants included physicians, theologians, and social scientists.

It was called a "Protestant Symposium on the control of Human Reproduction." Its organizers were eager for evangelicals to weigh in on several emerging public policy issues, one of which (abortion) later on became pivotal to the christianist agenda. The purpose of the conference was "to examine carefully the moral issues underlying the decision to perform an abortion, a sterilization, or to recommend the practice of [artificial] contraception."[96] Everyone at the conference (including me) believed that sex is taboo but that marriage transforms it. As the conference organizers put it, "Sexual intercourse is a gift of God and is to be expressed and experienced only within the marriage relationship."[97] Second, we affirmed the emerging Protestant view that contraception is not "forbidden or sinful . . . [if] it is in harmony with the total revelation of God for married life."[98] The third step in our logic was to acknowledge that abortion is a *"tragic moral choice* in which a lesser evil is chosen to avoid a greater one."[99] Accordingly, most conference participants supported the "necessity and permissibility for it [abortion] under certain circumstances."[100] My assigned task was to synthesize data and insights from social science with evangelical views on sterilization and abortion. I concluded that there are times when abortion is indeed an appropriate course of action—even for the evangelical.[101]

If, during the late 1960s, there was anything approaching an evangelical position on abortion that was both traditional and official, our conference statement surely expressed it. No evangelical wanted any woman ever to have an abortion. Nonetheless, most persons reluctantly agreed that the data supplied by researchers and by physicians (such as Fielding) who dealt every day with the horrendous sufferings of poor women required a response founded on human compassion. At the time, most evangelicals and other Americans would *not* have disagreed that abortion is indeed a "tragic moral choice in which a lesser evil is chosen to avoid a greater one." The "greater evil" meant the emotional and economic consequences of enforcing an unwanted delivery on the woman, on her child, and on her family. Disadvantaged women giving birth to children who in turn are likely to become disadvantaged can only harm the children, the women, their family, and our society. Hence, believed most conference participants, abortion is necessary and permissible (though regrettable) under certain circumstances. Several years after the conference, a desire for social justice coupled with human compassion provided at least some of the rationale behind the 1973 *Roe* decision restoring the entire United States to its pre-1800s prochoice climate.

Following *Roe,* christianist leaders began to veer away from the traditional "tragic moral choice/greater evil" principle and began instead to spin abortion as the "murder of unborn babies."[102] Those leaders rode the crest of that spin to gain control of the evolving Religious Right.

Their anti-abortion crusade helped feed their lust for political power. Up to that time, the moral choice of abortion had been placed in the same category as the moral choice/greater evil of taking a human life (soldier or civilian) in warfare, or as taking a human life via capital punishment, or by taking life in a police action. For example, in 1807, Britain launched a preemptive military attack against neutral Denmark. A third of Copenhagen was destroyed and 2,000 innocent civilians (women, children, and men) were killed. William Wilberforce, a devout Christian and an icon of today's evangelicals (discussed in chapter 6) "decided that, however horrible, [the devastation] was a necessary and just act of self-defense."[103] In effect, he placed that wholesale slaughter of innocent and blameless human beings within the realm of a tragic moral choice that he deemed necessary to avoid a greater evil.

But RR's leaders arbitrarily removed abortion from the moral choice/greater evil category without ever explaining their moral inconsistency—they continue to support the killing of humans in warfare or on death row. They conjured up the bizarre notion that terminating a zygote or fetus (whether or not either stage is human remains a matter of debate) is somehow uniquely different from killing persons in other circumstances—persons that are irrefutably human. To be sure, some of today's Catholics and Peace Church members remain staunchly consistent; such persons do not recognize the moral choice/greater evil dilemma under any circumstances—whether the termination of the fetus, or the killing of humans either in warfare or on death row.

Perhaps because they're uncomfortable over their moral inconsistency, christianists have opened yet another front in their goal of returning the United States to the domain of the back-alley butchers. The religious right's most recent (2007) spin is that:

> *Abortion, as a rule, is not in the best interest of the woman; that women are often misled or ill-informed about its risks to their own physical or emotional health; and that the interests of the pregnant woman and the fetus are, in fact, the same.*
>
> *The majority opinion in the [Supreme] court's 5-to-4 decision explicitly acknowledged this argument, galvanizing anti-abortion forces and setting the stage for an intensifying battle over new abortion restrictions in the states.*
>
> *This ferment adds to the widespread recognition that abortion politics are changing, in ways that are, as yet, unclear, if not contradictory.*[104]

The dishonesty underlying the christianists' latest spin is that abortion severely harms the woman. They allege that it's not in her best interest, and insist that the law should protect her by not allowing her to have an abortion. Never mind that the "evidence" on which their harm argument rests contains no merit whatever:

> *Women who choose to abort an unwanted pregnancy experience feelings of grief and loss, but there is no evidence that a single abortion causes significant mental health problems, a panel of the American Psychological Association reported [in 2008] after two years of study. The findings are almost identical to a similar review by the association in 1990. "The best scientific evidence published indicates that among adult women who have an unplanned pregnancy, the relative risk of mental health problems is no greater if they have a single elective, first-trimester abortion or deliver that pregnancy,"*[105]

In sharp contrast to the mythical christianist spin involving "harm to the woman," the research evidence paints a complex picture.[106] First of all, it is certain that no woman ever intentionally sets out to have an abortion. Second, faced with an unintended pregnancy, virtually every woman agonizes painfully over what to do about her tragic moral choice. She typically reasons that the choice to abort—though regrettable—is necessary to avoid a greater evil. To be sure, during their actual abortion experience, some women feel guilty and become stressed. Nevertheless time—the great healer—gradually cleanses their guilt and alleviates their stress. And, like CC Goldwater's mother, most of them eventually begin to feel good about themselves and their life. In the film, CC's mother remarks that although she agonized over her decision at the time, "I do not regret it for a moment."

If RR's latest spin somehow manages to further restrict abortions, then disadvantaged women (white, black, Asian, Latina) would end up with still fewer options than they have at present. Furthermore, even if new official restrictions are kept to a minimum, the misinformation alleging that abortion harms the woman may fool those who are less well-educated. The half truths may make them less willing to seek an abortion than if they'd they never heard the RR spin the first place. That is so even if their state continues to permit abortion and still pays for it. On the other hand, better-educated women sense immediately the sham of the harm argument. They fully appreciate the pain of the abortion option as well as its necessity in order to avoid a greater evil. Hence, despite agonizing over their decision, most of them would be as likely as ever to seek a legal abortion. Further, should legal options become restricted, better-educated women are just as likely as ever to have the means and the social network necessary to obtain a safe (though perhaps less than legal) abortion.

CONVERSATIONS ABOUT AN ABORTION-FREE SOCIETY

In 2005, New York State Senator Hillary Clinton launched a conversation in which persons of goodwill holding diverse viewpoints might reach out to one another and create an abortion policy we can all live with. One important reason for our conversation is that the majority of Americans want such a policy:

> Public opinion on the legality of abortion has remained relatively stable for well over a decade, with slight majorities of the public consistently saying they favor keeping abortion legal. Polling conducted between 1995 and 2008 reveals that support for keeping abortion legal in all or most cases has fluctuated between 49% and 61% over the 13-year time period. Fewer Americans have tended to express support for making abortion illegal in all or most cases, ranging from a low of 36% to a high of 48% over the same period of time.
>
> At the same time, large majorities have expressed support for the 1973 Roe v. Wade decision. . . . In October 1989, for instance, more than six-in-ten Americans (61%) said they would oppose seeing the U.S. Supreme Court completely overturn the Roe decision, while only one-in-three (33%) favored overturning Roe. Sixteen years later, in November 2005, two-thirds (65%) continued to express support for keeping Roe as the law of the land, while 26% supported overturning the decision.[107]

Persons of goodwill hope to restore a feature from the past—something old— but also add something new to the public policy debate on abortion. Something old means reestablishing the late 1960s (and pre-1800s) climate that existed in the United States as captured by the cited evangelical conference: Although "tragic," abortion was and should once again be viewed as a "moral choice in which a lesser evil is chosen to avoid a greater one." Advocates reject the peculiar

1970s "fetus as unique" argument because it is a radical departure from past traditions, defies the rules of logic, and punishes the "least of our sisters and brothers." *The ideal on which all persons of goodwill might agree is that no woman should ever need an abortion.* Accordingly, many advocates believe strongly that the tortuous path to an abortion-free society wends its way through the fields of contraception.

Simply discussing contraception by itself brings nothing new to the policy debate on abortion. What is new is to transfer contraception from the background of the debate and to place it front and center. Given that everyone agrees on the ideal of an abortion-free society and that contraception is an essential means of achieving it, progressive advocates argue that it is high time to assign the issue of contraception the pivotal place it requires: Our stated public policy objective should be to make contraception a defining issue in the life of every youth and every woman and man:

> *The safest and fastest way to reduce abortions and unwanted births is to assure that every sexually active woman is always protected by a contraceptive that suits her needs and health circumstances, unless and until she chooses to become pregnant.*[108]

Or, as I said above, beginning with the early teen years, every person should seek to cultivate sexual smarts. Pivotal to sexual smarts is the notion that One of my identities is "contraceptor." Essential to the identity of contraceptor is the notion that "I must and will do all I can to avoid facing the tragic moral choice of abortion—either for myself or my partner." Regrettably, it's hard to imagine many christianists going there—end of conversation.

Some evangelicals might, however, be willing to wrestle with questions such as these: If abortion is wrong for whatever reasons, then why not support the goal of making contraception a defining issue in the life of every citizen? Why not endorse the notion of sexual smarts and thus reduce drastically the numbers of women—especially the less advantaged—who must face the "tragic moral choice"? Persons of goodwill argue that the best way to reduce sharply the numbers of women (and men) having to face that "tragic moral choice" is to accept the reality that among the vast majority of persons around the world neither sex nor contraception is restricted to marriage. Nor do laws prohibiting abortion work—they simply punish less-advantaged persons. The American way to arrive at political arrangements is via compromise. The essence of any democracy is that citizens must give in order to get. Some evangelicals might—though reluctantly—accept the need to give up their *sex as taboo* ideal in order to get what they say they care most deeply about. Their bottom line would be the same as it is for all persons of goodwill—the ideal of a society as free as possible from the tragic moral choice of abortion.

What then is the bottom line for christianists refusing to surrender their *taboo* ideal even though doing so would surely move us closer toward the ideal of an abortion-free society? Why, in nondemocratic fashion, do christianists want it all? Given their refusal to meet progressive advocates halfway, it is entirely fair to question whether "taking life" or "harming women" are truly the underlying reasons for the RR opposition to abortion. Might there perhaps be something more profound at work? I am persuaded there is.

First, christianists are not republicans or democrats with a small r or d. And they are surely not conservatives in the historic sense of that term. Instead, the ancient gene for theocracy is alive and well among most christianists. They want it all because they envision a society that they can manipulate and whose every part fits into their grand scheme of things. More than anything else (including "baby-murder" or "damaged women") christianists are driven by two closely linked elements. On the political level is what Martin calls "the lust for power and the lure of battle."[109]

And, on the moral level, christianists perceive themselves as the custodians of the *sex as taboo* ideal. If christianists are obsessed with power, they are likewise consumed by their intense loathing of sex apart from heterosexual marriage. The ideal of responsible sex as a cause for celebration among all persons (including nonmarrieds) is for them both frightening and disgusting. Hence, they are determined to fight the notion of sexual smarts and all it entails. Christianists are hardly likely to accept the ideal of every citizen being a contraceptor. They reject that ideal, even though the more successful RR is in fighting sexual smarts, the greater the numbers of less-advantaged women it drives into abortion.

Hence, the question is indeed fair: What do christianists care most about? What do they *really* want? Alongside political power, what is their actual bottom line? Is it unborn babies, or damaged women, or when all's said and done, might it just be about plain old *sex?* My personal experiences within evangelicalism tell me that Kristoff is once again on target when he observes that "There is something about reproductive health—*maybe the sex part*—that makes some Americans [christianists] foam and go crazy."[110]

Andrew Sullivan says that doubt and uncertainty are hallmarks of a genuine conservative.[111] And Peter Beinart says the same thing about a genuine liberal.[112] Doubt and uncertainty about abortion had wracked the hearts and minds of conservatives and liberals alike long before the RR came along and abolished ambiguity. Even after it was criminalized during the 19th and 20th centuries, citizens of goodwill (including my fellow evangelicals) agreed—though with great apprehension—that the tragic choice of abortion is sometimes necessary and permissible in order to avoid a greater evil. And so it is today.

Accordingly, is it not scandalous that christianists—unlike genuine conservatives—hold not one shred of doubt toward their rigid take on abortion? How many of the least of our sisters—disadvantaged women and their children—are penalized unfairly by the christianist insistence that it and it alone knows the right thing to do about abortion for *every* citizen? Is it not horrendous that RR demonizes, persecutes, and sometimes murders doctors who perform abortions?[113] And is not the scandal intensified by RR's fierce antagonism toward the one strategy that has the greatest chance for reducing unwanted pregnancies—thus making the necessity of a tragic moral choice less common? Accordingly, because they are failing to love their neighbors as much as they love themselves, is it not appropriate to mark the christianist rigidity on sex and abortion as unwise at best and reckless at worst? And if so, is that not one more reason to assert that christianists lack the credentials necessary to occupy the moral high ground when it comes to sexuality in particular and families in general?

NOTES

1. Tomlin 2007.
2. For similar feelings among adolescents, see the Danish film *The Other Side of Sunday*. (Nominated for an Academy Award—Best Foreign Language Film 1996.)
3. Martin 1996:320–25; Barstow 2009.
4. Goldberg 2006b.
5. Sharlet 2008:322–35; Herzog 2008.
6. Tomlin 2007:127.
7. Martin 1996:102, italics added.
8. Mead 1967.
9. Lefkowitz and Gillen 2006. And see sexreally.com, a Web site devoted to sex among post-teens.
10. Pew Research Center, July 1, 2007, italics added. http://pewresearch.org.
11. Abma et al., 2004:39.
12. Levin and Kilbourne 2008; Olfman 2009; Maxwell 2008; Fisch and Baskin 2008.
13. Luker 2006; Regnerus 2007.
14. Luker 2006. Nevertheless, a recent discussion in my college class illustrates the tension that persists today between how we actually behave and our ambiguity over whether our behavior is right or wrong. Almost all the students are sexually active and

treat that reality as being rather ordinary and matter-of-fact. It's just a given—"no big deal." Some were cohabiting (sharing the same residence). Others were simply boy/ girlfriend (separate residences). One person was engaged, though not cohabiting. When I asked, "Why not?" she said her parents would not approve—they would not think it was the moral or right thing to do. The other students—including those who were cohabiting—concurred that their parents do not approve of cohabitation. I then asked all of them, "What about the fact that you're sexually active—do your parents approve?" Without exception, every student (including the engaged woman) agreed that their parents do *not* approve. However, even though their parents know they're active, we do not "discuss such things with our parents." And so I asked, "How do you feel? Do you feel that being sexually active is the right or moral thing to do?" Smiles, shrugged shoulders, and embarrassed looks were their responses to my question. They simply could not bring themselves to say in front of their peers, "What I'm doing *is* the moral or right thing to do."

I then shared the story line of the 1981 film *On Golden Pond* featuring Katherine Hepburn, Henry Fonda, and Jane Fonda. Jane's character brought her fiancé home to visit her parents, but her father (Henry's character) denied them permission to sleep in the same room because they were not married—it would not have been the right or moral thing to do. In order to gauge how much beliefs have or have not changed since that time I then asked the students what happens when they bring their partner home (cohabiter, boy/girlfriend, fiancé) to visit their parents: *Are you allowed to sleep in the same room?* Without exception, all said "no"—including the engaged woman. A man commented that unmarried couples sleeping together in the same room would show disrespect to their parents. When I next asked if, after the household retired, couples got together for a while, the students smiled and laughed nervously, admitting that was in fact what occurred.

15. Hebrews 13:4, KJV.
16. Frost 2008.
17. Gelles 1977.
18. Finkelhor and Yllo 1985.
19. Gelles 1977.
20. Coontz 2005.
21. St. John 8:1–11, KJV.
22. For a very funny, but highly incisive look at the inner soul of David, see Heller 1984.
23. 2 Samuel 11, KJV.
24. Acts 13:14, KJV.
25. Acton 1870/1968; Coontz 2005.
26. Bell 1966.
27. Scales 1986.
28. Luker 2006.
29. Freedman 2006a.
30. http://pewresearch.org/databank/dailynumber/?NumberID=371; viewed 18 September 2007.

31. Scales 1986:265.
32. Luker 2006:255.
33. Luker 2006:256, italics in original.
34. "Abstinence Classes Don't Stop Sex, Study Finds," April 13, 2007, as reported by the Associated Press and published in the *New York Times*.
35. Bakalar 2007.
36. Joannides 2009; Regnerus 2007.
37. Santelli et al., 2007.
38. Luker 2006:252.
39. Abma et al., 2004. "Positive Trends Recorded in US Data on Teenagers," July 13, 2007, by the Associated Press as reported in the *New York Times*.
40. Luker 2006:252.
41. Santelli et al., 2007. See also "Positive Trends Recorded in US Data on Teenagers," July 13, 2007, by the Associated Press as reported in the *New York Times*.
42. Marsiglio et al., 2006.
43. Santelli et al., 2007.
44. Santelli et al., 2007.
45. Santelli et al., 2007.
46. Eckholm 2009.
47. Santelli et al., 2009.
48. See Blow 2009 for a summary of recent data on the issue.
49. Regnerus 2007:141–42.
50. NPR's *Fresh Air,* July 31, 2008, Interview with Seth Rogen.
51. Mark Moring, posted January 22, 2008, 09:03 A.M., http://www.christianitytoday.com/ct/2008/february/10.35.html.
52. Abma et al., 2004. See Regnerus 2007:210 arguing in a very thoughtful manner that despite everything that's occurring today, "we may still wish to consider sex as suboptimal for adolescents [regardless of age]."
53. Lawes 1948.
54. Scott 2008; Winner 2005.
55. Lefkowitz and Gillen 2006.
56. Regnerus 2007:182.
57. Luker 1996, 2006.
58. Zernike 2006; Luker 1996, 2006; Henshaw and Kost 2008.
59. Altman 2008a.
60. Altman 2008b.
61. Centers for Disease Control 2009.
62. Lefkowitz and Gillen 2006:235; and see Joannides 2009.
63. Goldberg 2009.
64. Altman 2005.
65. Altman 2005.
66. Altman 2005.
67. Nagourney 2007.
68. Kristof 2006.

69. Kristof 2008c.

70. Kristof 2008b.

71. Zernike 2006.

72. Baker 2009.

73. Donnelly 2007. Donnelly draws from the research of Helen P. Epstein (2007) into HIV/AIDS in Uganda.

74. Susser 2009.

75. "Experts Plan Strategies to Prevent HIV," November 30, 2006. From the Associated Press as published in the *New York Times*.

76. Altman 2006.

77. Regnerus 2007:161ff.

78. Piehl 2007; Luker 1996, Kaplan 1997.

79. Luker 1996; Regnerus 2007.

80. Strayhorn and Strayhorn 2009. Being religious is based on how strongly respondents agree or disagree with a series of statements such as, "There is only one way to interpret the teachings of my religion," or "Scripture should be taken literally word for word," and so forth.

81. Solomon 2006.

82. Cited in Balmer 2006:ix.

83. "3 Indicted in Basement Liposuction Death," reported by the Associated Press in the *New York Times*, October 26, 2006.

84. Fielding 2008.

85. PBS, November 7, 2005.

86. See www.ncpublicschools.org/nclb/. This Web site offers information and resources for how the Elementary and Secondary Act (ESEA) of 1965, reauthorized in 2002 as the No Child Left Behind (NCLB) Act, is implemented in North Carolina.

87. Lerner 2005.

88. W. Cates, Jr., 1981.

89. See http://www.aclu.org/FilesPDFs/map.pdf.

90. St Matthew 25:40 KJV.

91. Pear and Liptak 2009.

92. Martin 1996:320–25.

93. http://christyhardinsmith.firedoglake.com/2009/07/19/what-do-gop-law makers-think-of-randall-terrys-violence-stoking/.

94. Mohr 1978:vii.

95. Mohr 1978:vii.

96. Spitzer and Saylor 1969:xvii.

97. "A Protestant" 1969: xxiv.

98. "A Protestant" 1969:xxv.

99. "A Protestant" 1969:xxv, italics added.

100. "A Protestant" 1969:xxv.

101. Scanzoni 1969.

102. Martin 1996:191ff.

103. Tomkins 2007:175.

104. Toner 2007.

105. Carey 2008.

106. Piehl 2007; Luker 1996.

107. "A Slight but Steady Majority Favors Keeping Abortion Legal, but Most Also Favor Restrictions," September 16, 2008, pewresearch.org.

108. Brody 2006. See Gawande 2007 for the same argument.

109. Martin 1996:237.

110. Kristof 2008a, italics added; see Herzog 2008, Goldberg 2009, and Sharlet 2008 for the same point.

111. Sullivan 2006:180.

112. Beinart 2006a, 2006b.

113. Wicklund 2007; Press 2006; Frosch 2007; Associated Press 2009; Barstow 2009.

Partnering: Love Is
Where It's At

In 1996, the religious right pressured the U.S. Congress to pass (and President Bill Clinton to sign) the Defense of Marriage Act, or DOMA.[1] Several years later, fearing the courts might overturn DOMA, christianists got President George W. Bush to propose an amendment to the U.S. Constitution establishing marriage as the "union of one man and one woman." In his 2004 proposal, Bush echoed the christianist spin:

> The union of a man and woman is the most enduring human institution, hon-oring—honored and encouraged in all cultures and by every religious faith. Ages of experience have taught humanity that the commitment of a husband and wife to love and to serve one another promotes the welfare of children and the stability of society. Marriage cannot be severed from its cultural, religious and natural roots without weakening the good influence of society. Government, by recogniz-ing and protecting marriage, serves the interests of all.[2]

Many citizens would no doubt nod their heads approvingly if asked by a poll-ster whether they agreed with Bush's homily. Their nodding, however, says more about the abysmal ways history and social science are taught in grades kinder-garten through 12 and in college than anything else. If Bush or his christianist allies wrote those statements on their SAT exam, they'd get a failing grade. No matter. Their political agenda is aimed at convincing citizens that the suppos-edly traditional marriage of the 1950s is the way things have always been done in every society since ancient times. Christianists argue that the 1950s marriage style expresses the Adam and Eve narrative—one man and one woman married to, and only ever having sex with, one another for life. What is more, christianists speak fondly of the "Judeo-Christian tradition," by which they mean that Jews and Christians alike have forever adhered to identical family values. Alas, as researchers tell us and the Old Testament itself reveals, the christianist arguments are bogus.[3]

A familiar Bible story sheds light on marriage traditions among the ancient Hebrews though, as a child, I had no idea what it was all about. Our Sunday school teachers didn't spoil the charm of the tale by passing on its less palatable aspects. They focused instead on the love Jacob had for Rachel and how much he'd sacrificed to marry her. Our teachers failed to mention that Jacob was on the run from his half-brother Esau who'd threatened to kill him because Jacob had cheated him out of his rightful inheritance. Their father Isaac gave Jacob another reason to get out of Dodge when he ordered him not to marry any of the local women. Jacob may perhaps have fancied them but it didn't matter. Isaac told him to run off to his uncle Laban, marry a first cousin, and be fruitful and multiply.[4]

Jacob did as he was told, and after a month informed Laban that he "loved Rachel" (Laban's younger daughter) because she was "beautiful and well favored."[5] Jacob was sexually attracted to Rachel and he also loved her—so much so in fact that he agreed to buy her via indenturing himself to Laban for seven years. At that time, says historian E. B. Cross, "the prevailing manner of marriage was by the purchase of a wife on the part of a man."[6] The man owned his women (wives, daughters) in precisely the same ways he owned his slaves, livestock, and lands. Despite the fact that she was his property, Jacob loved Rachel so much that (in charming Elizabethan prose) his seven years of labor "seemed unto him but a few days for the love he had to her."[7] Cross adds, "There is no reason for doubting the existence of sincere affection between a man and his purchased wife in those far off days" but the way he got her "savored of slavery."[8] In any case, when his indentured servitude was up Jacob demanded his payment, and Laban threw a huge wedding feast with plentiful food and bountiful booze.

In today's Western societies, the custom is that the clergy or legal official, with witnesses looking on, pronounces the couple as husband and wife. They are thus formally married—well, almost. A reception typically follows, after which the couple is allowed to go off on their honeymoon and finally have intercourse—the ideal being that she, though not he, is virginal. In any case, the couple must have intercourse for their marriage to be what the law calls consummated, or certified. If one or both partners claim(s) they did not have sex together then the law permits them to annul their almost-marriage. They were never husband and wife after all.

Sex likewise sealed the marriage bargain in Laban's culture and time (around 1800 B.C.). Following a sumptuous wedding feast, the culture's family values prescribed that the father, with kin and community watching, allowed the man to enter the daughter's tent minus a chaperone. The couple was permitted to have intercourse and they were thus officially married. Bad luck for Jacob, however, because Laban had conned him. It was dark outside and with no light in the tent Laban secretly switched his elder daughter Leah for Rachel. Between the darkness and the booze Jacob had no idea until morning that he'd had intercourse with Leah. Too bad. Like it or not, he was now officially married to Leah and not his intended Rachel!

INVENTING ONE HUSBAND AND SEVERAL WIVES

A furious Jacob confronted Laban, only to learn that Laban had somehow neglected to share a bit of vital news with him. Namely, their clan's tradition was to marry off their daughters by age—starting with the eldest. Hence, Rachel could not marry prior to Leah. No problem, said Laban, because Leah had just gotten married. All Jacob had to do was to indenture himself to Laban for seven additional years and he would sell Rachel to Jacob to be his second wife. Their society, as did virtually all cultures at that time, practiced polygyny (one man, multiple wives). Researchers tell us that throughout history "polygyny . . . is the marriage form found in more places and at more times than any other."[9] Ditto for Hebrew society: "The ancient Hebrew family . . . may be . . . described as . . . polygynous."[10] Cross adds that

> It might be supposed that throughout the Bible, which has been the basis of Christian thought, there would be consistent adherence to monogamy. This is not the case. Nowhere in the Old Testament do we find monogamy as the normal or ideal type of relation between men and women.[11]

In any event, Jacob shook hands with Laban and their polygynous deal was struck. Laban then allowed Jacob to enter Rachel's tent by himself. They had intercourse and their community recognized them too as husband and wife. And, it's no surprise to learn that, at least for a while, Jacob "loved [his wife] Rachel more than [his wife] Leah."

> In November 2007, "The polygamous leader of a fundamentalist Mormon sect was sentenced to 10 years to life in prison for forcing a 14-year-old girl to 'spiritually' marry her 19-year-old cousin and commanding the naïve bride to submit to sexual relations against her will. The defendant was convicted by a jury in September of two counts of acting as an accomplice to a rape."[12]

Leaders of the mainstream Mormon Church were much in the news during 2007 nervously assuring reporters that they no longer endorsed nor practiced polygyny. Nonetheless, the Mormon Church's founder, Joseph Smith, established polygyny among Mormons during the early 19th century.[13] And, later on in that century while the fledgling Mormon Church was struggling to take root in Utah, its members continued the practice. There were several reasons why they did so. One was the fact that there simply weren't enough men to go around. The Mormons shared a second important reason with Muslims who, by the way, still practice polygyny today—though they limit the man to no more than four official wives.[14] Nineteenth-century Mormons agreed with Muslims that the Old Testament portrays polygyny as the natural or normal or customary way to do things: Among the extended families and cultures of the Old Testament, traditional family values permitted a man to have several wives if he could afford them (which many could not).

Returning to our soap opera, we learn that after a time Jacob began to hate Leah because she was childless. The writer then tells us that God felt sorry for Leah because she was "hated [and so God] opened her womb." Leah then had three sons in a row, and thus convinced herself that because of her newfound childbearing prowess, "My husband will [finally] love me."

Meanwhile, back in her tent Rachel feared that because she wasn't getting pregnant, Jacob's love for her might be ebbing away. She sensed that Jacob would start loving Leah owing to the babies she was churning out. At that point our tale takes a bizarre twist which was, however, quite in line with that culture's traditional family values: Rachel followed a clan custom by asking Jacob to have intercourse with her slave Bilhah. The boy born to Bilhah was declared to be the official son and a legitimate heir of Jacob. Jacob kept on having sex with Bilhah, who then had another boy—the second legitimate son of Jacob. Not to be outdone in their frenzied competition for Jacob's love and approval, Leah asked him to have sex with her slave Zilpah, who then produced two more sons for Jacob. Leah later added additional sons of her own to what she called her "troop." Finally, this weird melodrama wraps up as we learn that God took pity on Rachel and caused her to bear a child of her own.

THE AGRICULTURAL REVOLUTION

Anthropologists tell us that long before the Hebrews and other ancient cultures appeared on the scene, the earliest humans wandered about in nomadic bands of hunters, fishers, and gatherers.[15] Sexual attraction was a reality but so was the fact that men were physically stronger than women. Hence, even if she were not attracted to him, a man could compel a woman to be one of his sexual partners. The stronger the man, the more partners he was likely to have. A collection of attractive partners served as a status symbol, showing off the man's physical strength and sexual prowess both in claiming women and, very importantly, in defending them from the claims of other men. Watching TV channels such as PBS, Discovery, or National Geographic we can observe similar patterns among today's primates and certain other animals as well.

For many humans the agricultural revolution undercut those patterns. They discovered they could drop seeds into the soil that would grow into food. Hence, they no longer had to be nomadic in order to survive. Though not immensely important before, land gradually became extraordinarily valuable. Land was treasured, not simply as a means of livelihood, but also as a source of wealth that went beyond mere survival. Hence, alongside women, land and wealth became additional symbols of men's power and status. Inevitably, men began to fight one another, not only for the most attractive women, but also for the land best suited to grow crops and graze livestock. The more allies the men had, the more likely they were to win. Their allies were drawn typically from their sons, fathers, brothers, and cousins. The term *extended family* was invented to describe those blood kin who, through intermarriages with other extended families, formed larger alliances called the clan or tribe.

Such was the tribe presided over, in turn, by men such as Abraham, Isaac, Laban, and Jacob. Given that land was such an intoxicating status symbol, how could such powerful men ensure their immortality—that their honor, prestige, and status would endure well beyond their lifetime? The obvious answer was to pass on their land and wealth to their son(s). To ensure that a man's property, and thus his prestige and status were passed on (solely) to his son(s), it became essential to tighten the man's control over the sexual activities of his female partners.[16] The term *wife* was invented to describe the woman (or women) who would be the unique repository for what the Old Testament calls the seed of her husband. It thus became indispensable that his wife (wives) be virginal prior to having sex with her husband.

If she were not a virgin she held no economic value for the man. A previously used woman could not guarantee that her child was also genuinely his—that her son (and thus his property) could not somehow be claimed by another man. If she lost her value to eligible suitors, her economic worth to her father would also decline precipitously. If Laban had not been able to certify that Rachel and Leah were in fact virginal, he could never have extracted the purchase price (14 years indentured labor) he got from Jacob for both daughters. Over time persons gradually came up with the term *marriage* to describe the partnership they themselves were inventing: Marriage was the partnership that joined a man with his virginal wives who were allowed to have intercourse only ever with him. The purpose of marriage was to produce sons to which he could pass on his property and wealth. Such customs assured his status and prestige and helped to maintain an orderly (i.e., one with minimal violence) society.

But, for his part, there were no economic or social reasons at all for the man to be monogamous either before or after his marriage(s). He could own as many wives and slaves as he was able to afford because each of them would give birth only to his children. Furthermore, he could have intercourse with as many nonfamily women as he wished, because if one of them got pregnant *her* child had no legitimate claim to *his* property. Incidentally, many of these same ancient family values come to life dressed in late 18th-century garb in the 2008 British film *The Duchess* (based on actual events) with Ralph Fiennes and Keira Knightley.

INVENTING ONE HUSBAND AND ONE WIFE (MEN EXEMPTED)

Those were some of the marriage and family values of the Old Testament world—the region we now call the Middle East. But the Greeks and the Romans started to tweak at least one of those traditions during the several centuries prior to the Christian era.[17] It slowly dawned on them that polygyny had a serious built-in flaw because it sometimes led to serious and occasionally violent clashes within extended families, clans, and tribes. The stories of Abraham and his sons and grandsons show how chaotic things could get when there is ambiguity over inheritance even among the men who do hold a legitimate claim to their father's property. In Jacob's case, for instance, does his property belong to Leah's sons or to Rachel's?

Eventually, the Greeks and Romans figured out that one way to reduce those sorts of highly disruptive family battles was to advocate monogamy—but not because monogamy was moral and polygyny was immoral. Instead, they endorsed it for pragmatic reasons: monogamy seemed more likely than polygyny to maintain order and reduce violence in society.[18] A man, they said, should have only one official wife—and only the legitimate sons of that wife were entitled to his land and wealth. Although that was an important change to be sure, most other things remained the same for men. Just as men in prior civilizations had mistresses and casual sex, the Greco-Roman cultures looked the other way when a man (whether married or not) took one or more mistresses or engaged in casual sex with slaves or other women or with men. It was not at all uncommon for men (married or not) to practice bisexuality—their sexual partners might well include both genders.[19]

The major change for the Greco-Roman wife was that she (unlike Leah and Rachel) no longer faced a threat to her unique status from a competing wife. She was now the officially recognized channel for his legitimate and thus most favored children. However, her sexual situation under monogamy changed very little from what it had been under polygyny. She must be virginal prior to her marriage, and afterwards she was formally forbidden to have sex with anyone except her husband. And the basis for her virginity and fidelity was the same as before: in order to protect her husband's wealth, status, and honor, she had to guarantee that her sons were in fact her husband's offspring. But as far as men were concerned, virginity and fidelity held no greater relevance than they'd held for Hebrew figures such as Jacob or David. Men continued to sow their seed whenever and wherever they wished.

As the centuries rolled by, a number of disconnects emerged between Christianity and the Greco-Roman world into which it was born. The practice of monogamy was not, however, one of them. Not only did the early Christians endorse monogamy for moral (not pragmatic) reasons, they began to take a dim view of the sexual freedoms practiced by Greco-Roman men. In sharp contrast to those pagan men, Christian men were expected to behave pretty much like Christian women: They should be sexually pure and thus virginal until marriage and faithful afterwards. Because sex was inherently evil apart from the cleansing properties of marriage, Christians believed that nonmarital sex was taboo for women and men alike.

Although the world around them agreed that a woman having sex was *verboten*, it was not because sex was inherently evil. A woman having sex with someone other than her husband (future or actual) dishonored him and tarnished the good name of his family. But for pagan men sex apart from marriage was neither inherently evil nor a basis of family dishonor. Prior to the Christian era, men sowed their seed freely and no one thought very much about it. There was no reason to hide the fact that two sexual standards prevailed—one for men and one for women. But the basis for their double standard was social and economic—it had nothing to do with the moral essence of sexuality.

While the Christian insistence on a single sexual standard may have been laudable, it was doomed to failure precisely because it ignored economic realities. The Christian Church disregarded the fact that a man's control of land, property, and wealth allowed him to be in charge of his life. Women simply did not possess that sort of control. Hence, no matter what the church has preached for two millennia, the sexual behaviors of most men throughout the entire

Christian era were pretty much the same as they'd been during the centuries before.[20] Only now they did it *sub-rosa*. By insisting that sex apart from marriage was inherently evil, the church succeeded in driving the formerly public double standard underground. A single man who wished to be thought of as decent and respectable could no longer afford to do premarital sex in an open and public manner. If he wished to make his way in the world he must avoid being seen as what the Brits called a "rake." Even more to the point, a married man could no longer afford to do extramarital sex in a public and open manner. He could not risk being seen was as what the Brits called a "bounder."

Down through the centuries, folk wisdom, stories, music, plays, journal accounts, and letters described what Kinsey and other researchers documented in the mid-20th century: The actual sexual behaviors of many men both before and after marriage fell far short of the church's standards of virginity and fidelity. The middle classes emerging during the late 19th and 20th centuries copied what the upper classes had always done—insisted that their families be cloaked with the appearance of propriety no matter what it covered up underneath. The sexual peccadilloes of unmarried or married men could be winked at unless they threatened public scandal.

A biographer of Winston Churchill's mother Jennie (the Princess Diana of her day) writes that at the turn of the 20th century, "Private lives were considered private, with only a single social rule—no scandal. Divorce meant scandal."[21] If, for instance, a wife finally got fed up with her husband's sexual transgressions and threatened divorce on grounds of infidelity her peers generally kept it from happening: "'We saw to it,' said Lady Warwick, 'that five out of every six scandals never reached the outside world.' . . . Social pressure converged on the couple to avoid the final step." Warwick's observation came in the midst of talking Jennie out of divorcing her politically famous, philandering, and syphilitic husband Randolph (Winston's father).

INVENTING A VARIETY OF PARTNERSHIPS

Thus far we've seen that long ago ordinary persons invented a distinctive partnership between men and women and called it marriage. It may have been either polygynous or monogamous. In either case, its purpose was to produce offspring to enhance both the man's social status and an orderly society. Sex and children were paramount to this partnership, but love, affection, and caregiving were incidental at best. Love may or may not have been present—it really didn't matter. Historian Stephanie Coontz tells us, however, that for thousands of years the partnership we call marriage has been evolving and thus changing.

What's finally happened now, she says, is that love has "conquered" marriage.[22] Over the centuries, people have been tweaking the pecking order of what's important. Though once incidental, people have elevated love to become far and away the single most important reason why they marry. At the same time, people have allowed the ancient reasons for marriage (producing offspring for men and society) to tumble in importance. Though sex remains near the top of the pecking order (close to love) its purpose has morphed from making babies to creating pleasure—making people feel good.

WHAT IS THIS THING CALLED LOVE?

Jacob could no more have understood the marriage between Jennie and Randolph than Randolph comprehended the marriages between Jacob and his wives. And Jacob could never have figured out why Randolph was allowed only one wife. And why, he might have wondered, was it scandalous for Randolph to have mistresses as well as casual sexual encounters? For his part, Randolph no doubt envied the fact that sexual encounters and multiple marriages (including sex with the slaves of his wives) were, in Jacob's day, normal, customary, and traditional.

But perhaps even more extraordinary is the contrast between Rachel and Leah on the one hand, and Jennie on the other. Although we're told that Jacob loved and fancied Rachel, the writer never tells us how Rachel or Leah felt about him. They may not even have liked him, much less loved him. We know that Jacob hated Leah, but we never discover if he felt better about her once she started having lots of babies. We do know, however, that both Rachel and Leah wanted Jacob to approve of and respect them. But the writer tells us nothing of the women's feelings for him because their feelings didn't matter—at that time women's feelings were simply unimportant.

Fast forward to Jennie and therein hangs a tale of the evolution of marriage from ancient times to the present. Jennie was a woman well ahead of her Victorian era peers—she was very much a prototype of the 21st-century woman. Her feelings mattered a great deal to her, and she wanted her feelings to matter to Randolph as well. She also wanted very much to be an autonomous woman. She coveted the same freedoms as Randolph to explore her world—but on her own terms. Reverse back to Rachel and Leah. They were, in effect, chattels—little more than baby machines whose chief purpose in life was to contribute to their husband's prestige and the enduring social status of his family. In essence, they bought Jacob's "love" with babies—the more sons they generated the more "love" they felt they deserved.

But what might Leah and Rachel have meant by "love?" What did Jacob mean? What did love mean to Jennie, or to Randolph? And what does love mean to 21st-century men and women? Throughout the centuries, philosophers, poets, novelists, and songwriters have grappled with the intricacies of love, but with little success. Perhaps the best we can do is echo Cole Porter when in 1929 he threw up his hands and wrote his pop tune, "What Is This Thing Called Love?" Or, in the equally well-known question of the 1949 musical (and movie) *South Pacific:* "Who can explain it, who can tell you why? Fools give you reasons; wise men never try." In 1955, Frank Sinatra sang that whatever it is, "Love goes together with marriage like a horse and carriage—you can't have one without the other." But today's performers (rock and roll, country) tend to dwell on darker and more realistic themes, for example, that love is as elusive, mysterious, and painful as it is desirable. Mary Evans describes love in magnet-like terms: "There is nothing that the human heart more irresistibly seeks than an object to which to attach itself."[23]

Although the profound meanings of love may never be entirely fathomed, we might at least try to pin down some of its more evident features. The pre-Christian Greek thinkers coined a number of words to describe the varied types of love they saw around them.[24] One word for love described the deep affection and caregiving expressed by family (extended and immediate) and also among close friends. A separate Greek term for love captured the divine-human dimension. Still another term for love was the familiar *eros,* and that's where things get messy.

Jacob was sexually attracted to Rachel and he also *loved* her meaning what? Alongside erotic feelings, did Jacob feel some sort of indefinable emotional feelings for Rachel? Cross says probably so—at least for a while. In addition, it seems that the more babies Rachel and Leah produced the more he loved them. Thus alongside sexual and emotional feelings, his love for them also included the idea of being pleased by certain activities they did on his behalf. On the other hand, we don't know if either Rachel or Leah loved Jacob. We can't tell if either one felt much sexual attraction to, or emotional connection with, or any sense of being pleased with, Jacob.

Fast-forward to the present. It is obvious that two persons (straight or gay) may be sexually attracted to one another but feel little or no emotional connection. Moreover, they may share few if any activities apart from intercourse. They are primarily sexual partners who hook up from time to time. Young adults today describe it as having a fuck-buddy, and it's quite possible to have more than one such buddy.[25] The partners are entirely free either to maintain their erotic connection, or terminate it, or add on additional facets. Those potential upgrades might include an emotional dimension, and/or an appreciation for shared leisure activities—hanging out together, partying with friends, and so on.

INVENTING THE RELATIONSHIP

If that kind of upgrading continues for a while, the couple may gradually start to define itself as having built or constructed a *relationship*. This is a relatively recent happening, having evolved since the 1960s. The partners typically intend to be sexually monogamous and are known to friends and family as a *couple* or an *item*. They are boyfriend and girlfriend. They might just as well of course be boyfriend and boyfriend or girlfriend and girlfriend. From the standpoint of social science—to say nothing of plain old common sense—being straight or gay/lesbian has nothing at all to do with constructing a relationship. As far as the research shows (and as far as I can tell by talking to and observing hetero- and homosexual couples of all ages), the sexual attraction, the emotional connection, the caregiving, and the sense of appreciation for shared activities are virtually identical among straights and gay/lesbians alike.[26] In essence, the feeling that "I love my partner" seems to be pretty much the same whether the couple is hetero- or homosexual.

Among both straights and gay/lesbians, partners are free to terminate their relationship at any time. Unlike the Sinatra ditty, there is no necessary connection at all between their love and anything like marriage. And, for straights and gay/lesbians alike, opting to maintain their relationship consists in large measure of efforts to build an ever-deeper emotional connection. Plato and other pre-Christian Greek philosophers believed that among the most treasured of life's experiences, none is greater than what Evans describes as bonding with a "soul-mate."[27] Though Plato never used that precise term, he believed that the intertwining of human beings at a profound emotional or psychological level—the fusion of their two inner selves—is a unique experience. Plato and his peers viewed that fusion as enormously gratifying and the wellspring of an incomparable sense of personal well-being.

Most Greeks felt, however, that this unique experience was the sole province of men with men. One of the proofs of women's innate inferiority was their perceived inability to bond with men at this deep emotional level. Consequently, most men sought out a soul mate from among other men. Neither his wife nor his mistresses were deemed eligible. Plato observed, "A man typically sought a marriage partner not to have conversations in which he could unburden his mind and pour out his ideas but to have children."[28] The notion that men bond with other men in a unique fashion—in a manner that is simply not possible between men and women—has in one form or another persisted down through the centuries. Even today the expression *guy thing* conveys the sense that men share some sort of mystical and rarefied bonding—a unique male camaraderie—from which women are necessarily excluded.

During the 1960s and 1970s, advocates began challenging the ancient notion that women and men could not bridge the chasm between them and bond as soul mates.[29] They argued that although women and men had forever inhabited different worlds, the past was past. Men and women, they said, were coming to share the same worlds of workplace and homeplace. Hence, there was no imaginable reason why they could not also strive to bond as soul mates, confidantes, and intimates. To be sure, trying to define or describe the soul mate experience is like defining or describing sex itself. There is absolutely no way to fully comprehend either experience unless and until one does it. Richard Kraut says that Plato thought of a soul mate this way:

> The best sort of lover is someone who is bursting with ideas about how to improve human life. Because he cannot fully understand or develop those ideas on his own, he needs a conversational partner who will help him nurture those [unformed ideas]. . . . In the best kind of eros, self-regard and dedication to others mutually reinforce each other.[30]

Simply being sexual partners (fuck-buddy) is a whole lot easier than being a soul mate, or confidante, or intimate. There is no such thing as the one-night stand or the no strings attached hook-up when it comes to being soul mates. It takes enormous amounts of time and lots of hard work, and there is no series of multiple orgasms to measure success. Nonetheless, among 21st-century adults one of the goals, if not *the* prime goal, of a relationship is to try to develop this sort of emotional bonding or connection with one's partner.[31] One of the indicators that their relationship is being successful is the perception by both partners that the depth of their emotional intimacy is growing and developing. The deeper their level of intimacy becomes, the more likely they are to maintain their relationship. On the other hand, if their soul mate bonding peaks and/or withers, the chances increase that one or both of them might gradually withdraw from their relationship. Today, many persons in the West believe that their efforts to cultivate this sort of intense emotional bonding are an essential part of what it means to be fully human and, needless to say, this quest is equally urgent among gay/lesbians and straights alike.

Thus far, we've seen that in the course of inventing the type of partnership known as the relationship, present-day persons (hetero or homo) incorporate sexual intercourse, an appreciation for shared activities, and emotional bonding in particular. But persons can and do experience any one of these three components apart from the other two. Good friends may, for instance, possess intense emotional bonding and shared activities but not be sexual. They might warmly embrace and even kiss each other and say "I love you," and tell others "I truly love my friend." But everyone understands that their love is not what the Greeks and others since have called *eros* or erotic love. The sexual component is indeed a distinctive element found at the core of what is meant by today's relationship as opposed to a strong friendship.

INVENTING COHABITATION

Furthermore, all of us realize that there are still more components or building-blocks that a couple might add in order to upgrade their partnership. A pre-1960s couple in love was expected to marry as a matter of course. Today, younger persons scoff at Sinatra's assertion that of necessity marriage follows love. Post-1960s, persons invented the relationship as a public indication of their love (including sexuality) quite apart from marriage. And while in the midst of experimenting with the notion of relationship, some persons started inventing yet another type of partnership as well.

Cohabitation represents the invention of a context for love that includes but extends well beyond the relationship. It is a way of life that persons on both sides of the Atlantic have invented in the relatively short span of several decades. Typically, it refers to unmarried heterosexual partners publicly sharing the same household on a continuing basis. But obviously, many gay and lesbian couples do in fact cohabit as well. Cohabitation is not simply love apart from marriage. It is love in a context that for all practical purposes looks very much like marriage. Research shows that the longer the couple cohabits the more their partnership becomes indistinguishable from that of married partners—particularly so when it comes to caregiving.[32] Recently, the male partner of a woman colleague of mine became seriously ill and was forced to endure a lengthy series of surgeries and other invasive treatments. They'd been cohabiting for 20 years, and her support, nurture, and attention towards him during his surgeries and recovery periods were precisely the same sorts of caregiving one would expect between spouses.

Although what we now call cohabitation is being invented primarily in the West, it turns out that certain other societies have over the centuries invented social arrangements that, analogous to cohabitation, are marriage-like in many (not all) respects. For example, a Shi'a Muslim man may, in addition to having as many as four permanent wives, have as many *temporary* wives as he can afford: "Temporary marriage is a contract between a man and an unmarried woman, be she a virgin, divorced, or widowed, in which both the period the marriage shall last and the amount of money to be exchanged must be specified. . . . At the end of the specified period the temporary spouses part company without any divorce ceremony."[33] Haeri adds that the purpose of the temporary marriage is sexual enjoyment, while the goal of the permanent marriage is procreation.

Prior to the 1960s, most Americans believed that living together in a non-married sexual relationship was a vile and ruinous thing to do—especially for the woman, who was viewed as cheap and a slut. Though some couples may have done so on the sly, almost none cohabited openly as is the practice today. Cohabitation was vilified as living in sin, and many landlords refused to rent to couples who confessed to being unmarried.[34] Indeed, as recently as 2006, officials in the St. Louis suburb of Black Jack threatened to evict an unmarried, cross-racial, heterosexual couple from a house into which they'd recently moved along with three children. Black Jack has an ordinance prohibiting more than three people from sharing a house together unless they're related by "blood, marriage or adoption."[35]

The chief reason why living together was believed to be a corrosive influence on society is because it publicly and unashamedly flaunted fornication (sex between unmarried persons) on a continuing basis. Although everyone knows that many people have secretly fornicated in the woods or behind closed doors, cohabitation puts sex on public display for all to see—especially the unsullied children of neighbors. It's as if cohabiters (hetero or homo) are discharging tiny airborne microorganisms into the atmosphere that infect and corrupt children and youth. Cohabiters undermine and destroy society, charge their critics, by turning the souls of innocents away from the 1950s model of marriage. Nevertheless, despite the fact that during the 1960s the allegedly reprehensible behavior of public and ongoing fornication was forbidden by law in virtually every state, growing numbers of couples first in Europe and then in North America started cohabiting anyhow.[36]

Today, only a few states continue to classify fornication as a felony offense. Widespread changes in state laws reflect the fact that cohabitation is no longer an uncommon form of behavior. One study concludes that in recent decades, cohabitation has "increased dramatically among both young people and old people."[37] According to the U.S. Census Bureau, the number of unmarried couples living together at any one point in time grew tenfold between 1960 and 2000. Between 1990 and 2000 the rate of increase was 72 percent.[38] By 2000, some

9.7 million Americans were cohabiting at the time they were interviewed. Equally significant is the fact that by 2000, 41 percent of all American women ages 15–44 had cohabited at least once in their life. And, among women aged 30–39, half had cohabited at some point in their life.[39]

Naturally enough, as growing numbers of citizens cohabit, people's ideas about cohabitation followed suit. Recent studies reveal that the majority of U.S. citizens no longer believe that cohabitation is a vile thing, no matter what people thought about it in the 1950s.[40] Quite the contrary, the percentages of persons (especially those who are younger) telling the pollster that cohabitation is a good thing, have risen steadily in recent decades. When the pollster asks today's citizens what they think about cohabitation, most seem to indicate that cohabitation is not a big deal—people no longer think it's worth getting all steamed up about.

Although one might presume so, by no means does being evangelical immunize against this particular social invention. A 2005 Gallup Poll revealed that 22 percent of U.S. evangelicals of all ages believe that "it's a good idea for a couple who intend to get married to live together first."[41] The comparable figure for Americans of all ages was 40 percent. A 2001 survey by the British Evangelical Alliance discovered that one-third of younger UK evangelicals (aged 18–35) "say they have no problem with cohabitation."[42] A similar survey in 1995 revealed that only 28 percent of younger UK evangelicals approved of cohabitation. Dismayed Alliance officials said the increase among their youth in such a brief time was "shocking." Officials took comfort, however, in the fact that their "number still trails far behind the 83 percent of non-Christians who approve of cohabitation." Nonetheless, the trend is causing them considerable anxiety. They can't help but wonder how much time will pass before cohabitation is as acceptable and as common among younger evangelicals as it is among the majority of citizens.

And, on this side of the pond, the National Association of Evangelicals (NAE) takes as dim a view of cohabitation as does its UK counterpart. The NAE views cohabitation as a clear and present danger to our republic. In 2000 the NAE declared that "marriage is a holy union of one man and one woman."[43] The NAE then added that, "Our nation is threatened by [among other things] a rise in cohabitation."

Based on the imagery of airborne microorganisms infecting innocents and destroying society, heterosexual cohabitation is as at least as great a hazard to our republic as is homosexual cohabitation. Indeed, it could be viewed as a much more serious threat owing to their vastly superior numbers. Heterosexuals, after all, account for at least 90 percent of the population. Why then do christianists focus so much attention and vitriol on homosexuals—at best only 10 percent of the population? If America is actually descending into moral quicksand, why not stalk the 90 percent who are most at fault for dragging us to oblivion? Why, for instance, did christianists and Bush stop with their 2004 amendment? Why not also propose an amendment that bans cohabitation among straights and gay/lesbians alike? Why not rid our society once and for all of the twin despicable moral evils of publicly tolerated fornication and publicly tolerated sodomy?

The answer lies, of course, with today's political realities. In their lust for power, christianist leaders realize that no votes can be gleaned by censuring a social pattern now taking hold among a large segment of the population. The religious right gets a lot more traction by demonizing a small minority of U.S. citizens. Chapter 4 argued that christianist abortion rhetoric is in essence an assault on disadvantaged and defenseless women—many of whom are black and Latina. Because homosexuals are likewise a minority of the population, the RR's leaders believe it's politically safe to assault them as well.

INVENTING *REAL* MARRIAGE IN TODAY'S WORLD

Mary Cheney, daughter of former Vice-President Dick Cheney, told Terry Gross, host of NPR's *Fresh Air,* that, "I've been married to Heather Poe for 16 years."[44] In her 2006 interview with Cheney, Gross wondered if homosexual marriages such as hers might undermine "real" marriage and thus the entire fabric of American society. At that remark Cheney bristled. She brusquely responded that she simply cannot fathom how her marriage could threaten anyone, much less our whole society. Several months later Cheney announced she was pregnant, and in 2007 gave birth to a boy that she and her spouse now parent together.

The root cause of the testy exchange between Cheney and Gross was Gross's term *real* marriage. Gross is well aware that persons on both sides of the Atlantic are inventing partnerships such as the relationship and cohabitation. Nonetheless she, like most citizens, seemed to have difficulty wrapping her head around the notion that marriage too is precisely the same type of thing—*it too is a social partnership that people invent or create.* The type of marriage our ancestors invented was based on the premise that prolific childbearing is the raison d'etre of marriage. Accordingly, it was necessary that the partners should carry around complementary biological equipment. Their copulation should result in reproduction to perpetuate the man's lineage and help make a stable society. Gross's comment implied that the way marriage was invented in ancient times still holds sway today: *Real* marriage happens when the heterosexual couple wiggles itself into the same suit of clothes worn by countless thousands of generations before it. Christianists and others argue that this is one suit humans do not have the luxury of tailoring. Our sole option is to adjust to its style and shape as best we can.[45]

"What's in a name? That which we call a rose, by any other word would smell as sweet" (*Romeo and Juliet,* act II, scene ii, lines 1–2). *Rose* is, of course, the common term for something quite uncommon—a flower whose beauty is magnificent and whose fragrance is unique. Shakespeare reminds us, however, that it's not the word *rose* that's unmatched and awe-inspiring, but rather the essential or fundamental qualities of a certain flower. Nature (helped along by skilled breeders) is forever enhancing the beauty and fragrance of that flower. When compared to its essential qualities, the name or label we happen to assign to the flower is irrelevant.

The essential nature of the flower we now call *marriage* is the same as it is for the relationship or for cohabitation—that indefinable something called *love.* Love is expressed in several ways, perhaps the most profound of which is emotional bonding with one's soul mate—a bonding that is equally powerful for straights and gay/lesbians alike. For some homo and hetero persons it is quite enough to express their bonding within the context of a relationship. Other couples choose to express their bonding via cohabitation, and that partnership turns out to be quite sufficient for them. They tend to feel that their soul-mate bonding would not be enhanced should they choose to marry. Moreover, a growing number of those cohabiting couples (homo and hetero) already share the activity of parenting, and they don't see how their parenting could be made any more effective should they marry.

Nonetheless, despite a long-term decline in marriage rates on both sides of the Atlantic, the majority of heterosexuals do indeed marry at least once. A 2007 Pew study found that "even though a decreasing percentage of the adult population is married, most unmarried adults say they want to marry."[46] (The percentage of married-couple households in the United States decreased from 52 to 49 between 2000 and 2005.[47]) Moreover, the fact that growing numbers of homosexuals are agitating for the right to marry terrifies christianists and led to their demands for DOMA.[48] But what is it about the label *marriage* that most people seem to covet? If, say, they are cohabiting (hetero or homo) and if their emotional bonding is becoming ever more profound, and if they are reasonably effective parents, what more could they possibly gain from marriage? And if, as the research studies show, parenting among both gay/lesbian and straight cohabiters is neither worse nor better than it is among married couples of the same social class, why covet the label of marriage?[49]

The answer starts with the fact that contemporary persons are transforming an onerous burden—a residue from pre-1960s marriages—into something quite different. Prior to the 1960s, divorce was illegal in some states and, in all cases, difficult and expensive to obtain. More to the point, separation and/or divorce were (as we saw in Jennie Churchill's case) perceived as scandalous. A stable marriage was judged to be a successful marriage. Men and women who suffered a broken marriage were thought to be lacking in moral fiber. In addition, children from a broken home were believed to be at greater risk for innumerable negative consequences. "For better or worse" meant precisely that— even when the worse far outweighed the better for both children and adults.

Today's couples (hetero and homo) value permanence or continuity, but not because it demonstrates moral virtue in any religious sense. Cultivating that most prized aspect of their bonding—namely, emotional intimacy—takes enormous amounts of time and energy. During the course of investing that much of their life in their partner, some cohabiting persons may gradually come to perceive that being with their soul mate is exceptionally rewarding. They might also sense that the rewarding process of struggling together to grow their intimacy deeper could very well continue indefinitely: As far as they can tell, their shared soul-mate experience is, like fine wine, expected to improve with age. They are thus prepared to make a commitment to one another—*the cohabiting partners (such as my colleagues above) pledge to continue cultivating their shared soul-mate experience for a lifetime.* Because most of us feel that having sex with someone other than our soul mate undermines that ongoing experience, we typically build monogamy into our commitment. A few such cohabiting couples (hetero or homo) choose to keep their commitment private, but most typically share their pledge with family and friends in an informal manner.

Some of those cohabiting couples (hetero or homo) believe that, in addition, a more public affirmation of their dedication would underscore their seriousness and reinforce their commitment. Accordingly, some cohabiting couples (especially in Europe) sponsor an open declaration of their commitment marked by a public event of some kind, including a celebration or party with family and friends.

Finally, other couples wish to take what many citizens believe to be the ultimate step—they want to sanction their public commitment via the law. In Western societies, we call that sanctioning *marriage*. Their formal proceedings may occur in either a jailhouse or a splendid cathedral or anywhere in between. I was once an official witness to a marriage ceremony performed by an armed deputy sheriff in the dark and dreary basement of his county jail with the cells as background. The 1997 film *The Boxer* opens with a bride complete in her lavish wedding gown and large bridal party being escorted into a British prison to marry a prisoner who appears in a formal tuxedo. Immediately following the vows, she and her party are whisked away to a wild celebration that lacks nothing except the groom, who remains in prison.

But no matter where the ceremony occurs, marriage is now perceived as the ultimate signal that the couple means business in terms of working together forever to nurture their shared soul-mate experience. During the festivities that typically follow, family and friends join with the *straight* couple in celebrating their good fortune at having a permanent soul mate. As of July 2009, a mere six states allowed homosexual couples to make that same sort of formal *and legal* affirmation of their love.[50]

During the times of the ancient Hebrews, marriage likewise triggered community festivities. But their merriment had nothing at all to do with the couple's mutual love, even if love were present. Love was entirely beside the point. Instead, the community paid attention to what the couple was now officially commissioned to do—produce male heirs ensuring the immortality of the man's family line. Because the couple had taken on this vital task, their community bestowed on them a great deal more esteem, prestige, respect, honor, and status *after* their marriage than they'd ever experienced beforehand. The fact is that both partners suddenly became special persons in their own eyes and in the eyes of their community. Moreover, being special applied to each of the wives a man might have. Jacob and all his wives now belonged, so to speak, to an exclusive club.

Today, we too celebrate marriage, though not because it transforms the couple (hetero or homo) into legitimate baby-makers. *But transform or morph them it does.* In the eyes of family, friends, and society, their legal certification represents an actual metamorphosis—caterpillar into butterfly. Like the TV ad showing how pathetic one looks *before* using a weight-loss pill, and how great one looks *after* using it, the community perceives that their marriage has had a similar pre–post impact on the partners. Because it is the legal and official confirmation of their commitment to cultivate their emotional bonding for a lifetime, marriage marks them as uniquely distinctive from, and more worthy of respect than, unmarried, that is, lesser mortals. Marriage thus has the effect of boosting their esteem, prestige, and social standing. In the eyes of most citizens (both married and single) married persons are respected more highly and regarded more positively than those who are not. Married persons have thus gained entrée into a select or exclusive club. Consequently, today's wedding celebration applauds the couple not only on their good fortune at having a soul mate, but also because of the honor and respect attached to their elevated social status.

THE REALITY OF TRANSITION

Needless to say, despite their vows to pursue forever their mutual quest for intimacy, many married and cohabiting couples (hetero and homo) do in fact split or transition. Transition carries with it none of the negative baggage conveyed by the D word. Divorce was a scandal, the husband and wife were viewed as morally suspect and, perhaps most shameful of all, they were accused of having failed at their marriage. It was quite common to point the finger at the guilty party—the spouse who was deemed most responsible for wrecking the marriage. If that turned out to be the adulterous husband, the wife was blamed for not keeping him happy in bed.

Today, instead of failure, we understand that the couple that is splitting is experiencing *transition* or *change*. In contrast to divorce, the idea of transition conveys positive feelings. A mid-life woman, for instance, recently told a National Public Radio reporter that she was now in the job market in order to support herself following what she called a "marital change."[51] One or both partners in the process of transition or change may feel that, for any number of reasons, their quest for emotional intimacy with their current spouse or cohabiter (hetero or homo) has reached its peak and/or is withering. It is always extremely painful and distressing for the partners to come to terms with the reality that they are no longer (if they ever were) soul mates. If children are in the picture, they too are likely to experience a certain amount of distress—at least for a while. Nonetheless, one or both partners may feel that it's healthier for their children (if any) and certainly for them to transition away from their partner. At the time of their marriage no one, of course, even dared think that the couple might not be together forever. After all, family and friends had gathered together to celebrate the couple's lifelong bonding and elevated social status.

Despite the fact that their marriage is emotionally unrewarding and perhaps even unhealthy, some couples remain together anyhow because often that is the path of least resistance. "Quiet desperation" was the phrase coined by one social scientist to capture the feelings of many 1950s spouses trapped in that situation.[52] But despair was much more likely to be tolerated then than it is now. Today, most persons perceive that increased maturity, growth, and development come from following a more active path. They believe that transitioning, though difficult and painful, is for many reasons the healthier route to follow. Furthermore, many persons hope they'll eventually be able to find someone with whom they can start cultivating a satisfying soul-mate experience. Needless to say, family and friends are typically distressed by the couple's transitioning. Nonetheless, many of them eventually come to realize, though perhaps reluctantly, that the couple's transitioning may ultimately be a good thing for all concerned.

DELINKING MARRIAGE FROM PARENTHOOD

That the elevated social status of a married couple (hetero or homo) has little if anything to do with producing children is documented in a 2007 report issued by the Pew Center. The study described what Pew called the "delinking of marriage and parenthood." For example, Pew found that in 2007 "just four-in-ten (41%) say that children are very important to a successful marriage, compared with 65% of the public who felt this way as recently as 1990."[53] Pew adds, "by a margin of nearly three-to-one, Americans say that the main purpose of marriage is the 'mutual happiness and fulfillment' of adults rather than the 'bearing and raising of children.'"

The book *Childless by Choice* gives us further insight into the "delinking" of marriage from parenthood. Thirty years ago, social scientist Jean Veevers argued that in North America and Europe there is a small but steadily growing minority of heterosexual women (most of whom are or want to be married) who choose to be child-*free*.[54] Unlike women who are child*less* owing to fertility problems, child-free women prefer, for any number of reasons, to rule out the identity of mother. Among those several reasons is their desire (like the child-free Roman Catholic nun) to devote maximum energies to serving the public household.[55] In any case, a 2008 U.S. Census Report suggests that Veevers may have spotted an important trend:

> Women are waiting longer to have children, and more women than ever are choosing not to have children at all. . . . Twenty percent of women ages 40 to 44 have no children, double the level of 30 years ago . . . and women in that age bracket who do have children have fewer than ever—an average of 1.9 children, compared with the median of 3.1 children in 1976.
>
> "A lot of women are not having any children," said Jane Lawler Dye, a Census Bureau researcher. . . . "It used to be sort of expected that there was a phase of life where you had children, and a lot of women aren't doing that now," Ms. Dye said. Women with advanced degrees are more likely to be childless, the study found. Of women 40 to 44 with graduate or professional degrees, 27 percent are childless, compared with 18 percent of women who did not continue their education beyond high school, the data show.[56]

These several studies from Pew, Veevers, and Census in no way diminish the worth or importance of children, as we see in Chapters 4 and 6. The idea of "delinking" marriage from parenthood is not some evil plot suddenly thrust on us by secular humanists. It is rather the continuation of the long-term trend begun in the 19th century—at the start of the industrial age. Recall from chapter 2 that for the first time in history effective contraceptive methods enabled ordinary citizens to figure out that marriage is far more than having as many children as God or nature might send. It is but a few short steps beyond that insight to the awareness that the partners' mutual love is far and away the most important reason for marriage. Children may or may not be present. If they are present, they deserve and demand the love and attention of parent(s), as well as the attention of others in their community. But they are no longer the raison d'etre for marriage—whether hetero or homo.

IN PURSUIT OF SINGLE BLESSEDNESS

Being Single on Noah's Ark is the title of a recent book in which the author asserts that "To be single in a couples' world is to be out of step with the prevailing belief about what constitutes a full life."[57] Cargan does not, however, mean that every person who is "out of step" (hetero or homo *and* not in a relationship, cohabiting, or married) goes about searching feverishly for a partner and thereby a "full life." Indeed, a 2006 Pew study found that, "Most young singles [nonpartnered] in America do not describe themselves as actively looking for romantic partners. Even those who are seeking relationships are not dating frequently. About half (49%) had been on no more than one date in the previous three months."[58] The authors added, "Only 16% of single [nonpartnered] Americans say they are hunting for a romantic partner."

Earlier chapters identified the 19th-century cult of true womanhood. But that same century also spawned its mirror opposite—"The Cult of Single Blessedness."[59] Louisa May Alcott (author of *Little Women*) was a member of that cult and in 1868 she wrote that "liberty is a better husband than love to many of us."[60] Those two cults stood at opposite ends of the continuum of a woman's autonomy during the 19th century. The married woman of that day must bury all thoughts of having any degree of independent control of her own life. But the woman who was both unmarried and advantaged was in complete charge of her own life—she was an autonomous person. Most of the women who identified with the cult of single blessedness came from advantaged families and were well educated. They were autonomous because they were economically self-sufficient. Most invested their life in serving the public household, that is, the greater good. They believed that having a husband and children would get in the way of their service to society and, in some cases, God.

In the urban North, causes such as abolition, women's interests (suffrage, education, and equality), abysmal housing and factory conditions of the urban poor, and horrific prison conditions were high on these women's list of priorities. Furthermore, it turns out that the cult of single blessedness existed also in

the South—in cities such as Savannah and Charleston. Apart from the abolition issue, those privileged women were similar to their advantaged Yankee sisters. There was, however, one major difference: the Northern woman achieved
autonomy by distancing herself from her extended family. Alcott, for instance,
distinguished herself as a famous writer. The Southern woman, on the other
hand, typically achieved autonomy under the auspices or sponsorship of her
well-to-do extended family.[61] She was able to convince her kin that it would be
in their best interest to indulge her idiosyncratic lifestyle. Their economic support and social connections made it possible for her (like Alcott) to carve out a
highly fulfilling life by pursuing the good of the public household rather than
any private household of her own.

Sexuality and unmarried parenthood are two major differences between single women (North and South) then and now. Women who belonged to the cult
of single blessedness were expected to be sex-free—to pursue passionlessness
as a way of life. It follows that they must also be child-free. The unmarried
mother of that era was scorned as a fallen woman and her children demonized
as bastards. Today, of course, sex is readily available to any nonpartnered woman
or man. That is no longer a big deal. However, the issue of being a never-married
mother is more complicated. On the one hand, it no longer bears the stigma it
once did. But on the other, chapter 4 explained that having a child is a potential
challenge to any woman's autonomy—particularly if she is nonpartnered and
economically less advantaged.

CHOOSING PARENTHOOD AND NO PARTNER

Nonetheless, some of today's nonpartnered women who are relatively advantaged appear to be creating a rather innovative pattern. They wish to be a
mother but, for a variety of reasons, prefer *not* to have a man in the picture:
"They are among a growing segment of women with jobs, often high-paying
professional ones, who have elected to bypass the storied progression from love
to marriage to motherhood."[62] They are well-educated, self-sufficient, autonomous women (most of whom are heterosexual) who choose, either via intercourse, or artificial insemination, or adoption, to become a solo-mother. But
they are not in the market for a partner. Instead, they "are choosing parenthood
without marriage and creating the new American family."[63] And because they
have only one, or perhaps a second, child, they seem able to provide quite well
for their child's economic and emotional needs.

From one perspective, we might say that there are vast differences between
the varied meanings of singleness today and what it meant to Louisa May Alcott

and her peers. But there is, on the other side, a striking similarity. And that is the awareness that enjoying a rich and full life does *not* compel a woman or man to conform to any predetermined cultural script. Personal fulfillment does not necessarily require a partnership (whether a relationship, cohabitation, or marriage). Nor does it demand children. One might have neither, or a partner without children, or children without a partner or, of course, both. Furthermore, regardless of one's personal situation, and whether living in present or past time, the quest for human fulfillment seems more achievable if a healthy dose of service to the public household is included in the mix.

HOMOSEXUALS AND ACCESS TO THE CLUB: MEMBERSHIP HAS ITS PRIVILEGES

I suggested that contemporary marriage is in essence a select club to which (in the United States) heterosexuals only may apply—except in a very few states. Club members enjoy the benefits of elevated prestige, respect, honor, esteem, and status—unique privileges that can be gotten nowhere else. That stark reality sheds a great deal of light on the current struggle over allowing homosexuals the right to marry. On January 1, 2008, New Hampshire became the fourth state to establish the civil union, which "gives same sex couples the same rights, responsibilities and obligations of marriage without calling the union a marriage."[64] As one of that state's legislators put it: "We are a citizen legislature and we legislated this into being." Another legislator announced that their next step is to replace the name civil union "with the word marriage—soon." And in fact New Hampshire did so the following year (2009). Several years earlier, neighboring Massachusetts had also changed the name and begun legalizing same-sex marriage. Connecticut followed in October 2008. New York does not yet permit same-sex marriage, but in May 2008 Governor Paterson

> directed all state agencies to begin to revise their policies and regulations to recognize same-sex marriages performed in other jurisdictions, like Massachusetts, California and Canada. . . . Gay couples married elsewhere "should be afforded the same recognition as any other legally performed union.". . . . Paterson described the move as "a strong step toward marriage equality." And people on both sides of the issue said it moved the state closer to fully legalizing same-sex unions in this state.[65]

Plainly, some public officials get it—they've figured out why homosexuals could never be fully content with lesser labels such as *civil union* or *domestic partnership* and so on. They would be dissatisfied even if those arrangements should offer every one of the legal perks (e.g., federal tax and social security benefits, emergency hospital visitation) now available to marrieds. The label *marriage* bestows a unique and elevated social standing on its occupants. The prestige, honor, and status attached to the name marriage convey enormous amounts of social, and thus personal, significance—benefits that can be gotten nowhere else. Denying a minority of citizens the right to join that exclusive club is thus discriminatory. It is social injustice which is, increasingly, being seen as a civil rights issue.

Not too long ago, most Southern states saddled marriage with the decree that only persons of the same race might apply for a license. But in 1967 the U.S. Supreme Court stripped away that decree by proclaiming that it was un-American to deny access to the club simply because the partners come from different races.[66] Given that we are now reinventing marriage to be all about a profound degree of love described as the bonding of soul mates, how can we possibly justify refusing entrée to the club simply because the partners belong to the same gender?

Nonetheless, despite the fact that gay and lesbian couples in a few states now have the legal right to marry, many citizens in those states and elsewhere in America do not yet perceive them as possessing a *real* marriage. That same hesitancy to appreciate homosexual marriage as *real* is found also among some citizens in Canada and in several European nations which have in fact already legalized it. It is very difficult to shake the ancient tradition that marriage is all about persons with complementary biological equipment connecting for purposes of childbearing. It is hard to come to terms with the fact that the historical trend of persons continually reinventing marriage is one vital part of our ongoing pursuit of happiness. It is not easy to admit out loud that whether persons are hetero or homo, marriage is no longer primarily about children.

Despite the many barriers to embracing the notion that homosexual and heterosexual marriage are equally *real,* growing numbers of (mostly younger) citizens are coming to terms with the fact that there is no compelling reason why homosexuals should not be entitled to participate fully in all of the legal privileges and obligations of marriage. Legislation affirming that homosexuals are married in precisely the same ways that heterosexuals are married is thus a *necessary* first step towards their full participation.

Although necessary, such legislation is however by no means *sufficient* to persuade all citizens that homosexual marriage is *real* marriage any more than the civil rights legislation of the 1960s and 1970s was sufficient to convince large numbers of white citizens that blacks are *real* people—as fully human as whites. Nonetheless, such legislation was essential because it created the social conditions prompting younger generations of whites to see past skin color and into the essential humanity of black persons. Likewise, homosexual marriage legislation is just as essential because it helps create a comparable social situation. This time around, the legislation encourages younger generations of heterosexual citizens to see past sexual orientation and into the basic humanity of homosexuals—"They are just like us!" Given that the essence of marriage is identical for straights and gay/lesbians alike, we shall eventually no longer think of hetero marriage as *real* and homosexual marriage as *other*. There will simply be *marriage* celebrated one and the same and for all citizens alike.

A PROGRESSIVE APPROACH TOWARD MARRIAGE

Americans flocked to the movies of the 1930s, 1940s, and 1950s to see love displayed as pure schmaltz. Most of it was romantic fluff—sappy, sentimental, and mushy. *Love Happy,* the title of a 1950 flick featuring Marilyn Monroe and Groucho Marx, says it all. Hollywood reinforced an airy mythology to which Americans desperately clung: they wanted to believe that any (straight) couple in the grip of their overpowering romantic love could marry and soar above and beyond all of the down and dirty, nitty-gritty, and disheartening realities of everyday life. But when today's progressives say that love "conquers" marriage they do not refer to the schmaltz of an earlier era. Obviously, such fairy tales were not what Plato had in mind when he identified *eros.* Hollywood fables were not in the picture when he described the powerful bonding with one's confidante or intimate—what we today call the soul mate.

Despite the gravity of *eros,* some christianists dismiss its significance by painting it as schmaltzy. They want citizens to believe that the ideal of love replacing children as the bottom line of marriage is little more than a feeble attempt to cling to Hollywood sentimentality. But christianists don't stop there. Not only do they come close to mocking that ideal, they also want us to believe that, unlike the 1950s love myths, what's going on today is ominous in the extreme. They want us to fear and abhor the notion that ordinary citizens (hetero and homo alike) are in fact disturbing what christianists see as the eternal pecking order of marriage. They want us to believe that the ideal of love replacing children at the core of marriage is yet another secular humanist plot to corrupt the moral fabric of American society. Such humanist revisions, they assert, are self-indulgent and decadent—leading inevitably to the collapse of America.[67]

It is quite true that exulting in love celebrates liberal ideals such as freedom, growth, change, and development. But just as powerfully, exulting in love applauds conservative ideals such as duty, accountability, stability, and obligation. Keeping a healthy balance between the two sets of ideals within the partnership we call marriage is, of course, an exceedingly tricky thing to do. As Plato saw it, a healthy balance occurs when "self-regard and dedication to others mutually reinforce each other."[68] Jesus captured the same spirit when he obliged us to love our neighbor as ourselves.

NOTES

1. National Conference of State Legislatures, June 2007. See http://www.ncsl.org/programs/cyf/samesex.htm.
2. Ibid.
3. Queen et al., 1985.
4. Genesis 28:1–4, KJV.
5. Genesis 29:17, KJV.
6. Cross 1969:60.
7. Genesis 29:20, KJV.
8. Cross 1969:61.
9. Coontz 2005:10; Zeitzen 2008.
10. Queen et al., 1985:109.
11. Cross 1969:60.
12. Dougherty 2007.
13. Ostling and Ostling 2007.
14. Haeri 1989. Muslim men are, however, allowed any number of concubines or mistresses, and also temporary wives.
15. Coontz and Henderson 1986; Westermarck 1922.
16. Coontz and Henderson 1986.
17. Pomeroy (1997:7–11) notes that there are as many differences as there are similarities between Greek and Roman families. But when it comes to the pragmatic benefits of monogamy over polygyny, they share a similar type of contrast with the Hebrews.
18. Queen et al., 1985:121; Pomeroy 1997; Lacey 1968; Coontz 2005.
19. Kraut 2008:286ff; Sowerby 1995/2009:71ff.
20. Coontz 2005.
21. R. G. Martin 1969:135.
22. Coontz 2005.
23. Evans 2003:1, citing William Godwin.
24. Kraut 2008.
25. Wolfe 2000. See http://www.urbandictionary.com/define.php?term=fuck-buddy.
26. Kurdek and Schmitt 1986a, 1986b; Bigner 2006.
27. Evans 2003:41.
28. Kraut 2008:300.
29. Cott and Pleck 1979.
30. Kraut 2008:309, italics in original.
31. Collins and van Dulmen 2006.
32. Warner et al., 2008.

33. Haeri 1989:2. See Amirrezvani 2007 for an engrossing fictional accounting of the custom.

34. Frost 2008.

35. "Mo. Town Denies Unmarried Couple Permit," April 17, 2006, from the Associated Press as reported by the *New York Times*.

36. Trost 1979.

37. Thornton and Young-DeMarco 2001.

38. U.S. Census Bureau. See http://census.gov.

39. Centers for Disease Control and Prevention, "Cohabitation, Marriage, Divorce, and Remarriage in the United States," Vital Health and Statistics Series 23, Number 22, Department of Health and Human Services, 2002.

40. Thornton and Young-DeMarco 2001.

41. Cited by *Christianity Today*, posted online January 5, 2006, http://www.ctlibrary.com/ct/2006/january/5.20.html.

42. Ted Olsen, "One-Third of Young British Evangelicals Approve of 'Living in Sin,'" *Christianity Today* Magazine Weblog, posted May 7, 2001, http://www.ctlibrary.com/ct/2001/mayweb-only/5-7-12.0.html.

43. A Christian Declaration on Marriage, National Association of Evangelicals, Washington, D.C., November 14, 2000. See http://www.smartmarriages.com/christian.declaration.html.

44. "Fresh Air," National Public Radio, npr.org, June 13, 2006.

45. Blankenhorn 2007.

46. "As Marriage and Parenthood Drift Apart, Public Is Concerned about Social Impact: Generation Gap in Values, Behaviors," July 1, 2007, Pew Research Center, available at pewresearch.org.

47. Roberts et al. 2007a.

48. Rauch 2004; Larocque 2006; Polikoff 2008.

49. Polikoff 2008.

50. "A Contentious Debate: Same-Sex Marriage in the US," July 9, 2009, Pew Research Center, pewresearch.org.

The states were Massachusetts, Iowa, Vermont, Connecticut, Maine, and New Hampshire. Pew adds that in "June 2009, President Barack Obama granted family medical leave and certain other benefits to the same-sex partners of federal workers. (The presidential memorandum did not include health insurance coverage, which would require congressional approval.)"

51. NPR *Weekend Edition*, August 1, 2009.

52. Goode 1963:380.

53. "As Marriage and Parenthood Drift Apart, Public Is Concerned about Social Impact: Generation Gap in Values, Behaviors," July 1, 2007, Pew Research Center, pewresearch.org.

54. Veevers 1980.

55. See Chapter 7 for a more detailed discussion of the child-free option.

56. Zezima 2008.

57. Cargan 2007:xi. See Stein 1981.

58. A research report by Lee Rainie and Mary Madden, *Not Looking for Love—Romance in America,* published on February 13, 2006, available at pewresearch.org.

59. Chambers-Schiller 1984:10ff; Adams 1976.

60. Chambers-Schiller 1984:xi.

61. Carter 2006.

62. Hertz 2006:xv.

63. Hertz 2006:iii.

64. From the Associated Press, as reported by the *New York Times,* January 1, 2008.

65. Peters 2008. Washington, D.C. also recognizes homosexual marriages from the states allowing it.

66. Larocque 2006; Polikoff 2008.

67. Galli, Mark, posted July 24, 2009, at http://www.christianitytoday.com, "Is the Gay Marriage Debate Over? What the Battle for Traditional Marriage Means for Americans—and Evangelicals."

68. Kraut 2008:309.

Parenting All Our Children: A Mission for Americans of Goodwill

Thus far, we've seen that growing numbers of ordinary citizens are crafting a progressive approach to families—one that works and makes sense for 21st-century society. The approach aims to blend liberal ideals such as innovation, freedom, and change with conservative ideals such as responsibility, obligation, and accountability. Americans have been following this approach to modify the ways we do gender, sexuality, and partnering. We are, of course, simply repeating what our forebears have always done—trying to make families better, struggling to make them work for us. Like our forebears we sometimes fail but sometimes we do okay. And we, like them, never stop trying. Some of us believe that those persistent efforts are paying off. We think that today's families are healthier than they were, say, 200 or 100 years ago, or at mid-20th century—especially if one happens to be a person of color, or a woman, or less privileged.

As in years gone by, the citizens most engaged in doing the changes tend to be relatively well off. There are several reasons why privileged persons pave the path of change. Perhaps the most basic is that they were and are keenly aware of the strong ties linking bread-and-butter issues with social issues. Recall that the 19th-century spread of the newer, highly effective artificial contraceptives was a social issue: many church and civic leaders condemned the use of the innovative methods as immoral and sinful. Nonetheless, citizens who were well off began using them anyhow because of their obvious economic benefits: the contraceptives helped make them more advantaged than they were to begin with. Thus, they saw the newer methods as a bread-and-butter issue. Soon thereafter, citizens who were not so well off understood the methods' economic benefits and started using them too. Eventually, citizens from every social class embraced the methods' bread-and-butter aspects and redefined their social aspects: They started reasoning that God and/or science had given them these methods to use in order make life better. Rather than being sinful, they were actually a blessing.

And today it is déjà vu all over again. Relatively advantaged (upper-middle-class) citizens (white, black, Latino/a, Asian) are struggling to craft ways of doing gender, sexuality, and partnering that make sense for this new century and its emerging information age. They too view the bread-and-butter and the social aspects of the changes as inseparable: the changes make economic sense *and* are the right or moral thing to do. In addition, advantaged Americans have always believed that they have an obligation toward less privileged citizens. Sometimes the obligation is seen as helping, sometimes as empowering, and often as a mixture of the two. Helping means handing out needed items such as food, clothing, shelter, and so forth. Helping is sometimes referred to as "giving people fish." In contrast, empowering citizens shifts the focus away from taking care of people and towards enabling them to take care of themselves. Empowering is referred to as coaching people on how to fish.

The 19th-century public schools were, for instance, aimed at providing opportunities for less advantaged citizens to gain the skills necessary to take care of themselves in the emerging industrial age. In the early 20th century, Margaret Sanger and her colleagues violated the law and risked prison by offering poor women the chance to obtain, and learn how to use, contraceptives. Sanger believed that empowering poor women to control and limit their family size is vastly preferable to giving food, clothing, and housing to families that simply kept on having more babies, which made them poorer still. Sanger understood that contraceptives were a means of coaching women on how to fish and thus made economic sense. It also made social sense—it was the right and moral thing to do.

Let's assume that the Americans who are now crafting a progressive agenda for families are at the same time persons of goodwill. As a result, they're likely to feel at least some obligation for the economic well-being of our less advantaged brothers and sisters. Let's also say that many privileged citizens are not too keen on simply giving fish to the less well-off. They would much rather empower them to catch their own fish. But how can we do that? Conservatives and liberals alike have offered numerous suggestions as to the best ways to empower less advantaged citizens of all ages. This chapter tackles one specific question: What is the role of the public schools (K–12) in empowering children and youth to participate in the 21st-century information age? What can K–12 do that makes the most economic sense? Let's say that Americans of goodwill respond that what makes the most economic sense is for K–12 to reform itself. And let's add that the reform should also make social sense—it should be the right and moral thing to do.

We all know of course that K–12 reform efforts are now well under way, but that reform is turning out to be a lot tougher than anyone imagined. It follows that suggesting that reform should also include opportunities for less advantaged youngsters to encounter a progressive approach to families would hardly make it any easier. Despite the difficulties of doing so, Americans of goodwill might nonetheless make that proposal. Their rationale for doing so is simple enough: it makes economic sense, and it also makes social sense—it is the right thing to do. The religious right would, of course, mount a fierce firestorm of opposition to the notion that K–12 should go anywhere near a progressive approach to families—even if it should make economic and social sense. But before we explore the connections between a progressive approach and K–12 reform we need to take a closer look at the broader question of reform.

THE K–12 OF YESTERDAY

During the agricultural age, illiteracy was commonplace among the masses of citizens because few required the Three Rs to survive. Free public education evolved slowly throughout the 19th century in response to the industrial age demand that every child must know the Three Rs. School was also viewed as a place to teach children the sorts of values and work habits necessary to make it during the industrial age. Among those was obedience—doing what you're told to do as well as you possibly can without asking why.

By the mid-20th century, American public education had developed a reasonable fit between its mission, the needs of its pupils, and the demands of the industrial society that encased it. I grew up, for instance, in all-white, but ethnically diverse, working-class neighborhood some two miles due north of Chicago's Loop. Most of its residents were either European immigrants or the children of immigrants. (My father was an immigrant and my mother, though born in the United States, had spent her formative years in Italy.) For $20 a month, my father rented a tiny flat on land now gentrified and filled with condos selling recently for upwards of a half-million dollars. We white, working-class boys and girls went to schools where the white, middle-class teachers (mostly women, single, and Anglo-Saxon) instilled in us the Three Rs. They also enforced a very strict code of discipline. In the classrooms, halls, and lunchrooms of those inner-city schools, order reigned supreme.

Among youngsters at that time, the word *gender* was as foreign as *astronaut*. Gender was never cited in books nor mentioned in class or in the media. Nevertheless, gender pervaded our entire school experience. Though implicit, it was a commanding force. While no one ever said it out loud, everything that went on within the schools was governed by what chapter 3 of this volume called the 19th-century gender model. That model fit the industrial age superbly. Everyone understood that the whole point of the schools was to prepare boys to get the kinds of secure, well-paying, working-class jobs held by our fathers. My father was a professional baker and a proud, card-carrying member of the AFL/CIO. We boys were instilled with the belief that with a solid job in hand, we could marry and support a wife and raise a family.

For girls, the schools' purpose was to prepare them to be devoted wives and attentive mothers. When they left school or graduated, girls might work for a while as sales-clerks or secretaries. But everyone knew that as soon as possible they would quit their jobs, marry, and become housewives and mothers. (If an unmarried girl became pregnant, she and the boy did the right thing—they got married and quit school to start their family.) Though never inscribed in any official document, the schools were in effect the breeding grounds for those closely linked patterns of social class and gender. But no one complained. It was a set of secure and comfortable arrangements that worked very well indeed. It's no wonder that christianists, as well as other citizens, look back on those days with fond nostalgia.[1]

Christianists complain bitterly that since the 1960s vile secularists and humanists have tried to manipulate the minds and hearts of American youth by undermining the traditional (mid-20th century) values that once permeated K–12. The RR identifies rulings by the U.S. Supreme Court in 1962 and 1963 "banning officially sponsored prayer and Bible readings in public schools" as one catalyst for America's spiral of descent into moral scurvy.[2] By the time my two sons were in school during the 1970s, the K–12 atmosphere was shifting dramatically. The now racially integrated public schools had become places where teachers and students spoke freely about the inequalities of race, class, and gender that had pervaded American society since the Pilgrims. Boys and girls—both white and black—were encouraged to think and behave quite differently than they had in the past. In particular, black children and white girls were urged to prepare themselves for college and career. The Family Protection Act that the RR got introduced into Congress in 1981 was a panicky reaction to the goings-on in K–12. Christianists were incensed that federal monies were being used to pay for educational materials that promoted feminist values. The RR wanted to put a stop to that foolishness and use federal dollars instead to pay for materials that promoted what the RR called traditional families and traditional roles for women.[3]

K–12 IN THE 21ST CENTURY

A visit to K–12 today might suggest that the battle is over and christianists lost. Fighting over class, racial, and gender inequities now seems passé. Teachers and students from diverse races/ethnicities do all they can to try to minimize those inequities. Although christianists deplore the fact that what chapter 3 called the 20th-century gender model is pretty much the norm in K–12, they tolerate it and focus instead on issues such as abstinence and intelligent design. But don't dismiss the RR just yet when it comes to the battle for the soul of K–12. Though one phase of that epic struggle may be winding down, its next phase might perhaps be heating up.

A PRIVILEGE GAP AMONG CHILDREN AND YOUTH

The 1968 Kerner Commission Report on the causes of the severe urban violence that then convulsed American cities produced a memorable phrase: *Our Nation Is Moving Toward Two Societies, One Black, One White—Separate and Unequal.* But many dramatic shifts have occurred since then, and the situation today is infinitely more complex than it was in the late 1960s. Rather than a simple racial dichotomy, what's surfacing instead is an economic fault line marked by uneven twists and turns. For example, a 2007 Pew survey reported that

> *African Americans see a widening gulf between the values of middle class and poor blacks, and nearly four-in-ten say that because of the diversity within their community, blacks can no longer be thought of as a single race.*[4]

Furthermore, recall what chapter 3 said about today's postindustrial, information age:

> *Girls and women, and boys and men from all social classes and all racial/ethnic groups must have the opportunity to participate fully in the abundance that the information age promises. Such abundance is not, however, solely or even principally material. Its abundance is equally intrinsic, intangible, or spiritual.*

It is obvious that some children and youth have ready access to that abundance. The majority of those privileged, upper-middle-class youngsters are white, but their ranks also include growing numbers of blacks, Asians, and Latinas/os. But on the other side, there are even larger numbers of youngsters (whites, blacks, Asians, and Latinas/os) that do not have ready access to such opportunities. Those youngsters are thus relatively less privileged. They are drawn largely from the middle-middle-class, the lower-middle/working class, and the working-poor/lower class. That is the broad swath of American families that observers have in mind when they talk about the "vanishing middle-class," or the "disappearing middle-class lifestyle."[5] In his 2007 testimony before Congress, economist Harley Shaiken remarked:

> *During a period of robust economic growth, record profits and the fastest sustained productivity increases since the 1950s, only a thin slice at the top of the economic heap is enjoying higher living standards.*[6]

And, in a later interview, he added: "We're building exit ramps from the middle class. But what is the path to the middle class for most Americans now? We need to figure out how to resume building entrance ramps."

Observers say that until recently, many U.S. families could maintain some semblance of a middle-class lifestyle—the American dream. Lacking that, they could at least feel confident that they *or their children* might one day realize the dream. But even prior to the severe economic downturn of 2008/2009, forces largely beyond their control were devouring the chances of many ordinary Americans to realize the dream. For example, U.S. census data show that over the past several decades, the gap in incomes between privileged families and less privileged families has been growing steadily wider.[7] On the privileged side of that gap, families with incomes that were already high are steadily adding still more dollars to their family's wealth. But on the other side of the gap, families with lower incomes are garnering fewer dollars each year, especially when inflation is taken into account. Hence, a social fracture seems to be occurring in our society that is potentially much more ominous than the scenario depicted by the Kerner Commission. On one side of the rupture is the minority of youngsters from all races able to tap into the opportunities offered by the postindustrial era. But on the other side are the majority of youngsters from all races less able to do so.

REINVENTING THE ENTRANCE RAMP

During recent decades, a number of observers have sharply criticized America's public schools. Their chief complaint is that K–12 no longer prepares youngsters below the upper-middle-class to function effectively in the global marketplace. As the marketplace evolves into being dominated by what chapter 3 called the mind-tech alliance, K–12 has not kept pace. In response to that critique, two broad types of solutions have evolved.[8]

One set of advocates believes that K–12 remains a sound entrance ramp into the information age. They readily admit, however, that the ramp has lots of potholes needing to be filled in. They believe the best way to plug the potholes is via rigorous standardized testing. The George W, Bush mantra, No Child Left Behind, was intended to assure less privileged parents that standardized testing is the ideal way to close the advantage gap their children face. Other advocates for a sound ramp suggest additional ways to fill in the potholes. These include improved teacher training, higher teacher salaries, more dollars spent per pupil, state-of-the-art facilities and technology, and so forth.

An alternative approach to what ails K–12 comes from advocates wondering just how sound the ramp actually is.[9] Rather than filling in potholes they're more inclined towards some sort of big idea solution—one in which Americans think about reinventing the entrance ramp. They start by asking a rather simple question: *What is an educated person?* When I put that query to college students I get puzzled looks implying the answer is obvious: it means someone who knows lots of stuff or information—facts, figures, and happenings. Like most Americans, they believe that a person who possesses information is by definition smart and well educated.

Students invariably point to TV quiz shows as examples of the widely held view that knowing lots of stuff equals being smart. The contestant able to answer the largest array of questions is assumed to be the smartest. The title of the popular show *Are You Smarter than a 5th Grader?* says it all. Its title connects being smart with grade level: a high school graduate should know more stuff than a fifth grader, and thus be smarter. In September 2008, for instance, the Georgia state school superintendent, Kathy Cox, won $1 million on that show. She was asked: "Who was the longest-reigning British monarch? She answered Queen Victoria."[10]

During the industrial age, knowing lots of stuff was an adequate entrance ramp for making it. Information was both necessary and *sufficient* to enter the ranks of relatively advantaged households. The mission of both K–12 and college was (and for the most part still is) to pour stores of knowledge into empty minds. Researchers who study this approach call it *lower-order* learning.[11] It is considered lower because the teacher (expert, guru, or sage-on-the-stage) gathers the information and (much like a parent bird dropping worms into empty mouths) simply drops it into the vacant minds of passive recipients. The student's chief obligation is to regurgitate bits of that information on subsequent tests.

However, no parent bird worth its weight in worms tolerates offspring passivity for very long. The parent bird soon insists that the juvenile bird should leave the nest, and then coaches it on how to gather its own worms. Unfortunately, K–12 and college alike remain, for the most part, gripped by the teacher-as-feeder model. By and large, neither K–12 nor college has yet replaced that model with some sort of teacher-as-coach model. Researchers call this latter approach *higher-order* learning, or *active* learning, or *discovery-based* learning.[12] Much like the parent bird, the teacher gradually sets aside the role of feeder and morphs instead into a coach enabling and guiding the students or players to gather and use their own information. Like the juvenile bird, the ultimate goal is for the players to become responsible for navigating their own journeys of exploration and discovery.

A recent experience offered a vivid contrast between lower-order and higher-order learning. During class discussion I referred to the religious right. At once Karen asked how I defined the RR. I was a sentence-and-a-half into my (lower-order, or feeder) response when Chris called out, "I have it." He was seated with his wireless laptop open in front of him and had keyed "religious right" into google.scholar. Chris did in fact have it, and he shared it with the rest of us. He'd gathered his own worms, thereby rendering my feeder role redundant.

Chris had demonstrated the first or *necessary* element of what it takes to be a player in the game called higher-order learning (HOL). He's learning where and how to discover trustworthy information that speaks to the question he's trying to answer. Influential advocates such as Ted Sizer favor initiating an HOL approach around grade five or six.[13] Accordingly, to reinvent K–12 means making HOL its predominant mode of learning. Advocates believe that the youngster must become proficient and adept at HOL in order to have a secure place on the entrance ramp into the information age. They say that HOL is the coin of the realm in this new era. In the 21st century, the first part of answering the question "what is an educated person" is that the person is actively engaged in the never-ending, lifelong process of cultivating mastery of HOL.

HUMANS AS BORN PROBLEM SOLVERS

If the first part of HOL is to discover trustworthy information that speaks to the question one is trying to answer, the second is the ability to use that information to solve that problem. Suppose I asked Chris and two of his fellow players to form a team to which I assign this problem: How and why do christianists differ from some of today's younger evangelicals in their approach to making society better? Their first task is to gather trustworthy information. The team's second task is to think through that information in order to craft a solution to their problem. Their critical thinking must be rigorous yet imaginative at the same time. Although careful writing does not guarantee critical thinking, writing that is thorough and painstaking typically enhances it. Hence, the team's solution should appear as a written document. The simpler part of the coach's role is to point them toward useful information. The far more demanding part of that role is to cultivate their critical thinking. One way the coach does that is to provide continual feedback to one draft after another of their written solution. The upshot is this: To say that a 21st-century person is educated is to assert that he or she is a problem solver; and a problem solver must have a working grasp of both aspects of higher-order learning.

Surviving entirely by their wits, our hunting and gathering ancestors were expert problem solvers—they practiced what we now call HOL. Next, throughout the agricultural age, the great masses of persons were either problem solvers or they perished. They learned through trial and error, or, as the chief apostle of HOL John Dewey once said, by doing. Anyone who's ever paid close attention to a preschool child would surely agree that every child is genetically encoded with an intense yearning to discover new things through her own efforts—efforts that are often imaginative, resourceful, and innovative. A preschool child's delight at learning how to figure stuff out for himself is among the most meaningful experiences of those early years. It's fascinating to watch small children express their intense and boundless curiosity. There's no doubt whatever that they love to learn by *doing*—through trial and error. Children are born problem solvers—it is as natural to them as breathing. Sadly, a curious thing happens to many children after doing time in K–12, typically when they reach grades five or six: the lively curiosity and love of learning that once drove them to explore and discover new things on their own initiative has evaporated. What happened?

Although the agricultural age required most persons to be problem solvers in order to survive, the industrial age did not. When Karl Marx wrote about the alienation of the 19th-century factory worker from work, he was describing something obvious yet profound. Instead of waking up every morning wondering (as their forebears had done for millennia) what surprises a fickle Mother Nature might thrust upon them, they woke up instead to something quite different: repetitive, mind-numbing tasks—the same-old, same-old, day in, day out. Problem solving was not on the radar screen for the vast majority of the industrial labor force—persons with lower-middle-class, working-class, and lower-class jobs.

It follows that during the industrial age K–12 had no need to make problem solving its central mission. Regrettably, despite the fact that we're now evolving into the 21st-century *post*-industrial age, the teacher-as-feeder model still holds sway. Small children literally bounce into K–12 with a lively curiosity and a love of learning, but in all too many cases their natural inquisitiveness soon gets lost in the shuffle and slowly dissipates. Though everyone agrees it's a pity, few do much about it.

Shaping the future sometimes requires drawing from the past, which in this case was the hunting and gathering and the agricultural eras. Today's *post-industrial* age demands that every person, now as then, should become a problem solver. Stifling (by either K–12 or college) the innate human urge to explore, discover, and create is no longer tolerable. Because we believe that humans are creative agents, we might reasonably conclude that stifling youngsters' urges to come up with new ways to solve problems is a moral or *spiritual* matter, though not in any sectarian sense. Holding back the problem-solving or creating part of their humanity is simply not the right thing to do. Furthermore, in the interest of social justice, releasing that urge could, over the long haul, achieve at least two objectives: One, it might help reduce socioeconomic disadvantage. Two, it could enable a broader range of persons than ever before to make contributions to the greater good.

But how expensive would it be to reinvent K–12 along these lines? For one thing, the United States squandered billions of dollars in an Iraqi escapade that most Americans now believe was ill-conceived, to say nothing of how miserably it was executed. Could not a fraction of those dollars have been devoted to reinventing K–12? Would that not be a sound investment in the lives of all our children and in America's future? Second, Sizer observes that "school, as Americans [now] conduct it, is expensive . . . On top of this is the fact that children of poorer families—presumably youngsters who might require more support—are generally found in the less supportive settings."[14] The grim fact is that the United States currently spends hundreds of millions of dollars on an educational system mired in the industrial age. Could citizens of goodwill lend their weight to initiatives aimed at diverting at least some of those dollars into figuring out ways to connect K–12 more meaningfully with the future?

Persons of goodwill who see themselves at the forefront of social justice might consider joining forces with the several groups (such as Sizer's) already intent on doing precisely that. Will Okun is a veteran high school teacher in Chicago's inner city. His observations (below) are drawn from the kinds of schools that are filled largely with youngsters (mostly black and Latina/o) of the working poor. Nevertheless, his essay conveys certain basic themes that are painfully familiar to virtually every teacher in almost every American public school from kindergarten through the senior year of college. Whether located in the inner-city or suburbia, our schools—K–12 and college—remain for the most part geared to the 20th-century industrial age. Lower-order learning prevails. Students are seldom, if ever, pushed to exceed the limits of what they believe they can do. Mediocrity reigns and the verdict of many observers is that we can find little or no intellectual curiosity or love of learning among our children and youth. The higher-order learning skills of most youngsters—including those from privileged households, to say nothing of those from less privileged families—are average at best. It is especially painful to discover that few students feel any compulsion to serve what chapter 3 called the public household:

> *Many urban schools are training workers rather than developing thinkers or community-minded activists. Most students enter our classrooms intent on earning a high school diploma (or hopefully a future college degree) for the sole purpose of improving their ability to obtain more lucrative or stable employment. The schools allow this passive mindset to fester. Our classes fail to foster intellectual curiosity. Our lessons are unable to motivate the students. We do not demand critical thinking. We do not offer materials that are relevant to the students' lives or communities. Even on days when I am not drilling test-taking techniques, I do not understand why I am teaching certain material. How can urban schools not address the myriad problems plaguing the surrounding communities? Why are we not providing our students with the tools and the knowledge to impact change in their families and in their communities? Why do we not attempt to make education relevant?*
>
> *Instead, many overworked teachers seek students' submission through mindless busywork. We secretly bear witness to the [fact that we] socially promote woefully uneducated children towards graduation. It is possible for a student to graduate high school with no academic abilities, critical thinking skills or social awareness. However, the roughly 50 percent of urban children who do reach graduation have demonstrated an ability to sedately sit at a desk for six to seven hours a day and dutifully perform often tedious and regimented assignments. These "molded" graduates are perfect for the menial labor force; too bad there are no jobs.*[15]

THE BIG QUESTION

What are the links, if any, between reinventing K–12 in order to grow problem solvers and a progressive approach toward families? Reasonable persons of goodwill might well argue that we should limit our mission to nurturing students' minds and simply ignore the spiritual side of their lives. That would be an attractive option if K–12 were solely about privileged, upper-middle-class youngsters because it would avoid stirring up the hornet's nest of christianist indignation. However, as Ted Sizer observes, a big failing of K–12 has been its inability to connect with youngsters below the upper-middle class. He echoes decades of social science research by asserting, "The best predictor of a child's educational success has always been and still is the economic and social class of his family rather than the school that she or he happens to attend."[16] He adds that the schools have never yet been able to figure out how to overcome the "accidents of family, wealth, and residence."

Children and youth within upper-middle-class families do in fact get the message loud and clear that there is a strong link between a progressive view of families (though not calling it that) and doing well within, and contributing to, society. They perceive the connections between, on the one side, gender, sexuality, and partnering and, on the other side, full participation in the information age. First, when it comes to gender, privileged women and men understand that above all, "I must be an autonomous person." Next, when it comes to sexuality, researcher Mark Regnerus identifies an "emerging sexual morality" which is "characteristic of the upper-middle-class."[17] He adds that it is "strategic" and "education-minded." Accordingly, as they approach sexual activity (whether during or after high school) the chances are that advantaged youths are highly motivated by a sense of urgency to prevent a happening (pregnancy, STD) that could easily spin life out of control.[18] Finally, privileged women and men comprehend fully that the whole point of being partnered (whether in a relationship, cohabitation, or marriage) is to experience the profound type of love that Plato extolled. These days, anything less makes no sense.

Though the message that privileged youngsters receive from parents, kin, and other adults may be silent and subtle, it is powerful nonetheless. Those youngsters absorb the reality that to do well in the information age it is *necessary* that they have opportunity, which their family provides them on an ongoing basis. But opportunity by itself is not *sufficient* in order to do well. What is *necessary and sufficient* is that opportunity must be pursued alongside wise or smart personal life choices. Research shows, however, that far too many less privileged youngsters fail to perceive those links.[19] That appears to be so even for talented youth such as Jean. Recall from chapter 4 that Jean is an African-American woman who grew up in a working-poor family with a mother and grandmother who'd each been a solo-parent. Her considerable talents earned Jean a much-coveted *opportunity*—an all-expenses-paid ticket to college.

On the smart-choice side of things, sex apart from marriage was unthinkable to Jean and contraceptives were as foreign to her (a south Florida resident) as snowshoes. Nevertheless, Jean and her boyfriend (a traveling musician) had intercourse and she got pregnant. But abortion, she told us, was out of the question. Our conversation indicated she was playing roulette with her chances of becoming an autonomous woman. Clearly, she hoped to marry her boyfriend. But in fact are marriage to him and parenting largely without him viable solutions for her? Would those kinds of life circumstances help or hinder her objective of participating fully in the information age? Would marriage and parenting largely without him increase her chances of repeating the strained and stressful life experiences of her mother and grandmother?

Recall the deafening silence of most Americans to the much publicized 2008 shotgun engagement of Republican vice-presidential hopeful Sarah Palin's 17-year-old pregnant daughter (Bristol) to the 18-year-old father. At the time, few citizens seemed willing to argue publicly that, in today's complex world, adolescent marriage is extremely dicey and, more to the point, adolescents have no business being parents. Intriguingly, not long after their child was born Bristol seems to have stumbled on those realities for herself and she broke off their engagement.[20] I have no firm answers to the quandaries facing Jean (or Bristol) in particular. But what of less privileged youngsters in general?

Up through the 1950s there was a close fit between K–12 and the prevailing model of gender, sexuality, and families. Why shouldn't there be a close fit between K–12 and today's patterns of gender, sexuality, and families? Shouldn't K–12 aim to fulfill the same type of mission within the *post*-industrial era that it accomplished so admirably within the industrial age? The teachers of K–12 did a good job of furnishing working-class youngsters with both opportunity *and* also linking it with messages about smart life choices. Why should K–12 not perform a similar mission today, even though the nature of both opportunity and of smart life choices has morphed dramatically? Would this perhaps be one means of helping to place less privileged youngsters on the same level playing field as their more privileged peers?

Keep in mind that blending a progressive approach into a reformed K–12 does not imply some sort of isolated add-on like most of today's largely irrelevant and often laughable family life/sex education courses. Instead, imagine a school, or rather, a learning center, in which problem solving permeates the very atmosphere breathed by coaches and players alike. Players come to understand that problem solving is the hub of their learning center and that there are several spokes attached to that hub. One spoke is their current academic pursuits. A second spoke attached to the hub is families (gender, sexuality, partnering). Those features are part of their life right now and will remain so throughout the foreseeable future. A third spoke is the marketplace they shall one day enter. All three spokes join together in one central hub. Hence, day in and day out the players get up close and personal with the crucial reality that their learning center is all about problem solving—whether that is nurtured through their academics, or in their personal relationships, or later on in the marketplace.

INTELLIGENT DESIGN

The damage that christianists inflict on less advantaged youngsters is not limited to families. The RR also impairs them by insisting that K–12 should teach intelligent design. Since the mid-20th century end of racial segregation, a number of christianist churches have established (mostly white) K–12 academies: The Bible assures them that if they "train up a child in the way he should go, when he is old he will not depart from it."[21] Not content with controlling the minds of their own children, they set their sights on holding sway over K–12 as well. Although the courts have recently been ruling against christianist efforts to impose intelligent design on K–12, by no means has the RR given up its century-long crusade against evolutionary biology.[22] Despite the christianist spin that it's not possible, a few evangelicals and some mainstream people *do* believe in evolution, yet do *not* believe that it clashes with or threatens faith. Perhaps the best known of these is the evolutionary biologist Francis Collins, an evangelical who is director of the National Human Genome Research Institute and also of the National Institutes of Health.[23] In a 2008 interview with the Pew Group, Collins described, in rather poetic terms, the harmony he's fashioned between his faith and his evolutionary biology:

> *If you see God as the creator of the universe—in all of its amazing complexity, diversity and awesome beauty—then science, which is, of course, a means of exploring nature, also becomes a means of exploring God's creative abilities. And so, for me, as a scientist who is also a religious believer, research activities that look like science can also be thought of as opportunities to worship.*[24]

When Pew asked him why only a quarter of Americans accept "evolution through natural selection" Collins blamed it on what he termed the "lousy efforts" of our schools over the past 150 years to communicate science in general and evolution in particular. We can be certain, however, that less advantaged youngsters were more likely than upper-middle-class youngsters to be deprived of an accurate comprehension of science—including evolution. Evolution is not just one more subtopic on a crowded biology syllabus, as christianists falsely claim. Biological science *is* evolution, and evolution *is* biological science, and bundled together with them *is* higher-order learning. To think in scientific terms is to think in terms of higher-order learning. To cultivate HOL is to cultivate scientific thinking. Scientific thinking is all about problem solving. But intelligent design undermines students' HOL because it is based on the false premise that the big problems are solved! It is, as the courts have said, nothing other than camouflaged creationism. In short, when christianists trivialize evolution, they trivialize all of science *and* higher-order learning at the same time.

It may have been acceptable during recent decades for much of K–12 to be content with "lousy efforts" at coaching science, evolution, and HOL, and thus to shortchange youngsters who were less than privileged. Such injury can, however, no longer be tolerated in the information age. Assaulting evolution in the name of intelligent design undermines the capabilities of less advantaged youngsters to cultivate their HOL. While privileged youngsters are amused by and shrug off intelligent design, their less advantaged peers are more likely to swallow it whole. Sadly, succumbing to that falsehood weakens their HOL capabilities. Those weakened capabilities in turn lessen their chances to do well in the 21st century, and also reduce their opportunities to serve the public household effectively.

AN EVANGELICAL DILEMMA

I've said repeatedly that being evangelical is not the same thing as being christianist. The distinction pivots around imposing the will of the divine on society. Though an evangelical may believe the same things as a christianist about gender, sexuality, and partnering, the evangelical is typically reluctant to impose those views on others via the law or politics. But intimidating outsiders is, of course, what a christianist is all about. With the death in 2007 of christianist firebrands such as Jerry Falwell and D. James Kennedy, and the aging of leaders such as Pat Robertson and James Dobson, there's a sense of generational change in the evangelical air. The tension between some younger evangelicals and christianists surfaced in late 2006 when Joel C. Hunter stepped down as president-elect of the Christian Coalition, a religious right group founded some years earlier by Robertson. Hunter wanted to maintain the coalition's opposition to matters such as abortion and same-gender marriage, but also to enlarge its agenda to address "economic and environmental concerns."[25] The coalition, however, took a rather dim view of his expanded agenda, and both sides agreed Hunter should resign.

It turns out that during the George W. Bush administration, the RR's leaders struck a deal to trade votes with that wing of the GOP seeking to enhance the economic well-being of the most affluent segments of American society at the expense of the less privileged. Christianists agreed to back the economic agenda of privileged citizens in exchange for their support of the christianist agenda for families. Today, that unholy alliance causes some younger evangelicals a good deal of shame and embarrassment. They hope to undo the dreadful legacy of the religious right, which they believe clings like unwanted barnacles to their evangelical faith.[26] Their chagrin is one reason why they aim to connect their faith with the economic well-being of ordinary citizens. Indeed, if there is anything at all that today's younger evangelicals agree on, it is the moral necessity of helping less advantaged citizens both here and abroad.

In his witty essay "Evangelicals a Liberal Can Love," N. D. Kristof observes that some evangelicals do "superb work on poverty, AIDS, sex trafficking, climate change, prison abuses, malaria and genocide in Darfur."[27] He adds that a "recent CBS News poll found that the single issue that white evangelicals most believed they should be involved in was fighting poverty." His essay, describing several evangelical outreach efforts in Africa, triggered memories of my childhood encounters with the many foreign missionaries our church supported. We youngsters spent countless hours watching out-of-focus black and white slides and grainy 16-millimeter black and white movies about their mission work in Africa and elsewhere—work that included getting the natives saved as well as giving them food, medical care, and schools. Evangelicals do indeed have a long record of helping disadvantaged people in other countries.

Helping the disadvantaged also took place here at home. When I was a college student in Chicago my peers and I spent a lot of time serving persons who were then called the "less fortunate." The formula we followed in order to serve men (mostly) at the very bottom of the economic ladder (homeless alcoholics on Skid Row) was known as "soap, soup, and salvation." We steered them into storefront missions that provided—free of charge—a hot shower, clean clothing, warm food, and a clean bed for the night. The man's sole obligation was to listen to the sermon and then, hopefully, make his way to the altar and get saved.

We also served people just above them on the economic ladder—poor women and children who, for the time being at least, had some sort of residence. Although not requiring soap, those families were much in need of soup in the form of food, clothing, and other necessities. They also, we strongly believed, needed salvation. It never occurred to us *not* to evangelize those lost souls. The children of those families were our particular target. The purpose of serving both adults and children—whether on Skid Row or in low-income neighborhoods—was never an end in itself. Like our overseas missionaries, our service was the means to a much greater end—the salvation of their eternal souls. "Scratch an evangelical and find a proselytizer" is an old cliché bearing an essential truth.

In any case, some of today's evangelicals are quite keen on helping less advantaged citizens, and that is one reason many of them support the federally funded program called faith-based initiatives.[28] Critics complain, however, that those tax-supported programs are simply a smokescreen for evangelical efforts to proselytize—get people saved. But evangelicals defending those initiatives protest (too?) loudly that such charges are false. They are willing, they say, to serve citizens' earthly needs without leaning on them to get converted. Evangelicals claim they're able to repress their innate urge to proselytize and focus instead on people's bread-and-butter needs. In any event, though today's younger evangelicals affirm their desire to help disadvantaged persons, helping is by no means the same thing as empowering.

For example, are evangelicals prepared to empower today's less privileged children and youth by supporting the type of K–12 reform that includes a progressive approach toward families? Younger evangelicals heaped praise, and rightly so, on the 2006 film *Amazing Grace* because it showed the link between the Christian faith of the British politician William Wilberforce and his late-18th-century efforts to abolish the African slave trade.[29] Simply serving the urgent earthly needs of Africans was, for him, a lofty moral purpose in and of itself. Wilberforce was *not* interested in getting either the slave traders or the Africans saved, and he ignored the missionaries' strategy of imposing Christian ethics on the Africans. Some evangelicals are praising Wilberforce and urging their colleagues to follow his stellar example of making the world a better place. He believed, they say, that serving the earthly needs of endangered Africans was by itself a worthy moral crusade. He was content, they add, to fulfill Jesus' command to love my neighbor as much as I love myself.

But are evangelicals prepared to follow Wilberforce that far when it comes to the bread-and-butter needs of today's less advantaged youngsters? Are they primed to set aside any efforts to get them saved? And more to the point, are they able to quell the insistent urges welling up within them—their instincts to oppose learning centers that incorporate a progressive approach to families? Are they equipped to live with the tension they'd inevitably endure between social justice on the one side and what they believe to be biblical teachings on the other? Though they themselves might be quite ambivalent about many aspects of a progressive approach, would they be persuaded that allowing it to happen anyhow might perhaps serve the economic well-being of less advantaged youngsters? Would they, akin to Wilberforce, feel that when all's said and done, the right thing to do is enable those youngsters' long-term bread-and-butter interests?

Wilberforce himself is not a consistent guide as to how today's evangelicals might resolve their dilemma of social justice versus biblical teachings. As political battles over the slave trade wound down, England was entering the early 19th-century industrial revolution. At that point, Wilberforce came face-to-face with a new personal dilemma pitting social justice against biblical teachings. His critics charged that he resolved his dilemma by ignoring social justice: "Wilberforce," they said, "was familiar with all that went on in the hold of a slave ship but ignored what went on at the bottom of a [British] mineshaft."[30] And, like christianist leaders who got in bed with the U.S. economic elite at the expense of less privileged Americans, Wilberforce was accused of "defending the oppressed abroad and the oppressors at home; [and of advocating] compassion for slaves, [but supporting] repression for [British] workers."[31]

Early 19th-century British workers were suffering the horrific downsides of industrialization, and Wilberforce was eager to help them by giving them fish. But he staunchly resisted their efforts to catch their own fish. In reaction to the workers' demands that they be allowed more active participation in the burgeoning prosperity being enjoyed by Wilberforce and his wealthy peers, he became influential in "outlawing unions, introducing imprisonment without trial, [and] reducing the freedom of speech and assembly."[32] He refused adamantly to empower British workers. Wilberforce was unalterably opposed to sharing social and political influence with the working classes. He did not want the workers to possess the sort of economic clout that might enable them to control their own destiny.

But how was it possible that he "should do all in his power to improve the condition of the poor, while fearing their attempts to take that power to themselves"?[33] Why did he believe in helping the poor, but did *not* believe in empowering them? The distressing answer, says Tomkins, is that although Wilberforce argued that depriving slave ship captains and Southern U.S. plantation owners of their livelihood was God's will, requiring British factory owners to share some of their power and profits with their workers was decidedly *not* God's will. Wilberforce argued that the workers' efforts to gain greater control of their own work life, and thus to have some semblance of becoming independent persons, "was an assault on Christian values and society."[34]

Wilberforce's ambivalence must resonate with some of today's evangelicals. Some could reason that empowering less privileged women and men like Jean via a progressive approach within K–12 might be "an assault on Christian values and society." But on the other side, some evangelicals might conclude that they should instead attempt the reinvention of K–12 the way Wilberforce dealt with the slave trade but *not* the way he handled the plight of British workers. Those evangelicals might argue that social justice should be preeminent: "Our goal," they might say, "should be to work towards the goal of empowering today's less advantaged youngsters. And, as much as it makes us squirm, we're willing to give up any ideas of proselytizing them. Furthermore, as painful as it is, we would not stand in the way of a progressive approach to families be-coming one part of a reinvented K–12 experience."

A recent class discussion highlights the ambivalence felt by some younger Christians regarding a progressive approach. One of the students (Ann) said, "I'm an observant Roman Catholic, yet right now I'm comfortable with this pro-gressive approach to families. But if one day I had a daughter of middle-school age, how would I feel if, say, the 'sex as celebration' theme became part of her school experience?" My response to Ann's uncertainty was twofold: first, she and her daughter would no doubt have talked about that issue long before she ever got to middle school. Ann herself could, I noted, look up (and so could her daughter) the social science research showing that the chances of a privileged adolescent girl (such as hers) contracting an STD and/or facing a pregnancy are extremely low.[35] Her daughter would be more keenly aware than less privi-leged youngsters that a pregnancy could potentially play havoc with her plans to become an autonomous woman, and thus to participate fully in the infor-mation age.

Ann was concerned first of all, and rightly so, about "my child." We agreed that loving her daughter implies that Ann might enable her to embrace some version of the sexual smarts theme described in chapter 4: if and when sexual intercourse occurs at all (the older she is, of course, the better), it should occur only within a context of responsibility. And, among other things, responsi-bility requires that her daughter would surely view herself as an effective con-traceptor.

At that point, Ann and I moved on to think about the next step: How far are we privileged citizens prepared to carry the lofty ideal of parenting *all* our chil-dren? What obligations if any do we have to less privileged youngsters such as Jean? What does it mean to love the children of our less privileged neighbors as much as we love our own? Does loving them imply that we would want them to have, among other things, the same opportunities as our own children to con-sider carefully all aspects of a progressive approach to families?

THE ANCIENT TRADITION OF THE CARING COMMUNITY

During the mid-1990s, Hillary Clinton floated the ideal that Americans of goodwill might in one way or another assume the responsibility of parenting *all* our children. She adapted the traditional African proverb that "It takes a village to raise a child" as the title of her book, which highlighted citizens' obligations for the well-being—not only of one's private household—but also of our public household. In reaction to her efforts, Clinton took a lot of flak from christianists who mocked her by alleging she had no clue that to raise a child properly takes a *family*—by which of course they meant the 1950s variety.

Alas, we've seen repeatedly that christianists seem unaware of the histories of families throughout the centuries, and how much they've changed over time. The fact is that the concept of *village* is, as the African proverb implies, an ancient tradition.[36] During the millennia of the agricultural age, most nuclear families survived within the bosom of their extended family. Chapter 1 explained that an array of blood-linked nuclear families typically lived nearby each other, and helped each other out in every way possible. Those networks of mutual support sometimes absorbed nuclear families and other persons that were not blood-related. Anthropologists such as Margaret Mead called them "fictive kin."[37] Although parents and their biological children obviously shared a unique bond, everyone in the community, or village, felt some degree of responsibility to look out for *all* our children—whether blood-linked or not.

The industrial age and the spread of large urban areas put an end to that traditional type of caring community, thereby transferring, for the first time in history, huge burdens for their children's well-being solely onto parents' shoulders. It was no longer customary for parents to share those burdens with members of their (now nonexistent) helping network. Hence, most parents had no choice but to try to care for their children largely on their own. The ancient tradition of looking out for all our children was pretty much swallowed up by a preoccupation that might be expressed as "looking out for my own children because if I don't no one else will." An old tradition slowly withered while a new tradition—the one we're now familiar with—gradually replaced it.

But not entirely! Even now when a nuclear family finds itself overwhelmed by forces beyond its control, its community (blood and/or fictive kin) may sometimes step in to help out. Recall from chapter 4 the innovative ways in which some of today's poor African women and adolescents are being empowered to cope with HIV/AIDS. One activist observed that the cure for HIV/AIDS "lies in the strength of women, families and communities who support and empower each other to break the silence around AIDS and take control of their sexual lives."[38] Those women (and men) are in fact adapting the ancient African proverb that "It takes a village." In their case, the caring community mobilizes to protect women and their children from the scourge of HIV/AIDS. A woman acting on her own could not possibly bring about the kinds of innovations necessary to ensure her family's well-being.

Intriguingly enough, evangelicals have always been effective at creating a sense of community within their own churches. The type of community they typically create is a quasi-extended family, or fictive kin.[39] The middle-class church in which I grew up was indeed my fictive-kin family, enabling me, among many other things, to make my transition from the working class into the middle class. There were a number of privileged adults in that church who treated me *as if* I were in fact a member of their blood family. As I look back on it, I'm convinced that the adults in my fictive kin network felt they had a responsibility to less advantaged youngsters—children and youth beyond their own family. They were concerned for all our children, and that included me. I often wonder if Jean's life might perhaps have taken a different turn if she'd had the same chances I'd had to belong to a set of caring fictive kin. That assumes of course that her fictive kin would have been able and willing to convey to her, among other things, the significance of sexual smarts.

Today, research reveals that "poor children, on average, arrive in kindergarten far behind their middle-class peers."[40] Families and communities that I called working poor or lower class are for a host of reasons unable to prepare their children adequately for the K–12 experience. Accordingly, if we intend to reinvent K–12 along the lines of an HOL model, we should begin by paying special attention to the unique needs of lower-class youngsters. Fortunately, some advocates are hard at work doing precisely that. One of them is Geoffrey Canada. He

> *runs the first and so far the only organization in the country that pulls together under a single umbrella integrated social and educational services for thousands of children at once. Canada's agency, the Harlem Children's Zone, has a $58 million budget this year, drawn mostly from private donors; it currently serves 8,000 kids in a 97-block neighborhood of Harlem.*[41]

Canada is, in effect, recreating a village: "As students progress through an all-day prekindergarten and then through a charter school, they have continuous access to community supports like family counseling, after-school tutoring and a health clinic." He and his colleagues are experimenting with a wide range of programs "all designed to mimic the often-invisible cocoon of support and nurturance that follows middle-class and upper-middle-class kids through their childhoods. The goal, in the end, is to produce children with the abilities and the character to survive adolescence in a high-poverty neighborhood, to make it to college and to graduate."[42]

The Harlem Children's Zone operates very much like the old-time village. When the household finds itself, because of overwhelming forces beyond its control, unable to prepare its youngsters adequately for K–12, its fictive kin step in and compensate for its powerlessness. The community aims to prepare youngsters for the K–12 schools created within their zone. Because those are charter schools, Canada and his colleagues are free to experiment with creative ways to develop lower-order learning among their youngsters. Furthermore, the hope is that eventually they'll be able to experiment with ways to cultivate HOL among their charges.

Rather than conceiving of schools and families as separate entities as we've done for 200 years, Canada blurs their boundaries and blends them together into a village in search of the common good. Hence, it seems to me that some persons of goodwill with a commitment to social justice might wish to consider developing additional 21st-century caring communities. Such a community would focus on the urgent need of preparing poor children for, and sustaining them through, K–12. It turns out that Barak Obama favors expanding faith-based initiatives.[43] Accordingly, might some evangelicals be willing to experiment with a faith-based Children's Zone for poor children—minus any hint of proselytizing? Furthermore, would some evangelicals struggle with ways to make HOL an essential part of those zones? Might they even go so far as to eventually incorporate a progressive approach toward families?

YOUTH BEYOND THE WORKING POOR

Next, let's move on to the majority of youngsters who are adequately prepared for the lower-order learning they'll likely encounter in K–12. A full-blown Children's Zone would not seem to be called for in terms of upper-middle, middle-middle, and lower-middle/working-class youngsters. Nevertheless, the concept of a village participating with the school or learning center as it experiments with ways to make HOL a reality would seem to be a useful policy initiative. Recall the discussions Ann and I had about her uncertainty over folding a progressive approach to families into school reinvention. She and I eventually concluded that the village concept might help to make such innovations less threatening and perhaps more palatable.

Specifically, persons of goodwill might form caring community groups or villages that emerge as one vital part of school reinvention. The village might, for example, participate with officials and coaches during the initial stages of the invention of the learning center. Together, they could help flesh out the center's central mission in the new century—cultivating HOL among all youngsters with particular concern for those in the middle-middle and working classes. The village might also help figure out how to blend that mission with an emerging 21st-century approach to gender, sexuality, and partnering. Once a center is up and running, the village would continue working with officials and coaches helping to solve the innumerable and often unforeseen problems that are bound to arise in the wake of such an innovative undertaking.

Canada does his experiments among charter schools in hopes they would serve as a model that other school districts might one day follow and adapt to their own circumstances. Likewise, renovating the school experiences of children beyond the lower class might also be initiated within certain types of charter schools or learning centers. Here too the hope is that those kinds of centers might serve as a model for other schools to follow and adapt.

ADULT-FRIENDLY NETWORKS

Thus far, our focus on youngsters has ignored the fact that during the agricultural age, helping networks of blood and fictive kin were adult-friendly as well as child-friendly. Adults of all ages who were not married had important duties—both economic and caring—to fulfill. Single women (the maiden aunt) in particular carried out a wide range of responsibilities. Older persons too had important duties—often attending to small children while parents and older siblings labored at their varied tasks. Solo-parents (widows, mostly) were also obliged to contribute in whatever ways they could. There was, as chapter 1 noted, a meaningful niche for virtually every adult (and child) in the community.

Fast-forward to the 21st-century villages we just described that are obviously child-friendly. But they could be adult-friendly as well: they could be places of caregiving and mutual support among participating adults.[44] They would likely include couples (married or cohabiting, and either straight or gay/lesbian) with children. In addition, the villages would likewise seek to involve couples who opt to be childfree (or who are childless), or whose children have left home. Solo-parents (of either gender) would also be very much a part of the village, and so would persons living alone—regardless of age or sexual orientation. Finally, today's village would also want to include the growing numbers of older adults now living longer and healthier lives. Many of them have the potential for making contributions that are as substantial as, though different from, the significant inputs made by older persons during the agricultural era.

In short, could the 21st-century village be an ancient tradition whose time may perhaps have come again?[45] During the agricultural age, its prime mission was to ensure the survival of both its nuclear families and its unmarried persons. Today, the principal function of the caring community would be to participate actively in the reinvention of K–12 for youngsters beyond the lower class. The major share of its caring is likely to be vertical—adults fulfilling their responsibility to try to nurture all our children. But could such a setting also supply opportunities for horizontal caregiving and mutual support as well? Would some adults reach out to other adults, hoping to affirm one another while at the same time pursuing their shared quest to make 21st-century learning center work for all our children?

NOTES

1. Martin 1996:367.
2. Martin 1996:77.
3. Martin 1996:230–31.
4. "Blacks See Growing Values Gap between Poor and Middle Class—Optimism about Black Progress Declines," November 13, 2007, Pew Research Center: Social and Demographic Trends, pew.org.
5. Eckholm 2008; "Inside the Middle Class: Bad Times Hit the Good Life," April 9, 2008, Pew Research Center, pew.org.
6. Herbert 2008.
7. Kenworthy 2008; Herbert 2008; Johnston 2007.
8. Sizer 2005.
9. Sizer 1992, 1996, 2005; Scanzoni 2005.
10. Rimer 2008.
11. Sizer 1992, 1996; Scanzoni 2005.
12. Michaelsen et al., 2008; Scanzoni 2005.
13. Sizer 1992, 1996.
14. Sizer 2005:xii.
15. Okun 2008.
16. Sizer 2005:xii.
17. Regnerus 2007:182.
18. Luker 1996, 2006.
19. Luker 1996, 2006; Regnerus 2007.
20. Seelye 2009.
21. Proverbs 22:6, KJV.
22. Forrest and Gross 2007; Bowler 2007; Petto and Godfrey 2007.
23. Collins 2006.
24. "The 'Evidence for Belief': An Interview with Francis Collins," April 17, 2008, pewresearch.org.
25. Banerjee 2006.
26. Kuo 2006a,b; Freedman 2006b; Wallis 2005, 2008.
27. Kristof 2008a.
28. Wuthnow 2006; Kuo and Diiulio, Jr., 2008.
29. Tomkins 2007.
30. Eric Williams, cited by Tomkins 2007:219.
31. Tomkins 2007:219.

32. Tomkins 2007:220.

33. Tomkins 2007:221.

34. Tomkins 2007:221.

35. Luker 1996, 2006.

36. Scanzoni 2000.

37. Mead 1967; Scanzoni 2000.

38. Donnelly 2007. Donnelly draws from the research of Helen Epstein (2007) into HIV/AIDS in Uganda.

39. Wallis 2008:222ff.

40. Tough 2008a, 2008b.

41. Tough 2008a.

42. Tough 2008a.

43. "Media Coverage of the Faith-Based Initiative in the First Six Months of 2001 and 2009," August 12, 2009, pewresearch.org.

44. Scanzoni 2000, 2004.

45. Waters 2003.

Ten Guidelines for Healthy Families in the New Century

One way to get a snapshot of what the pre-1960s family was all about is to watch an old sitcom like *Ozzie and Harriet* or a movie like *Mr. and Mrs. Bridge*. But if we search for an image of everything the family was *not* we could do no better than view some of the nine films featuring Katherine Hepburn and Spencer Tracy. Two that are specially worth seeing today are *Woman of the Year* (1942) and *Adam's Rib* (1949). Americans flocked to the Hepburn-Tracy films even though, paradoxically, what they watched was as foreign as Mars. And perhaps that was the films' magnetism: what people saw was entirely alien, exotic, and bizarre. It must have been a science fiction experience—great fun but everyone knew it was sheer fantasy and could never happen in real life! But occasionally science fiction portends the future and becomes reality. And that appears to be true for the work of those two artists. Deftly using the tools of comedy to ease the pain of agonizing change, they gave Americans a taste of what to expect several decades down the road.

PEOPLE MATTER MORE THAN ANYTHING

"The Normal American Family" was the title of a mid-20th-century essay by a preeminent social scientist of the time.[1] By *normal* he meant both ideal and typical. He put into words what almost everyone believed about the 1950s family style. We've since traveled quite a distance in terms of what we actually *do* when it comes to families. But, oddly enough, that deep-rooted 1950s model of the family remains the official or publicly recognized yardstick against which our behaviors are evaluated. That older image of what's normal and best still hovers over us: it measures what we do as good or bad, worthy or unworthy, desirable or undesirable.

That 1950s family image is, of course, strongly advocated by the religious right, or christianists. But throughout the book I've argued that the demands of the 21st-century information age require us, first, to upgrade our image of families: We're searching for a more contemporary picture of what's best and ideal. This newer image is called *progressive* because it seeks to blend essential ideals from both the liberal (e.g., freedom and growth) and the conservative (e.g., responsibility, accountability, and order) traditions. Second, we need to develop public policies and programs that support that upgraded or progressive model. Although all citizens stand to benefit from a fresh image of families as well as from updated policies and programs, the need is greatest among relatively less advantaged adults and youngsters from every racial and ethnic group—those living below the upper middle class.

In the 1993 movie *Mrs. Doubtfire,* Robin Williams told his children (on the sly from his ex-wife, played by Sally Field) while in drag (his children didn't recognize him) that there is no longer only one type of normal family. He told them there are now many different kinds of families (divorced, blended, single-parent, cross-racial, same-gender, and so forth), all of which may be equally positive. Williams was, of course, correct in asserting that there are various ways people live, and that one specific way of doing family is not necessarily better or worse than any other.

The paradox is that at the same time we've been producing that much variety, citizens have also been forging a coherent set of principles or guidelines by which to evaluate the various ways of doing families. The guidelines might be thought of as a gauge judging any and all of the ways people are crafting families. So far, the evolving guidelines have been largely implicit or tacit—unspoken and perhaps only dimly understood even by those trying to sort them out. But when taken as a whole this emerging set of guidelines gives rise to an image of families that could be considered both desirable and workable for our new century. We might even go so far as to say that this progressive cluster amounts to a new gauge as opposed to the 1950s yardstick. That former gauge endorsed one specific arrangement—it prescribed just one particular way to live. But as early as 1970, psychologist H. A. Otto posed a question showing that way back then some people were beginning to weigh the relative merits of the old versus some new kind of yardstick:

> *To what extent does the American family structure contribute to the optimum*
> *development of the human potential of its members? This is perhaps the key*
> *question for the assessment of any alternative structure.*[2]

The premise of his question is simple: *The purpose of families is to serve people,*
and not the other way around. Back then most people believed, and christianists
still believe, that citizens are obliged to serve and work for The Family. In 1981,
for instance, the RR got the Family *Protection* Act introduced into Congress in
order to safeguard the 1950s family from feminists. Later on, in 1996, the RR
lobbied our federal government to pass the *Defense* of Marriage Act. During that
second go-round they aimed to protect The Family from homosexuals.

But Otto proposed a 180-degree turn in our thinking. Accordingly, let's say
that a new gauge should consist of a set of guidelines that "contributes to the op-
timum development of the human potential of its members." In effect, making
everyday life better for ordinary citizens should be the foundation of a 21st-
century, progressive image of families. What's more, *the issue of human devel-*
opment takes priority over any specific ways of doing family (whether single-parent,
dual parent, cohabiting, divorced, blended, same-gender, and so on). Christianists insist that they alone occupy the moral high ground because they declare that the
right thing to do is to defend The Family. But the contrary, and to me much
more compelling, argument is to assert that the moral high ground belongs instead to those who advocate that people matter much more than any specific ways
of doing families: The right thing to do is to ensure that families—no matter
what precise form they take—serve people. That is the bottom line.

JEAN, GENDER, AND SEXUALITY

The set of guidelines I have in mind is drawn from prior chapters, and each
one does indeed cultivate human growth and betterment. The flip side is that
they also facilitate the greater good, or public household. As background for the
guidelines, let's consider a series of mostly imagined conversations with Jean.
Recall from chapters 4 and 6 that in 2007 several college students and I had an
actual discussion following class. Jean (a gifted African-American) was among
them and she told us that despite her awesome scholarship, she'd soon be
dropping out of college in order to give birth. Both her mother and grandmother
had been solo-parents, and she'd grown up being part of what chapter 3 called
the working poor. At semester's close, I lost track of Jean and never heard from
or saw her again. But from time to time I think about her and wish I'd had

opportunities to speak with her further both as sociologist and as friend. If I had been able to speak with her, I can imagine a scenario something like the following.

I'd begin by reminding her of our class discussions about autonomy (chapter 3). Autonomy, we'd agreed, is the sense that as fully as possible one should be in charge, or in control, of one's own life. Developing a sense of autonomy is a lifelong process commencing during the earliest days of childhood. It is a vital part of our growth and development into a whole and healthy human being. It starts when important figures in one's life (e.g., parents, sibs, kin, teachers, clergy, friends) convey to the girl or boy that, "Whatever else you intend to be or do, you must first of all be in charge of your own life. And, guess what? You're not too young to start—the process begins today." To be sure, autonomy in its fullest sense relies on economic independence, which children and most adolescents don't fully possess. Youngsters can, however, start developing autonomy by doing things that reinforce it, and especially by avoiding things that undermine it.

I'd ask Jean if important persons in her life had encouraged her to cultivate autonomy and my hunch is she'd respond, "Yes and no." In 1966 Jeanne Noble wrote about the "Negro woman's role as a working citizen."[3] She argued that during slavery, and after Emancipation, and on into the mid-20th century, most black women had no choice but to make work central to their existence if they and their children were to survive. Hence, Jean might say that she'd learned that lesson from her mother and grandmother very early in life. She'd likely add that in school her obvious abilities caught the eye of her teachers, who made it clear to her that while economic self-sufficiency is *necessary* for autonomy, it is not sufficient. From them she'd heard the additional notion that, in the postindustrial era, meaningful work supplying intrinsic satisfactions is a large part of what it means to be autonomous. And autonomy, they'd emphasized, is an essential part of being fully human.

I might also ask Jean if she felt that her (evangelical) religion had thwarted her quest for autonomy—given its insistence on abstinence-only and its resistance to the use of effective contraception by singles. Had I asked this question in the spring of 2007 during our actual conversation when she was first pregnant and still in college, I suspect she'd affirm that "my religion has *not* ill-used me." At that point in time, she'd likely blame herself for ignoring her independence and autonomy: "If I'd obeyed my church and refused intercourse with my boyfriend (an itinerant rock musician), all would now be well." But had I been able to query her the following year (summer and fall of 2008) as to whether her religion had served her well, her response might have been quite different. By then, my hunch is that she'd have come to view her world through a different set of lenses.

By that time Jean might have been parenting her infant with the help of her (former) boyfriend's mother who, let us imagine, had stuck with her despite the fact that Jean broke up with her son. Jean might also have been working part-time and trying to squeeze in a class or two at her community college. She might say she's had a lot of time to ponder her unanticipated and stressful life experiences, and she's changed her mind about several things. For one thing, like any number of evangelicals before her, Jean might have reluctantly started questioning her religion.[4]

For example, let's assume that Jean now believes that her religion let her down owing to its archaic views of gender. Its 1950s image is terribly remote from the information age reality that before anything else, the woman (and man) must be autonomous. The 1950s image continues to exalt visions of marriage and motherhood as being a woman's highest calling.[5] In my imagined scenario, Jean explains that prior to getting pregnant, she saw herself as being en route to a good (i.e., lucrative) job. It had never dawned on her, she says, that unprotected sex might have anything at all to do with that long-term goal. In addition, because she defined work strictly in material terms (despite her teachers' counsel) it never occurred to her that work could exist on the same moral plane as being a wife and mother: she failed to perceive that work (like parenthood) might perhaps be a spiritual vocation. Hence, once she got pregnant, it was unimaginable to think that a mere material goal (work) could stand in the way of a spiritual goal—her high calling as a mother. The upshot was that Jean dismissed the abortion option and gave up college and its bountiful scholarship. She set out to be a mother and, comparable to Bristol Palin, a wife as well.

In our imagined conversation, Jean and I reflect on Palin's initial intention to marry Levi Johnston (the father of her child), and Jean comments that some things are far worse than being a solo-parent. Palin herself must have arrived at that same conclusion because in March 2009, following the birth of their child, she broke off her engagement to Johnston.[6] Jean explains that once she came to the disturbing realization that marriage to her boyfriend would have multiplied her problems, she too decided to end their relationship. Because he was indifferent to her long-term goal of autonomy he would have been, she adds ruefully, far more of a hindrance than a help. He believed that she (the mother) should take on the role of parent with him (the man) playing (whenever possible) a supportive role. When she tried to discuss the issue with him it became plain that he would never consent to cultivate the *identity* of parent, and to participate as fully as she in the life of their child. Most basic of all, their discussions (such as they were) made her realize that he was not prepared to engage in the kinds of agonizing negotiations necessary to sort out the competing demands of her career, his career, and their child.

As our imagined conversation continues, Jean adds that her religion also let her down owing to its unbending insistence on sex as taboo. Because she'd been told that sex apart from marriage was morally wrong, she could not bring herself to ask her boyfriend to use condoms. Her religion boxed her in—it squeezed her into a no-win situation: She felt that having sex was dreadfully wrong, but getting pregnant was just as bad, and trying to prevent it via condoms was even worse! The unhappy result was that she found herself in the same boat as teens in the recent national study that found an unexpected link between being religious and pregnancy: the more religious the teens were, the more likely they were to have gotten pregnant.[7] Jean adds she now agrees with Bristol Palin who, in a February 2009 TV interview said:

> *"Everyone should be abstinent but it's not realistic . . . [Sex] is more and more accepted among kids my age." Palin added that she wished she could have delayed her pregnancy "like 10 years so I could have a job and education and my own house."*[8]

In our imagined conversation, Jean's traumatic experiences have led her to conclude, though reluctantly, that what makes intercourse right or wrong is not marriage but responsibility. She says she wishes she'd understood then what seems so obvious to her now. If she'd used her sexual smarts, having sex with her boyfriend would have turned out quite differently. She would have insisted on condom use (and also used a hormonal method) based on her (and his) obligation to act responsibly. Accordingly, she's become convinced that it's never too early for an adolescent to start cultivating the identity of contraceptor—even if the adolescent is not now, nor has any plans to become, sexually active. Hence, we might assume that Jean finally realizes that possessing sexual smarts is an essential part of becoming a fully autonomous person.

GUIDELINES 1, 2, AND 3: AUTONOMY, WORK, AND SEXUALITY

Recall that we're searching for a set of guidelines that might help us craft a 21st-century, progressive image of families. Hence, what guidelines might we glean from our actual and imagined conversations with Jean, as well as from the full range of ideas discussed in chapters 3 and 4?

The first guideline that strikes us is that *autonomy and sexuality are two sides of the same coin*. To be an autonomous woman or man requires that she or he must possess sexual smarts and thus practice sexuality in a responsible manner. Failure to be sexually responsible might jeopardize one's own quest for autonomy, as well as the quest of one's partner. Responsibility covers all of the facets of sexual smarts detailed in chapter 4. Marriage is *not*, however, a precondition for sexual responsibility. Married and unmarried persons alike may be equally responsible or *irresponsible* when it comes to sexuality.

A second guideline is that *autonomy, work, and parenting are three sides of the same coin.* To be an autonomous woman or man requires that she or he practices an occupation which *at the very least* promises economic self-sufficiency. Throughout the millennia of the agricultural age, both genders understood that survival (to say nothing of their independence as a family) required productive work from each of them. Neither she nor he was a stranger either to the obligations or the intrinsic satisfactions (e.g., problem solving) of work. But industrial-age religious ideology tarnished the meaning of work for women. At the same time, it diminished the importance of parenting for men relative to its mounting significance for women. The information age, however, restores something old—the ancient obligation that both genders should work. It also adds several new ideas, chief of which is that both parents—the man in particular— should cultivate the identity of parent.

The information age offers to women, as well as men, the kinds of mind-tech occupations that, because of their focus on problem solving, promise high levels of intrinsic (not necessarily lucrative) satisfactions. Hence, the woman is obliged to work—but not just to be economically independent, as basic as that is. In addition, she owes it to herself to seek as fully as possible the intrinsic or spiritual satisfactions of work. Pursuing those satisfactions shows that she loves herself as much as she loves her neighbor (partner, child). Cultivating those satisfactions is an essential part of what it means to be fully human. They are vital to her growth and development as a whole person.

And while women are being drawn into the information age world of work, men are likewise being drawn into the emerging world of children. As she relinquishes her 19th-century option *not* to work, he likewise sets aside his 19th-century option *not* to parent as actively as she does. Loving his neighbor (partner) as much as he loves himself happens as he affirms and cultivates her identity of worker just as much as he affirms and cultivates his own identity of worker. Furthermore, he shows that he loves both of his neighbors (child as well as partner) when he affirms and cultivates his identity of parent just as much as she affirms and cultivates her identity of parent. And, by pursuing the intrinsic or spiritual satisfactions of parenting, he shows that he loves himself. Cultivating those satisfactions is an essential part of what it means to be a whole person. They are vital to his human growth and development.

That brings us to the third guideline we're gleaning from chapters 3 and 4: *just as negotiation and problem solving are increasingly central to the information age world of work, they are equally pivotal to the world of 21st-century families.* The fact that each gender possesses the identity of worker and of parent does not necessarily require that both partners should always participate simultaneously in both activities to the same degree. Flexibility, improvisation, and compromise are the watchwords. Nonetheless, what cannot ever be sacrificed is the woman's capability to be economically self-sufficient, alongside her basic human need to treasure the intrinsic satisfactions of work. Nor can the man's basic human need to take pleasure in the intrinsic satisfactions of parenting be let go. Given these several constraints—operating all too often at cross-purposes—partners should expect that quite frequently their negotiations will be tough and unsettling. That no-nonsense reality is built into the DNA of this third guideline.

These first three guidelines are very much in play throughout the 2007 film *2 Days in Paris*. Perhaps that's why the film was marketed as postromantic. The older romantic notions of male-female relations were derived from the myths and fairy tales built into 1950s images of The Family. Today's romantic films have morphed a bit and are sometimes referred to as chick-flicks.[9] If we keep in mind that they too are fairy tales, they can be fun to watch. But adolescents and youth who happen to take today's romantic images too seriously do themselves no service. That is particularly so if, like Jean, they are also less privileged. It seems to me that they are much better served by carefully considering these several emerging postromantic guidelines. Such guidelines are foundational to an updated and contemporary image of families—an image much more in synch with postindustrial society.

GUIDELINES 4–10: LOVE, PARTNERS, CHILDREN, AND THE PUBLIC HOUSEHOLD

To say that an emerging image of families debunks romantic fairy tales is not to say that families shaped by postromantic ideals are devoid of love. Quite the opposite is true. If anything, love now plays an even more significant role than it did in the old-time normal family.

For example, let's say that the fourth guideline of a progressive image of families is that *autonomy and love are two sides of the same coin.* I've already implied their coupling by what I said earlier: the man who genuinely loves his partner will enter fully into her quest for autonomy—just as she enters into his because she loves him. Moreover, his love for his partner is one (not the sole) reason why he cultivates his identity as parent.

Ever since the pre-Christian Greek thinkers began probing its mysteries, it's been clear that love has no facile meaning. The best we can hope for is to pin down some of its more salient facets. Chapter 5 explains how Plato and his colleagues identified three broad kinds of love. One is the divine-human dimension. A second is human love that is not sexual or erotic—for example, the love between parents and offspring, and among siblings and kin, or the love that marks an intense friendship. Third is *eros*—love with a sexual component. Plato believed that emotional intimacy is the most vital and valuable facet of *eros*. *Soul mate* is the term used today to try to capture the depth of what we mean when we say "my lover is also my confidante and intimate." During Plato's time, many men believed that the most profound levels of emotional intimacy are achieved mainly with their male lover(s). To be sure, the man was also obliged to have intercourse with his wife in order to get children and heirs. Plato did, however, concede the possibility that a man might on occasion experience emotional intimacy with a woman lover (including his wife)—though that was thought to be far less common than intimacy among male lovers.

Throughout the intervening centuries our views have obviously matured so that today most people in the West understand that emotional intimacy has nothing at all to do with gender or sexual orientation. Growing numbers of persons (especially those who are better educated) demand it—they believe it is requisite. They feel that emotional intimacy is the bottom line—the *sine qua non*—of erotic love, whether one is straight, gay, or lesbian. Intimacy is a powerful bonding agent—it is after all the blending or fusion of two human souls. But where does that leave autonomy? Can one be fused at such a profound level with another human being and still be in charge of one's own life? Or does fusion result in a loss of control? That is no doubt the basic dilemma facing the contemporary couple—whether in a relationship, or cohabiting, or married. Ideally, we want to believe that it's possible to have both, and that's why I suggest that autonomy and love are two sides of the same coin.

On one side, autonomy implies that the couple is able to negotiate the often rival demands of work, household chores, children (if any), and other matters in ways that permit him and her, her and her, or him and him to retain the freedom to pursue what's important to each person. On the other side, emotional intimacy implies that in the course of resolving those issues, each partner shares more and more of one's inner self with one's partner, thereby enriching the other partner as well as oneself. Hence, at the same time that their mutual enrichment binds them more tightly than ever before, each feels that his or her own quest for freedom is being affirmed.

And that brings us to the fifth guideline: *all partnerships are created equal in terms of their inherent worth or value—though some are perceived socially as more equal than others*. Whether the couple is in a relationship, or is cohabiting (straight or gay/lesbian), or is married, the partners may experience a profound degree of love marked by emotional intimacy, and they may at the same time be autonomous persons. In effect, love and autonomy are the bottom-line criteria for judging the inherent worth of any eros-based partnership—whether it is marriage, or cohabitation, or a relationship.

Nevertheless, many people continue to define marriage per se as unique—existing in a class by itself, despite the fact that it is *not* inherently better or worse than the two other types of partnerships. It continues to enjoy far more prestige and social status than either a relationship or cohabitation. Marriage is still perceived as an exclusive social club to which heterosexuals only may apply for membership (except in a very few states). Most homosexuals are thus denied the elevated social status, prestige, and honor attached to legal marriage—privileges available to all other citizens. Christianists continue to lead the charge against granting that social and civil right to homosexuals. Unhappily, their mean-spirited crusade against homosexuals flies in the face of the 21st-century standard that families must serve people. The RR's refusal to recognize that love and autonomy are identical among both hetero- and homosexuals alike relegates the latter to second-class status, thereby making their chances for robust human growth and development that much more challenging. To mend that rupture in our social fabric, homosexuals must have the same legal access as heterosexuals to that exclusive club called marriage.

In the past, children were a primary reason why marriage was viewed as a superior social status reserved for heterosexuals only. But chapter 5 cited a Pew study revealing that as time goes by more and more Americans are ranking love over children as their main reason to marry. That gradual separation of marriage from children parallels the separation of marriage from sexuality begun in the 1960s.

The sixth guideline is that *love and autonomy govern the transitions between being partnered and partner-free*. In the past, persons who refrained from divorce were said to possess moral fiber and fortitude. Conversely, persons who divorced were thought to be morally suspect. It was common to hear of marriages that failed while others were successful. The sole criterion of success/failure was stability/divorce. That criterion fit perfectly well with the older ideal that men and women must serve marriage; the prevailing wisdom was that the family was some sort of fixed institution that was somehow bolstered by stable, and weakened by unstable, marriages. Today, in contrast, we realize that marriages that do not further human development are unhealthy for the partners, and for their children (if any), and for the larger society. We now understand that persons seek *eros*-based partnerships in hopes of cultivating emotional intimacy—of fusing with one's soul mate. Equally important—especially for women—is that their partnership must simultaneously further their autonomy as well.

But both goals take time, and so it makes sense to continue embracing the traditional ideals of continuity and stability. And that is one reason why marriage retains its elevated social position. Given that intimacy and autonomy are the lofty goals we seek, and given that they require much time and energy, continuity becomes both necessary and desirable. Nevertheless, though the ideal of permanence is viewed as an essential part of marriage, it is not seen as vital for the two other types of partnerships. Hence, we assume that if the partners genuinely mean business regarding their twin goals, they will no doubt marry. We expect them to evolve upward from a relationship to cohabitation and eventually to marriage.

Not incidentally, that link between seriousness of purpose and marriage is part of the overall argument as to why homosexuals cannot be denied the right to marry. Gays and lesbians have in the past suffered from negative stereotyping and overt discrimination. Hence, to assert that marriage is the prime indicator of serious human purpose, and then to deny to a whole class of marginalized persons the opportunity to demonstrate their seriousness, only serves to reinforce their second-class class status.

Though persons in the West continue to embrace continuity, we have surely reinvented it. We now understand that permanence per se has no particular merit. It is no longer viewed as an end in itself, but rather as one means to a most desirable end—the cultivation of love and autonomy. However, if one or both partners perceive that over time those goals are *not* being achieved, they may conclude that it is necessary to transition or move out of their current partnership—whether a relationship, or cohabitation, or marriage. One may feel obliged to oneself, and/or to one's partner, and/or to one's children (if any), to transition even though it is frequently a sad occurrence. It is particularly distressing if one's partner does not wish their partnership to end. However, for those partners seeking transition, their ending is not a failure but is seen instead as a *positive* or good thing—the means to a larger purpose. It allows the persons to once again begin the terrifying search for a partnership that promises to sustain the cultivation of both love and autonomy. However, according to a recent Pew study, by no means is everyone is eager to start searching—at least not right away.

And that study brings us to the seventh guideline of a progressive image of 21st-century families: *being partner-free is created equal with being partnered.* The Pew study revealed, "Only 16% of single [non-partnered] Americans say they are hunting for a romantic partner." Pew added that although the majority of unmarried Americans say they eventually hope to marry, the fact is that the percentage of married-couple households has been declining steadily in recent decades. Currently, among all U.S. households, less than half (49%) contain a married couple. Could it be that growing numbers of single Americans feel in synch with Louisa May Alcott's 1868 observation that "liberty is a better husband [partner] than love to many of us"? Alcott, along with other well-educated, autonomous women of her day, embraced what they called the "Cult of Single Blessedness." Until the late 20th century, it was almost impossible for a woman to be autonomous and married at the same time. Consequently, for well over a hundred years a handful of privileged women on both sides of the Atlantic opted for autonomy over marriage.[10] And, while things have changed a great deal in recent decades, their basic insight remains timeless—autonomy always beats a love-free partnership of any type hands down.

Until the late 20th century, women who opted for singleness were expected to abstain from sex, and surely to relinquish all thoughts of parenting. Now, of course, sex is readily available to single women and men alike, and parenting too is a live option, as we shall see in a moment. Nonetheless, what the partner-free person lacks is the unique blending of *eros* with emotional intimacy; and also the prestige and social status attached to being in a partnership of whatever type—especially marriage.

Hence, in order to compensate, the partner-free person may, in addition to liberty, seek the kinds of distinctive emotional satisfactions vital to women of earlier generations who coveted single blessedness. Those satisfactions were captured by the profound *eros*-free love enjoyed among handfuls of very close friends including both genders, and the same holds true today.[11] Those kinds of emotional satisfactions are, by the way, a central feature of the 2008 film *The Women.* In addition to those emotional satisfactions, women of earlier generations who were partner-free typically devoted their considerable energies to serving the public household. Other partner-free persons eager to serve the greater good pursued the vocation of nun or priest. Today, devoting one's life to serving the public household in whatever capacity remains a viable option for partner-free persons of either gender.

This seventh guideline probes deeper into the links between *eros*-based love and autonomy discussed earlier. At its core, it raises this question: Is it possible to love—in the sense of profound emotional intimacy—apart from autonomy? And if it is *not* possible, why would anyone ever want to enter into or remain within any type of partnership where autonomy and love are not fused? Wouldn't that dreadful situation do untold damage to one's growth and development as a human being? Wouldn't every person be infinitely better off to become or remain partner-free unless and until (as perhaps Jean or Bristol Palin might have sensed) there is a realistic possibility of their fusion?

It would seem that the message, "It's okay to be partner-free," is especially relevant for less advantaged girls and women. Compared with their more advantaged sisters autonomy may loom as less of a realistic option. Hence, lacking ready access to the intrinsic satisfactions that autonomy supplies, a less advantaged girl or woman might be tempted to wonder, "What else is there besides a man?" The best response to that question is for the girl or woman to recall our imagined scenario with Jean in which she finally came to realize that a man may all too easily get in the way of a woman's quest for economic independence, to say nothing of her autonomy.

Children are, of course, another typical response to the question, "What else is there besides a man?" Children obviously offer many intrinsic satisfactions, and there is a certain mystique attached to being a mother even when a man is not around. Recall, however, that unmarried childbearing tends to be associated with socioeconomic disadvantage—especially among adolescents. There is almost universal consensus that, in today's postindustrial society, adolescents (whether married or not, and regardless of their economic status) have no business being parents. Even among adult women, the challenge of being a solo-parent is formidable indeed.

And that discussion flows into the eighth guideline of a progressive image of 21st-century families: *autonomy and parenthood are two sides of the same coin— whether one is partnered (married, cohabiting, relationship) or not.* In the past, becoming a solo-parent was largely unintentional: the woman did not set out to get pregnant. As Jean told us, "It just happened." The woman may not have had access to abortion or else like Jean had the option but chose not to exercise it. In any event, the woman eventually found herself the solo-parent of an unplanned child. In many cases, women (like Jean) caught in those circumstances tended not to be economically self-sufficient, much less autonomous.

Turning to a somewhat different scenario, a married or cohabiting woman may have planned her pregnancy, and expected that she and her partner would parent their child together. But either they transitioned or he died and she too found herself as a solo-parent. Her child had been planned, but being a solo-parent was not—it was unexpected. In all too many cases, the solo-parent was not economically independent, much less autonomous.

In sharp contrast to the situation of a less advantaged woman who becomes a solo-parent unintentionally, some adult women are now deliberately electing it. Chapter 5 showed that in recent years, some well-educated, autonomous women "are choosing parenthood without marriage and creating the new American family."[12] In effect, those women are saying that it's okay for a woman (or man) to be a parent without having a partner *if at the same time she or he is also autonomous*. Or, at the very least, she or he must be economically independent. These adult women are making the same argument about parenting that chapter 3 made about sexuality: what makes parenting right or wrong is *not* marriage or its absence. What makes parenting right is responsibility; what makes it wrong is *ir*responsibility.

In the 21st-century information age, a responsible parent must at the very least be economically self-sufficient and, ideally, an autonomous person. That is obviously the case for a woman or man who elects to have a child but no partner. Moreover, it is equally true for the partner-free woman who becomes pregnant unintentionally and must ponder her abortion option. If she is neither independent nor autonomous, which is the responsible thing to do: bring an unplanned child into the world or have an abortion? Finally, even when a couple (married or cohabiting) sets out to have a child, there is no guarantee they shall remain partnered until the child reaches, say, age 18. Hence, the responsible thing is to be certain that each partner is an autonomous person prior to the pregnancy and birth, and to endeavor to remain so throughout the years following. Autonomy does not necessarily demand that both parents be continuously involved in economic activities—only, as chapter 3 points out, that great care is taken to negotiate arrangements that do not compromise either partner's autonomy.

The theme of responsibility pervading the previous eight principles likewise inspires the ninth guideline: *being child-free is created equal with being a parent*. Earlier chapters showed that prior to the 19th-century spread of effective contraceptive methods, most married persons believed they must passively bow to as many children as God might send. But by the mid-20th century, the norm had changed: it became laudable for a married couple to have as many children as, but not more than, it could afford.[13] Persons who were intentionally child*less* were seen as selfish and perhaps emotionally stunted. However, in this century we now understand that, partnered or not, opting to be child-*free* is a *responsible* choice. It has the potential to benefit oneself and one's partner, as well as the public household.

Chapter 5 showed that in fact growing numbers of U.S. women are choosing either to be child-free or at least to be "child-minimum" (having one child). As a researcher put it: "A lot of women are not having any children. . . . It used to be sort of expected that there was a phase of life where you had children, and a lot of women aren't doing that now." Like the 19th-century use of contraception that began among advantaged persons and spread eventually to the less advantaged, being child-free is more frequent among women who are better educated. It is likely that in this new century more women (and men) than ever before will become better educated. And, as that happens, it follows that the proportions of U.S. child-free women (married or not) will likely increase.

In the past it was assumed that anyone could be a parent because, after all, everyone had once been a child. If one needed a bit of help, one could always read how-to-parent books or take parenting classes. It was well known that some persons were good parents and others not. In particular, most women were thought to be better at parenting than most men. The quirky idea that sometimes it is wiser *not* to parent than to parent was seldom if ever seriously discussed—unless of course the couple applied for an adoption, in which case the serious question of whether they could at the very least be satisfactory parents dominated the conversation. Despite decades of research revealing that all too many biological parents abuse, damage, neglect, or simply ignore their children, few persons seem willing to consider the odds that they may in fact lack the talents and/or temperament to be at least a satisfactory parent.

Today, it appears that a small but growing number of better-educated women and men are now weighing those odds. They may, for instance, recognize that for them and their partner, having a child (or more than one) would place undue strains on their capabilities to negotiate their competing career and relationship demands alongside the demands of being effective parents. They sense that because a child (or children) in that situation would not be served in the best ways possible, it would *not* be responsible to have that child. They believe that by being child-free (or child-minimum) they avoid doing a disservice to that child. They are thus being guided by the ancient wisdom that "first of all, one should do no harm."

There is yet another reason why exercising the child-free (or child-minimum) option is becoming an increasingly responsible course of action, namely, the carbon footprint that each human being invariably makes. In recent years, we've heard a great deal about the huge amounts of resources consumed by the average American over the course of a single year. Every American child is a potential contributor to the growing levels of carbon being discharged into the atmosphere, thus increasing the dangers of global warming. Two researchers recently concluded that:

> *Having children is the surest way to send your carbon footprint soaring. . . . The study found that having a child has an impact that far outweighs that of other energy-saving behaviors.*

> *Take, for example, a hypothetical American woman who switches to a more fuel-efficient car, drives less, recycles, installs more efficient light bulbs, and replaces her refrigerator and windows with energy-saving models. If she had two children, the researchers found, her carbon legacy would eventually rise to nearly 40 times what she had saved by those actions.*
>
> *"Clearly, the potential savings from reduced reproduction are huge compared to the savings that can be achieved by changes in lifestyle," the report states.*
>
> *The impact of children varies dramatically depending on geography: An American woman who has a baby will generate nearly seven times the carbon footprint of that of a Chinese woman who has a child, the study found.*[14]

Hence, when reflecting on the greater good, would it not be responsible at least to consider being child-free, or perhaps to have only one child? Because of immigration, the United States is in no danger of becoming either a declining or a graying population. And, for those persons wishing to parent and yet reduce the global warming implications attached to childbearing, there is the option to adopt. The pool from which to draw eligible children includes the United States as well as other countries around the globe.

That discussion brings us to the tenth and final guideline of a progressive picture of 21st-century families: *responsibility requires paying careful attention, not simply to one's private household, but to the public household as well.* Bringing a child into the world is, as we just saw, not simply a private matter. Childbearing always has a range of broader social implications—an issue typically overlooked by christianists as they strive (via their antichoice agenda) to force unplanned (and typically less advantaged) children into the world.

In any case, once they're with us, chapter 6 noted that caring for all our children (from all social classes, not just the upper middle class) includes paying special attention to the public schools (K–12). Throughout the book, I've argued that the christianist agenda weakens the capabilities of less advantaged youth and adults to empower themselves. Conversely, a progressive approach to families—as captured, say, by these 10 principles—seeks to empower youngsters and adults. But empowering youngsters also requires among other things a distinctively relevant K–12 experience that, in conjunction with this entire set of guidelines, fits them for the postindustrial age. Regrettably K–12 carries on, for the most part, as if its mission was still to prepare youngsters for the fading industrial age.[15]

The K–12 experience occupies a special niche in the overall christianist agenda. The religious right is not, however, much interested in shifting K–12 from what chapter 6 called lower-order to higher-order (active, discovery-based) learning. It seeks instead to enlist K–12 as an agent to help impose its schema on the larger society. Chapter 2 noted that what we now call the RR jelled in the 1960s over disputes with regard to K–12. Christianists were offended that while Bible readings and prayers were being excised from K–12, courses on sex education were being introduced. In a very real sense, K–12 was the first battle-field in what eventually came to be known as the culture war. And it remains a combat zone today with disputes over abstinence-only (AO) and intelligent design (ID). Recent court decisions have, for the time being at least, curbed christianist efforts to impose ID on K–12.[16] When it comes to AO, however, the situation is nowhere nearly as hopeful.

Despite research revealing that AO is at best folly and at worst fraudulent, AO still prevails in K–12. The puzzle is what would replace it. Reviving the older liberal policy of simple risk reduction is not a viable option. Hence, it seems to me that the first step in replacing AO is to make clear that it is locked into the 1950s family—a style of family that does 21st-century children and youth no fa-vors. Notably, youngsters from less advantaged households suffer most from that disservice. Conversely, the interests of all youngsters would be better served by asking them—within the context of K–12 learning centers—to think about the set of guidelines being considered here. This progressive approach to fam-ilies would not be an isolated part of those learning centers, but would instead be one vital segment of the broader effort to shift K–12 toward what chapter 6 called active learning.

The long-term objective of that broader effort is to empower youngsters to function effectively within the emerging information age. And it so happens that this set of 10 guidelines dovetails with that objective. The theme of autonomy that pervades each of them is especially significant. It turns out that youngsters within the upper middle class are already aware—at least implicitly—that there is a close fit between a progressive approach to families and effective participa-tion in the information age. Over time, the awareness of that fit will likely be-come more explicit, and eventually filter down to less advantaged youngsters. It seems to me that the latter's well-being, alongside the interests of the public household, would be better served if that process could be expedited. One way to begin doing that is to discard AO in K–12 and instead make the linkages be-tween progressive families and effective participation in postindustrial society much more explicit.

"To whom much is given much is required," is a core value shared by all people of goodwill, whether they profess faith or not.[17] And that sense of duty is surely one of the core values of the public household. Concern for the interests of less advantaged youngsters is one way to express this value, as we just saw. Another way was described in chapter 3: as fully as possible, one should view one's own occupation as a means to serve the greater good. Effective participation in the information age is *not* aimed at assisting more citizens to pile up lots of money. It is aimed instead at enabling more citizens to reap a greater share of the intrinsic satisfactions of work. And one of its very important compensations stems from service to others.

To be sure, some occupations may seem less well suited than others to the possibility of serving the public household. In such situations, one might seek for ways to serve the greater good alongside one's occupation. In any case, lurking behind this 10th principle is the hope that not too many years down the road most students, when asked what they expect to do following graduation, will no longer respond (as I reported in chapter 3), "I don't know—just makes lots of money." Plainly, the 1950s image of the family did little or nothing to stem our obsession with the material face of work to the exclusion of its non-material face, including service to others. That is so even though the Judeo-Christian tradition warns against the corrosive effects of materialism. It seems to me that, in many respects, the progressive approach to families described here harmonizes with *progressive* interpretations of that religious tradition.[18] And that is especially so when it comes to this 10th principle—service to the public household.

STEALING CHRISTIANIST THUNDER: MAKING LIFE BETTER FOR PEOPLE

Benjamin Franklin has been called the "First Scientific American," and some historians rank him as an actual genius.[19] One author cleverly described him as "stealing God's thunder" owing to his invention of the lightning rod.[20] Prior to Franklin's invention, the practice in Britain and America was to permit a house to burn to the ground if set on fire by lightning. The town's fire brigade monitored the burning house while soaking houses on either side with water to prevent them from catching fire. Theirs was the same logic used not too long ago by certain RR leaders charging that HIV/AIDS was God's way of punishing homosexuals. Similarly, in Franklin's day, it was thought that the inhabitants of a house struck by lightning were being punished by God. Hence, no mere mortal must ever dare thwart God's purpose and thus incur his wrath by dumping water on the fire. "Nonsense," responded Franklin, and promptly proceeded to invent the simple device (which he refused to patent) that has since made life a whole lot better for millions of people around the globe.

Because Franklin was a deist, it seems unlikely to me that he thought of himself as stealing *God's* thunder. He would instead, I suspect, see himself as pulling the rug out from under the narrow-minded traditionalists of his day whom he openly disdained on numerous grounds—chief among which was his impatience with their mindless arguments. As a child of the Enlightenment as well as a deist, Franklin believed that God gives people Reason to figure out new ways of doing things—ways that might perhaps have a chance of making life better for everyone.

Christianists are among today's narrow-minded traditionalists, and I trust it's accurate to say that this set of 10 guidelines steals their thunder or pulls the rug out from under them. Or, we could switch the metaphor from pulling rugs to missing clothes. Recall the children's tale when the king parades in front of his dutiful subjects clad only in his underwear while commanding them to admire his exquisite (though nonexistent) clothing. The citizens loudly praise their monarch's fashionable garments until at last one small boy suddenly cries out, "But the emperor has no clothes!" For "emperor" insert "Religious Right." For any number of reasons christianists are set on forcing the rest of us to kowtow to their make-believe moral superiority. But it is finally high time to state the obvious: There is nothing there except a pathetic attempt to coerce the rest of us into saying that there is.

NOTES

1. Parsons 1965.
2. Otto 1970:4–5.
3. Noble 1966:535.
4. Ehrman 2005; Lobdell 2009; Reece 2009; Schaeffer 2008.
5. Rosin 2007.
6. Seelye 2009.
7. Strayhorn and Strayhorn 2009.
8. "On the Record," Fox News, hosted by Greta Van Susteren, February 16, 2009.
9. See http://www.urbandictionary.com/define.php?term=chick+flick.
10. Chambers-Schiller 1984; Carter 2006.
11. Waters 2003.
12. Hertz 2006:iii.
13. Rainwater 1960.
14. Galbraith 2009.
15. Sizer 2005.
16. Goodstein 2005.
17. A paraphrasing of St Luke 12:48, KJV.
18. MacFee 2008.
19. Chaplin 2006.
20. Dray 2005.

References

"A Protestant Affirmation on the Control of Human Reproduction." 1969. In *Birth Control and the Christian*, eds. W. O. Spitzer and C. L. Saylor, xxiii–xxxi. Wheaton, Ill.: Tyndale.

Abma, J. C., G. M. Martinez, W. D. Mosher, and B. S. Dawson. 2004. "Teenagers in the United States: Sexual Activity, Contraceptive Use, and Childbearing 2002." National Center for Health Statistics. *Vital Health Statistics* 23, no. 24. Hyattsville, Md.: Centers for Disease Control and Prevention.

Acton, William. [1870] 1968. *Prostitution*. 1968 edition: Ed. Peter Fryer. New York: Praeger.

Adams, Margaret. 1976. *Single Blessedness—Observations on the Single Status in Married Society*. New York: Basic Books.

Allen, Frederick Lewis. 1997. *Only Yesterday: An Informal History of the Nineteen Twenties*. New York: Wiley.

Allyn, David. 2000. *Make Love, Not War: The Sexual Revolution—An Unfettered History*. New York: Little, Brown.

Alston, Margaret. 1995. *Women on the Land—The Hidden Heart of Rural Australia*. Kensington NSW Australia: UNSW Press.

Altman, Lawrence K. 2005. "U.S. Blamed for Condom Shortage in Fighting AIDS in Uganda." *New York Times* (30 August).

Altman, Lawrence K. 2006. "U.N. Official Assails South Africa on Its Response to AIDS." *New York Times* (19 August).

Altman, Lawrence K. 2008a. "Sex Infections Found in Quarter of Teenage Girls." *New York Times* (12 March).

Altman, Lawrence K. 2008b. "H.I.V. Study Finds Rate 40% Higher than Estimated." *New York Times* (3 August).

Alvarez, Lizette. 2009. "G.I. Jane Breaks the Combat Barrier as War Evolves." the *New York Times* (16 August).

Amirrezvani, Anita. 2007. *The Blood of Flowers: A Novel*. Boston: Little, Brown.

Andersen, Karen. 1981. *Wartime Women: Sex Roles, Family Relations and the Status of Women during WWII*. Westport, Conn.: Greenwood.

Associated Press. 2009. "Minnesota Abortion Clinic Rammed by SUV—Man Arrested." Reported by *New York Times* (22 January).

Atwood, Margaret. 1985. *The Handmaid's Tale*. New York: Houghton-Mifflin.

Bailey, Beth L. 1989. *From Front Porch to Back Seat: Courtship in Twentieth-Century America*. Baltimore: Johns Hopkins University Press.

Bakalar, Nicholas. 2007. "Adolescence: Abstinence-Only Programs Not Found to Prevent HIV." *New York Times* (14 August).

Baker, Peter. 2009. "Obama Reverses Rules on US Abortion Aid." *New York Times* (24 January).

Balmer, Randall. 2006. *Thy Kingdom Come: An Evangelical's Lament*. New York: Basic Books.

Banerjee, Neela. 2006. "Pastor Chosen to Lead Christian Coalition Steps Down in Dispute over Agenda." *New York Times* (28 November).

Barr, James. 1977. *Fundamentalism*. Philadelphia: Westminster Press.

Barstow, David. 2009. "An Abortion Battle, Fought to the Death." *New York Times* (26 July).

Basch, Norma. 1986. "The Emerging Legal History of Women in the United States: Property, Divorce, and the Constitution." *Signs* 12: 97–117.

Bauer, Gary L., ed. 1986. *The Family: Preserving America's Future*. Washington, D.C.: The White House Working Group on the Family.

Beinart, Peter. 2006a. "The Rehabilitation of the Cold-War Liberal." *New York Times* (30 April).

Beinart, Peter. 2006b. *The Good Fight: Why Liberals—and Only Liberals—Can Win the War on Terror and Make America Great Again*. New York: HarperCollins.

Bell, Robert R. 1966. *Premarital Sex in a Changing Society*. Englewood Cliffs, N.J.: Prentice-Hall.

Bennetts, Leslie. 2007. *The Feminine Mistake: Are We Giving Up Too Much?* New York: Hyperion Books.

Bigner, Jerry J., ed. 2006. *An Introduction to GLBT Family Studies*. New York: Haworth Press.

Blades, Joan, and Kristin Rowe-Finkbeiner. 2006. *The Motherhood Manifesto—What America's Moms Want and What to Do about It*. New York: Nation/Avalon.

Blank, Rebecca M. 1997. *It Takes a Nation—A New Agenda for Fighting Poverty*. Princeton, N.J.: Princeton University Press.

Blankenhorn, David. 2007. *The Future of Marriage*. New York: Encounter Books.

Blow, Charles M. 2009. "By the Numbers—Love Shouldn't Hurt." *New York Times* (12 February).

Bowler, Peter J. 2007. *Monkey Trials and Gorilla Sermons—Evolution and Christianity from Darwin to Intelligent Design*. Cambridge, Mass.: Harvard University Press.

Brock, Peter. 1968. *Pacifism in the United States: From the Colonial Era to the First World War*. Princeton, N.J.: Princeton University Press.

Brody, Jane E. 2006. "New Devices and Effective Options in Contraception." *New York Times* (17 October).

Brookhiser, Richard. 1999. *Alexander Hamilton, American*. New York: Free Press.

Brookhiser, Richard. 2006. *What Would the Founders Do? Our Questions, Their Answers*. New York: Basic Books.

Brooks, David. 2006. "Where the Right Went Wrong." *New York Times* (22 October).

Burke, Peter J., and Jan E. Stets. 2009. *Identity Theory*. New York: Oxford University Press.

Butterfield, L. H., Marc Friedlaender, and Mary-Jo Kline. 1975. *The Book of Abigail and John—Selected Letters of the Adams Family 1762–1784*. Cambridge, Mass.: Harvard University Press.

Carey, Benedict. 2008. "Abortion Does Not Cause Mental Illness, Panel Says." *New York Times* (13 August).

Cargan, Leonard. 2007. *Being Single on Noah's Ark*. Lanham, Md.: Rowman & Littlefield.

Carter, Christine Jacobson. 2006. *Southern Single Blessedness—Unmarried Women in the Urban South, 1800–1865*. Urbana, Ill.: University of Illinois Press.

Casper, Gerhard. 1995 (22 September). "On Playing Hamlet." Stanford, Calif.: Stanford University, Office of the President.

Cates, W., Jr. 1981. "The Hyde Amendment in Action. How Did the Restriction of Federal Funds for Abortion Affect Low-Income Women?" *Journal of the American Medical Association* 246 (10): 1109–12.

Centers for Disease Control and Prevention. 2002. "Cohabitation, Marriage, Divorce, and Remarriage in the United States." *Vital Health Statistics* 23, no. 22. Department of Health and Human Services.

Centers for Disease Control and Prevention. 2009. "Sexual & Reproductive Health of Persons 10–24 Years, US, 2002–2007." *Morbidity & Mortality Weekly Report* 58 (17 July).

Chambers-Schiller, Lee Virginia. 1984. *Liberty, a Better Husband. Single Women in America: The Generations of 1780–1840*. New Haven, Conn.: Yale University Press.

Chaplin, Joyce E. 2006. *The First Scientific American: Benjamin Franklin and the Pursuit of Genius*. New York: Basic Books.

Cheatham, Harold E., and James B. Stewart. 1990. *Black Families*. New York: Transaction Books.

Chevalier, Tracy. *The Virgin Blue*. London: Plume, 1997.

Cohen, Patricia. 2007. "Signs of Détente in the Battle between Venus and Mars." *New York Times* (31 May).

Cohen, Roger. 2007. "Secular Europe's Merits." *New York Times* (13 December).

Collins, Francis. 2006. *The Language of God: A Scientist Presents Evidence for Belief.* New York: Free Press.

Collins, W. Andrew, and Manfred van Dulmen. 2006. "Friendships and Romance in Emerging Adulthood: Assessing Distinctiveness in Close Relationships." In *Emerging Adults in America—Coming of Age in the 21st Century,* eds. Jeffrey Jensen Arnett and Jennifer Lynn Tanner, 219–34. Washington, D.C.: American Psychological Association.

Coontz, Stephanie. 2005. *Marriage, a History—How Love Conquered Marriage.* New York: Penguin.

Coontz, Stephanie, and Peta Henderson. 1986. *Women's Work, Men's Property—The Origins of Gender and Class.* London: Verso Press.

Correll, Shelley J., Stephen Benard, and In Paik. 2007. "Getting a Job: Is There a Motherhood Penalty?" *American Journal of Sociology* 112: 1297–1338.

Cott, Nancy F. 1979. "Passionlessness: An Interpretation of Victorian Sexual Ideology, 1790–1850." *Signs* 4: 162–81.

Cott, Nancy F., and Elizabeth H. Pleck. 1979. "Introduction." In *A Heritage of Her Own—Toward a New Social History of American Women,* eds. Nancy F. Cott and Elizabeth H. Pleck, 9–24. New York: Simon & Schuster.

Cross, Earle Bennett. 1969. "The Hebrew Family in Biblical Times." In *Marriage and the Family,* eds. Jeffrey K. Hadden and Marie L. Borgotta, 60–73. Itasca, Ill.: Peacock.

Currell, Susan. 2009. *American Culture in the 1920s.* Edinburgh, UK: Edinburgh University Press.

Dermott, Esther. 2008. *Intimate Fatherhood—A Sociological Analysis.* New York: Routledge.

Deutsch, Francine M. 1999. *Halving It All—How Equally Shared Parenting Works.* Cambridge, Mass.: Harvard University Press.

Dillon, Sam. 2008. "Teach for America Sees Surge in Popularity." *New York Times* (14 May).

Dionne, E. J., Jr. 2008. *Souled Out—Reclaiming Faith and Politics after the Religious Right.* Princeton, N.J.: Princeton University Press.

Donnelly, John. 2007. "The Plague of Nations." *New York Times* (29 July).

Dougherty, John. 2007. "Polygamist Sentenced to 10 Years in Prison." *New York Times* (21 November).

Dray, Philip. 2005. *Stealing God's Thunder—Benjamin Franklin's Lightning Rod and the Invention of America.* New York: Random House.

Ducat, Stephen J. 2004. *The Wimp Factor—Gender Gaps, Holy Wars, and the Politics of Anxious Masculinity.* Boston: Beacon Press.

Eckholm, Erik. 2008. "Blue-Collar Jobs Disappear, Taking Families' Way of Life Along." *New York Times* (16 January).

Eckholm, Erik. 2009. "'07 US Births Break Baby Boom Record." *New York Times* (19 March).

Ehrman, Bart. 2005. *Misquoting Jesus—The Story behind Who Changed the Bible and Why.* San Francisco: HarperCollins.

Einhorn, Catrin. 2008. "At College, a High Standard on Divorce." *New York Times* (4 May).

Elkin, Stanley. 1983. "Alfred Kinsey: The Patron Saint of Sex." *Esquire* (December). Reprinted in *Kinsey—Public and Private,* ed. Bill Condon, 85–88. New York: Newmarket Press, 2004.

Epstein, Helen P. 2007. *The Invisible Cure: Africa, the West, and the Fight against AIDS.* New York: Farrar, Straus & Giroux.

Erzen, Tanya. 2000. "Liberated Through Submission? The Gender Politics of Evangelical Women's Groups Modeled on the Promise Keepers." In *The Promise Keepers—Essays on Masculinity and Christianity,* ed. Diane S. Clausen, 238–54. Jefferson, N.C.: McFarland.

Evans, Mary. 2003. *Love: An Unromantic Discussion.* Malden, Mass.: Blackwell.

Fairchilds, Cissie. 2007. *Women in Early Modern Europe: 1500–1700.* New York: Pearson.

Ferreira, M. Jamie. 2009. *Kierkegaard.* Malden, Mass.: Wiley-Blackwell.

Fielding, Waldo L. 2008. "Repairing the Damage, Before Roe." *New York Times* (3 June).

Finkelhor, David, and Kersti Yllo. 1985. *License to Rape: Sexual Abuse of Wives.* New York: Free Press.

Fisch, Harry, and Kara Baskin. 2008. *Size Matters: The Hard Facts about Male Sexuality That Every Woman Should Know.* New York: Three Rivers Press.

Ford, Ford Maddox. [1915] 1989. *The Good Soldier.* New York: Random House/Vintage.

Forrest, Barbara, and Paul R. Gross. 2007. *Creationism's Trojan Horse—The Wedge of Intelligent Design.* New York: Oxford University Press.

Freedman, Samuel G. 2006a. "Muzzling Sex Education on Anything but Abstinence." *New York Times* (19 July)

Freedman, Samuel G. 2006b. "The Disillusionment of a Young White House Evangelical." *New York Times* (28 October).

Frosch, Dan. 2007. "Albuquerque Has Renewal of Attacks on Abortion." *New York Times* (28 December).

Frost, Ginger S. 2008. *Living in Sin: Cohabiting as Husband and Wife in Nineteenth-Century England.* Manchester, UK: Manchester University Press.

Galbraith, Kate. 2009. "Having Children Brings High Carbon Impact." *New York Times* (7 August).

Gathorne-Hardy, Jonathan. 2000. *Sex, the Measure of All Things—A Life of Alfred C. Kinsey.* Bloomington, Ind.: Indiana University Press.

Gawande, Atul. 2007. "Let's Talk about Sex." *New York Times* (19 May).

Gelles, Richard J. 1977. "Power, Sex, and Violence: The Case of Marital Rape." *The Family Coordinator* 26: 339–47.

Gerth, H. H., and C. Wright Mills. 1958. *From Max Weber—Essays in Sociology.* New York: Oxford University Press.

Giberson, Karl W. 2008. *Saving Darwin—How to Be a Christian and Believe in Evolution.* New York: HarperOne.

Gilgoff, Dan. 2007. *The Jesus Machine—How James Dobson, Focus on the Family, and Evangelical America Are Winning the Culture War.* New York: St. Martin's.

Gitlin, Todd. 1993. *The Sixties—Years of Hope, Days of Rage.* New York: Bantam.

Goldberg, Michelle. 2006a. *Kingdom Coming: The Rise of Christian Nationalism.* New York: Norton.

Goldberg, Michelle. 2006b. "Sinners in the Hands of an Angry GOP." *Salon* (29 March).

Goldberg, Michelle. 2009. *The Means of Reproduction: Sex, Power and the Future of the World.* New York: Penguin.

Goldin, Claudia, and Maria Shim. 2004. "Making a Name: Women's Surnames at Marriage and Beyond." *Journal of Economic Perspectives* 18: 143–60.

Goldin, Hannah. 2006. "Working It Out." *New York Times* (15 March).

Goode, William J. 1963. *World Revolution and Family Patterns.* New York: Free Press.

Goodstein, Laurie. 2005. "Judge Bars 'Intelligent Design' from Pa. Classes." *New York Times* (20 December).

Goodstein, Laurie. 2006. "Evangelicals Fear the Loss of Their Teenagers." *New York Times* (6 October).

Gordon, Michael. 1978. *The American Family—Past, Present and Future.* New York: Random House.

Graff, E. J. 2007. "The Opt-Out Myth." *Columbia Journalism Review* (March/April).

Graham, Billy. [1953 (27 September)] 2004. "The Bible and Dr. Kinsey." Original article, *St. Paul Pioneer Press.* Reprinted in *Kinsey—Public and Private,* ed. Bill Condon, 125–27. New York: Newmarket Press.

Greenhouse, Steven. 2009. "Recession Drives Women Back to the Work Force." *New York Times* (19 September).

Haeri, Shahla. 1989. *Law of Desire: Temporary Marriage in Shi'i Iran.* Syracuse, N.Y.: Syracuse University Press.

Halberstam, David. 1993. *The Fifties.* New York: Villard Books.

Halliwell, Martin. 2007. *American Culture in the 1950s.* Edinburgh, UK: Edinburgh University Press.

Harris, Gardiner. 2007. "Teenage Birth Rate Rises for First Time Since '91." *New York Times* (6 December).

Heller, Joseph. 1984. *God Knows.* New York: Dell.

Henshaw, Stanley K., and Kathryn Kost. 2008. *Trends in the Characteristics of Women Obtaining Abortions, 1974 to 2004.* New York: Guttmacher Institute.

Herbert, Bob. 2008. "Where's the Big Idea?" *New York Times* (9 February).

Hertz, Rosanna. 2006. *Single by Chance, Mothers by Choice—How Women Are Choosing Parenthood without Marriage and Creating the New American Family.* New York: Oxford University Press.

Herzog, Dagmar. 2008. *Sex in Crisis: The New Sexual Revolution and the Future of American Politics.* New York: Basic Books.

Hilley, Joe. 2008. *Sarah Palin—A New Kind of Leader.* Grand Rapids, Mich.: Zondervan.

Himes, Norman E. 1936/1970. *Medical History of Contraception.* New York: Schocken Books.

Hirshman, Linda R. 2005. "Homeward Bound." *The American Prospect* (21 November).

Hirshman, Linda R. 2006. "Unleashing the Wrath of Stay-at-Home Moms." *Washington Post* (18 June): B01.

Hoffer Eric. 1951. *The True Believer: Thoughts on the Nature of Mass Movements.* New York: Harper & Row.

Horrell, Sara, and Jane Humphries. 1998. "Women's Labor Force Participation and the Transition to the Male-Breadwinner Family, 1790–1865." In *Women's Work—The English Experience 1650–1914,* 172–206. New York: Arnold Press.

Hunter, Malcolm L., Jr., David B. Lindenmayer, and Aram J. K. Calhoun. 2007. *Saving the Earth as a Career—Advice on Becoming a Conservation Professional.* Malden, Mass.: Blackwell.

Hyland, Paul, ed. 2003. *The Enlightenment Reader: A Sourcebook and Reader.* London: Routledge.

James, Lawrence. 2006. *The Middle Class—A History.* London: Little, Brown.

Jesella, Kara. 2007. "Mom's Mad. And She's Organized." *New York Times* (22 February).

Joannides, Paul. 2009. *Guide to Getting It On—For Adults of All Ages.* Lanham, Md.: National Book Distribution/Goofy Foot Press.

Johnson, David R., and Laurie K. Scheuble. 1995. "Women's Marital Naming in Two Generations: A National Study." *Journal of Marriage and the Family* 57: 724–32.

Johnston, David Cay. 2007. "Income Gap Is Widening, Data Shows." *New York Times* (29 March).

Jones, James H. 1997. *Alfred C. Kinsey: A Public/Private Life.* New York: Norton.

Kaplan, Elaine Bell. 1997. *Not Our Kind of Girl—Unraveling the Myths of Black Teenage Motherhood.* Berkeley: University of California Press.

Kazin, Michael, ed. 2008. *In Search of Progressive America.* Philadelphia: University of Pennsylvania Press.

Kelley, Donald R. 1972. "Martyrs, Myths, and the Massacre: The Background of St. Bartholomew." *American Historical Review* 77: 1323–42.

Kennedy, David M. 1970. *Birth Control in America: The Career of Margaret Sanger.* New Haven: Yale University Press.

Kenworthy, Lane. 2008. *Jobs with Equality.* New York: Oxford University Press.

Kinnaman, David, and Gabe Lyons. 2007. *Unchristian—What a New Generation Really Thinks about Christianity.* Grand Rapids, Mich.: Baker Books.

Kinsey, Alfred C., W. B. Pomeroy, and C. E. Martin. 1948. *Sexual Behavior in the Human Male.* Philadelphia: Saunders.

Kinsey, Alfred C., W. B. Pomeroy, C. E. Martin, and P. H. Gebhard. 1953. *Sexual Behavior in the Human Female.* Philadelphia: Saunders.

Kirsch, Jonathan. 2008. *The Grand Inquisitor's Manual—A History of Terror in the Name of God.* New York: HarperOne.

Kowalski, Gary. 2008. *Revolutionary Spirits—The Enlightened Faith of America's Founding Fathers.* New York: BlueBridge.

Kraditor, Aileen S. 1968. *Up from the Pedestal—Selected Writings in the History of American Feminism.* Chicago: Quadrangle Books.

Kraut, Richard. 2008. "Plato on Love." In *The Oxford Handbook of Plato,* ed. Gail Fine, 286–310. New York: Oxford University Press.

Kristof, Nicholas D. 2006. "Race Against Death." *New York Times* (4 June).

Kristof, Nicholas D. 2008a. "Evangelicals a Liberal Can Love." *New York Times* (3 February).

Kristof, Nicholas D. 2008b. "Can This Be Pro-Life?" *New York Times* (9 October),

Kristof, Nicholas D. 2008c. "Rejoin the World." *New York Times* (1 November).

Kuo, David. 2006a. *Tempting Faith: An Inside Story of Political Seduction.* New York: Free Press.

Kuo, David. 2006b. "Putting Faith before Politics." *New York Times* (16 November).

Kuo, David, and John J. Diiulio, Jr. 2008. "The Faith to Outlast Politics." *New York Times* (29 January).

Kurdek, Lawrence A., and Patrick Schmitt. 1986a. "Early Development of Relationship Quality in Heterosexual Married, Heterosexual Cohabiting, Gay and Lesbian Couples." *Developmental Psychology* 22: 305–9.

Kurdek, Lawrence A., and Patrick Schmitt. 1986b. "Relationship Quality of Partners in Heterosexual Married, Heterosexual Cohabiting, and Gay and Lesbian Couples." *Journal of Personality and Social Psychology* 51: 711–20.

Lacey, W. K. 1968. *The Family in Classical Greece.* Ithaca, N.Y.: Cornell University Press.

Lantz, Herman R. 1976. *Marital Incompatibility and Social Change in Early America.* Thousand Oaks, Calif.: Sage.

Larocque, Sylvain. 2006. *Gay Marriage: The Story of a Canadian Social Revolution.* Toronto: James Lorimer.

Larson, Rebecca. 2000. *Daughters of Light: Quaker Women Preaching and Prophesying in the Colonies and Abroad, 1700–1775.* Chapel Hill, N.C.: University of North Carolina Press.

Lasch, Christopher. 1977. *Haven in a Heartless World: The Family Besieged.* New York: Basic Books.

Lawes, Frank A. 1948. *The Sanctity of Sex.* Chicago: Good News.

Ledgin, Norm. 2000. *Diagnosing Jefferson: Evidence of a Condition that Guided His Beliefs, Behavior, and Personal Associations.* New York: Future Horizons.

Leeman, Richard W. 1989. "Believing and Make-Believing: Christian Metaphors for and against Prohibition." *Metaphor and Symbolic Activity* 4:19–37.

Lefkowitz, Eva S,, and Meghan M. Gillen. 2006. "'Sex Is Just a Normal Part of Life': Sexuality in Emerging Adulthood." In *Emerging Adults in America—Coming of Age in the 21st Century,* eds. Jeffrey Jensen Arnett and Jennifer Lynn Tanner, 235–56. Washington, D.C.: The American Psychological Association.

Leonhardt, David. 2006. "Scant Progress on Closing Gap in Women's Pay." *New York Times* (24 December).

Lerner, Sharon, 2005. "Post-Roe Postcard: Is Ole Miss Our Future? Having All but Out-lawed Abortion, Mississippi Has Become a Laboratory for Antichoice Strategists. Prochoicers Are Beginning to Take Notice." *The Nation* (7 February).

Levin, Diane E., and Jean Kilbourne. 2008. *So Sexy So Soon—The New Sexualized Child-hood and What Parents Can Do to Protect Their Kids.* New York: Ballantine

Lind, Michael. 2009. "America Is Not a Christian Nation." *Salon* (14 April).

Lindner, Christopher. 2003. *The James Bond Phenomenon—A Critical Reader.* Manches-ter, UK: Manchester University Press.

Lindsay, D. Michael. 2007. *Faith in the Halls of Power—How Evangelicals Joined the American Elite.* New York: Oxford University Press.

Lindsey, Brink. 2007. *The Age of Abundance—How Prosperity Transformed America's Poli-tics and Culture.* New York: HarperCollins.

Lipset, Seymour Martin. [1955] 2002. "The Sources of the 'Radical Right.'" Reprinted in *The Radical Right* (3rd ed.), ed. Daniel Bell, 307–72. New Brunswick, N.J.: Trans-action.

Lobdell, William. 2009. *Losing My Religion: How I Lost My Faith Reporting on Religion in America—and Found Unexpected Peace.* New York: Collins.

Lopez, Claude-Anne. 2000. "My Life with Benjamin Franklin." *Yale Bulletin & Calendar* 28 (23 June).

Luker, Kristin. 1996. *Dubious Conceptions—The Politics of Teenage Pregnancy.* Cambridge, Mass.: Harvard University Press.

Luker, Kristin. 2006. *When Sex Goes to School: Warring Views on Sex—and Sex Educa-tion—Since the Sixties.* New York: Norton.

MacAfee, Norman (ed.). 2008. *The Gospel According to RFK: Why It Matters.* New York: Basic/Perseus.

Macklin, Eleanor D., and Roger H. Rubin, eds. 1983. *Contemporary Families and Alterna-tive Lifestyles.* Thousand Oaks, Calif.: Sage.

Madden, Thomas F. 1999. *A Concise History of the Crusades.* New York: Rowman & Lit-tlefield.

Mansbridge, Jane J. 1986. *Why We Lost the ERA.* Chicago: University of Chicago Press.

Marsden, George M. 1991. *Understanding Fundamentalism and Evangelicalism.* Grand Rapids, Mich.: Eerdmans.

Marsden, Lee. 2008. *For God's Sake—The Christian Right and US Foreign Policy.* New York: ZED Books.

Marsiglio, W., A, Ries, F. Sonenstein, K. Troccoli, and W. Whitehead. 2006. *It's a Guy Thing: Boys, Young Men, and Teen Pregnancy Prevention.* Washington, DC: National Campaign to Prevent Teen Pregnancy.

Martin, Ralph G. 1969. *Jennie: The Life of Lady Randolph Churchill.* Englewood Cliffs, N.J.: Prentice-Hall.

Martin, William. 1996. *With God on Our Side: The Rise of the Religious Right in America.* New York: Broadway Books.

Masci, David. 2008a. "An Overview of the Same-Sex Marriage Debate." *Pew Forum on Religion and Public Life* (10 April).

Masci, David. 2008b. "The Evidence for Belief: An Interview with Francis Collins." *Pew Forum on Religion and Public Life* (17 April).

Masci, David, and Gregory A. Smith. 2006. "God Is Alive and Well in America." *Pew Forum on Religion and Public Life* (4 April).

Mathews, Donald G. 1977. *Religion in the Old South*. Chicago: University of Chicago Press.

Maxwell, Sharon. 2008. *The Talk—What Your Kids Need to Hear from You about Sex*. New York: Penguin.

McCulley, Carolyn. 2004. *Did I Kiss Marriage Goodbye? Trusting God with a Hope Deferred*. Wheaton, Ill.: Crossway Books.

McHugh, Kathleen Anne. 1999. *American Domesticity—From How-To Manual to Hollywood Melodrama*. New York: Oxford University Press.

Meacham, Jon. 2006. *American Gospel—God, the Founding Fathers, and the Making of a Nation*. New York: Random House.

Meacham, Jon. 2007. "A Nation of Christians Is Not a Christian Nation." *New York Times* (7 October).

Mead, Margaret. 1967. "The Life Cycle and Its Variations: The Division of Roles." *Daedalus—Toward the Year 2000, Work in Progress* 96: 871–75.

Michaelsen, Larry K., Michael Sweet, and Dean X. Parmelee, eds. 2008. *Team-Based Learning: Small Group Learning's Next Big Step*. San Francisco: Jossey-Bass.

Miles, Rosalind. 1988. *The Women's History of the World*. New York: Harper & Row.

Mintz, Steven, and Susan Kellogg. 1988. *Domestic Revolutions: A Social History of American Family Life*. New York: Free Press.

Modell, John. 1989. *Into One's Own: From Youth to Adulthood in the United States*. Berkeley: University of California Press.

Mohler, R. Albert, Jr. 2000. "Against an Immoral Tide." *New York Times* (19 June).

Mohr, James C. 1978. *Abortion in America: The Origins and Evolution of National Policy*. New York: Oxford University Press.

Munger, Michael, and Thomas Schaller. 1997. "The Prohibition-Repeal Amendments: A Natural Experiment in Interest Group Influence." *Public Choice* 90: 139–63.

Nagourney, Adam. 2007. "McCain Stumbles on HIV Prevention." *New York Times* (16 March).

Noble, Jeanne L. 1966. "The American Negro Woman." In *The American Negro Reference Book*, Ed. John P. Davis, 514–41. Englewood Cliffs, N.J.: Prentice-Hall.

Norris, Floyd. 2009. "In This Recession, More Men Are Losing Jobs." *New York Times* (14 March).

O'Beirne, Kate. 2006. *Women Who Make the World Worse—How Their Radical Feminist Assault Is Ruining Our Schools, Families, Military, and Sports*. New York: Sentinel.

Okun, Will. 2008. "The Schools." *New York Times* (19 February).

Olfman, Sharna, ed. 2009. *The Sexualization of Childhood*. Westport, Conn.: Praeger.

"On the Record." 2009. Fox News, hosted by Greta Van Susteren, February 16.

Osterud, Nancy Grey. 1991. *Bonds of Community: The Lives of Farm Women in Nineteenth-Century New York*. Ithaca, N.Y.: Cornell University Press.

Ostling, Richard N., and Joan K. Ostling. 2007. *Mormon America: The Power and the Promise*. New York: HarperOne.

Otto, Herbert A. 1970. "Introduction." In *The Family in Search of a Future*, ed. H. A. Otto, 1–13. New York: Appleton, Century, Crofts.

Palmquist, Steven. 1993. *Biblical Theocracy: A Vision of the Biblical Foundations for a Christian Political Philosophy*. Hong Kong: Philopsychy Press.

Paris, Ginette. 1992. *The Psychology of Abortion*. Putnam, Conn.: Spring Publications.

Parsons, Talcott. 1965. "The Normal American Family." In *Man & Civilization: The Family's Search for Survival*, ed. S. M. Farber et al., 31–50. New York: McGraw-Hill.

Pear, Robert, and Adam Liptak. 2009. "Health Bill Might Direct Tax Money to Abortion." *New York Times* (20 July).

Peril, Lynn. 2006. *College Girls: Bluestockings, Sex Kittens, and Coeds, Then and Now*. New York: Norton.

Peters, Jeremy W. 2008. "New York to Back Same-Sex Unions from Elsewhere." *New York Times* (29 May).

Petto, Andrew J., and Laurie R. Godfrey, eds. 2007. *Scientists Confront Intelligent Design and Creationism*. New York: Norton.

Phillips, Kate. 2006. "Lone Muslim Congressman Speaks Out." *New York Times* (21 December).

Piehl, Norah, ed. 2007. *Abortion*. New York: Greenhaven/Thomson/Gale.

Polikoff, Nancy D. 2008. *Beyond (Straight and Gay) Marriage: Valuing All Families under the Law*. Boston: Beacon Press.

Pomeroy, Sarah B. 1997. *Families in Classical and Hellenistic Greece—Representations and Realities*. New York: Oxford University Press.

Press, Eyal. 2006. *Absolute Convictions*. New York: Henry Holt.

Queen, Stuart A., Robert W. Habenstein, and Jill S. Quadagno. 1985 (rev. ed.). *The Family in Various Cultures*. New York: Harper & Row.

Rainwater, Lee. 1960. *And the Poor Get Children*. Chicago: Quadrangle.

Rauch, Jonathon. 2004. *Gay Marriage—Why It Is Good for Gays, Good for Straights, and Good for America*. New York: Owl Book/Henry Holt.

Reece, Erik. 2009. *An American Gospel: On Family, History, and the Kingdom of God*. New York: Riverhead/Penguin.

Reed, Ralph. 1996. *Active Faith*. New York: Free Press.

Regnerus, Mark D. 2007. *Forbidden Fruit: Sex and Religion in the Lives of American Teenagers*. New York: Oxford Press.

Reiss, Ira L. 1960. *Premarital Sexual Standards in America*. New York: Free Press.

Rice, John R. 1941. *Bobbed Hair, Bossy Wives and Women Preachers: Significant Questions for Honest Christian Women Settled by the Word of God*. Murfreesboro, Tenn.: Sword of the Lord Publishers.

Rimer, Sara. 2008. "For the Georgia Schools Chief, Geography and History Pay Off." *New York Times* (9 September).

Roberts, Sam, Ariel Sabar, Brenda Goodman, and Maureen Balleza. 2007a. "51% of Women Are Now Living Without Spouse." *New York Times* (16 January).

Roberts, Sam, with Cristina Maldonaldo. 2007b. "For Young Earners in Big City, Gap Shifts in Women's Favor." *New York Times* (3 August).

Rohter, Larry, and Tom Zito. 1977. "Rock Idol Elvis Presley Dies at 42." *Washington Post* (17 August).

Rosenmann, Ellen Bayuk, and Claudia Klaver, eds. 2008. *Other Mothers: Beyond the Maternal Ideal.* Columbus: The Ohio State University Press.

Rosin, Hanna. 2007. *God's Harvard—A Christian College on a Mission to Save America.* New York: Harcourt.

Rossi, Alice S. 1970. "Sentiment and Intellect: The Story of John Stuart Mill and Harriet Taylor Mill." In *Essays on Sex Equality: John Stuart Mill and Harriet Taylor Mill,* ed. Alice S. Rossi, 1–64. Chicago: University of Chicago Press.

Santelli, John S., Laura Duberstein Lindberg, Lawrence B. Finer, and Susheela Singh. 2007. "Explaining Recent Declines in Adolescent Pregnancy in the United States: The Contribution of Abstinence and Improved Contraceptive Use." *Contemporary Sexuality* 41: 8–12.

Santelli, John S., Mark Orr, Laura D. Lindberg, and Daniela C. Diaz. 2009. "Changing Behavioral Risk for Pregnancy among High School Students in the United States, 1991–2007." *Journal of Adolescent Health* (July): 343–60.

Scales, Peter. 1986. "The Changing Context of Sexuality Education: Paradigms and Challenges for Alternative Futures." *Family Relations* 35: 265–74.

Scanzoni, John. 1969. "A Sociological Perspective on Abortion and Sterilization." In *Birth Control and the Christian,* eds. W. O. Spitzer and C. L. Saylor, 313–26. Wheaton, Ill.: Tyndale House.

Scanzoni, John. 1971. *The Black Family in Modern Society: Patterns of Stability and Security.* Boston: Allyn & Bacon, 1971. Revised and reissued in 1977. Chicago: University of Chicago Press.

Scanzoni, John. 1972. *Sexual Bargaining: Power Politics in American Marriage.* Englewood Cliffs, N.J.: Prentice-Hall, 1972. Revised and reissued in 1982. Chicago: University of Chicago Press.

Scanzoni, John. 1973. "The Christian View of Work." In *Quest for Reality—Christianity and the Counter-Culture,* ed. Carl F. H. Henry, 122–39. Downers Grove, Ill.: Intervarsity Press.

Scanzoni. John. 1979. *Love and Negotiate—Creative Conflict in Marriage.* Waco, Tex.: Word Books.

Scanzoni, John. 1995. *Contemporary Families and Relationships: Reinventing Responsibility.* New York: McGraw-Hill.

Scanzoni, John. 2000. *Designing Families: The Search for Self and Community in the Information Age.* Thousand Oaks, Calif.: Pine Forge Press/Sage.

Scanzoni, John. 2002. "A Personal and Intellectual Journey." In *Pioneering Paths in the Study of Families: The Lives and Careers of Family Scholars*, eds. Suzanne K. Steinmetz and Gary W. Peterson, 405–26. New York: Haworth.

Scanzoni, John. 2004. "Household Diversity: The Starting Point for Healthy Families in the New Century." *Handbook of Contemporary Families—Considering the Past, Contemplating the Future*, ed. Marilyn Coleman & Lawrence H. Ganong, 3–22. Thousand Oaks, Calif.: Sage.

Scanzoni, John. 2005. *Universities as if Students Mattered: Social Science on the Creative Edge*. New York: Rowman & Littlefield.

Schaeffer, Frank. 2008. *Crazy for God—How I Grew Up as One of the Elect, Helped Found the Religious Right, and Lived to Take All (or Most of It) Back*. New York: Perseus.

Schuking, Levin L. 1970. *The Puritan Family: A Social Study from the Literary Sources*. New York: Schocken Books.

Scott, Dan. 2008. *Naked and Not Ashamed: How God Redeems our Sexuality*. Eugene, Ore.: Harvest Press.

Seelye, Katherine Q. 2009. "Canceled Palin Wedding Becomes a Public Matter." *New York Times* (13 March).

Sharlet, Jeff. 2008. *The Family—The Secret Fundamentalism at the Heart of American Power*. New York: HarperCollins.

Sharpe, Pamela, ed. 1998. *Women's Work—The English Experience 1650–1914*. New York: Oxford University Press.

Shorter, Edward. 1975. *The Making of the Modern Family*. New York: Basic Books.

Simpson, Ruth. 2009. *Men in Caring Occupations—Doing Gender Differently*. New York: St. Martin's/Palgrave.

Sizer, Theodore R. 1992. *Horace's School—Redesigning the American High School*. Boston: Houghton Mifflin.

Sizer, Theodore R. 1996. *Horace's Hope—What Works for the American High School*. Boston: Houghton Mifflin.

Sizer, Theodore R. 2005. *The Red Pencil: Convictions from Experience in Education*. New Haven, Conn.: Yale University Press.

Smith, Jean Edward. 2007. "When Government Was the Solution." *New York Times* (21 May).

Soland, Brigitte. 2000. *Becoming Modern: Young Women and the Reconstruction of Womanhood in the 1920s*. Princeton, N.J.: Princeton University Press.

Solomon, Deborah. 2006. "Questions for CC Goldwater—Goldwater Girl." *New York Times* (27 August).

Sowerby, Robin. 1995/2009. *The Greeks—An Introduction to Their Culture* (2nd ed.). New York: Routledge.

Spates, James L. 1976. "Counterculture and Dominant Culture Values: A Cross-National Analysis of the Underground Press and Dominant Culture Magazines." *American Sociological Review* 41: 868–83.

Spitzer, Walter O., and Carlyle L. Saylor. 1969. "Introduction: A Protestant Symposium on the Control of Human Reproduction." In *Birth Control and the Christian*, eds. W. O. Spitzer and C. L. Saylor, xvii–xxii. Wheaton, Ill.: Tyndale House.

Stack, Carol. 1974. *All Our Kin: Strategies for Survival in a Black Community*. New York: Harper & Row.

Stein, Peter J. 1981. *Single Life: Unmarried Adults in Social Context*. New York: St. Martin's Press.

Steiner, Leslie Morgan, ed. 2006. *Mommy Wars—Stay-at-Home and Career Moms Face Off on Their Choices, Their Lives, Their Families*. New York: Random House.

Steinfels, Peter. 2008. "Religious Right May Be Fading, but Not the 'Culture Wars.'" *New York Times* (16 February).

Strasser, Susan. 1982. *Never Done: A History of American Housework*. New York: Pantheon.

Strayhorn, Joseph, and Jillian C. Strayhorn. 2009. "Religiosity and Teen Birth Rate in the United States." *Journal of Reproductive Health* 43: 1–22.

Sullivan, Andrew. 2006. *The Conservative Soul—How We Lost It, How to Get It Back*. New York: HarperCollins.

Susser, Ida. 2009. *AIDS, Sex, and Culture—Global Politics and Survival in Southern Africa*. Oxford/UK: Blackwell-Wiley.

Tademy, Lalita. 2001. *Cane River*. New York: Warner Books.

Thomas, Sherry. 1981. *We Didn't Have Much, But We Sure Had Plenty—Stories of Rural Women*. New York: Anchor/Doubleday.

Thornton, Arland, and Linda Young-DeMarco. 2001. "Four Decades of Trends in Attitudes Toward Family Issues in the United States: The 1960s Through the 1990s." *Journal of Marriage and Family* 63: 1009–37.

Tomlin, Graham. 2007. *The Seven Deadly Sins and How to Overcome Them*. Oxford, UK: Lion House.

Tomkins, Stephen. 2007. *William Wilberforce—A Biography*. Grand Rapids, Mich.: Eerdmans.

Toner, Robin. 2007. "Abortion Foes See Validation for New Tactic." *New York Times* (22 May).

Tough, Paul. 2008a. "24/7 School Reform." *New York Times* (7 September).

Tough, Paul. 2008b. *Whatever It Takes—Geoffrey Canada's Quest to Change Harlem and America*. Boston: Houghton-Mifflin.

Trost, Jan. 1979. *Unmarried Cohabitation*. Vasteras Sweden: International Library.

Veevers, Jean. 1980. *Childless by Choice*. Toronto: Butterworth.

Wall, Helena M. 1990. *Fierce Communion: Family and Community in Early America*. Cambridge, Mass.: Harvard University Press.

Wallis, Jim. 2005. *God's Politics: Why the Right Gets It Wrong and the Left Doesn't Get It*. San Francisco: HarperCollins.

Wallis, Jim. 2008. *The Great Awakening: Reviving Faith und Politics in a Post-Religious Right America*. New York: HarperCollins.

Warner, Judith. 2005. *Perfect Madness—Motherhood in the Age of Anxiety.* New York: Riverhead/Penguin.

Warner, Judith. 2007. "A Warm Welcome for 'Dad Lit.'" *New York Times* (17 May).

Warner, Judith. 2009. "Families to Care About." *New York Times* (19 March).

Warner, Ralph, Toni Ihara, and Frederick Hertz. 2008. *Living Together: A Legal Guide for Unmarried Couples* (14th ed.). Berkeley, Calif.: Nolo Press.

Waters, Ethan 2003. *Urban Tribes: A Generation Redefines Friendship, Family, and Commitment.* New York: Bloomsbury.

Weatherford, Doris. 1994. "Mercy Otis Warren." In *American Women's History: An A to Z of People, Organizations, Issues, and Events.* New York: Prentice Hall.

Weisberger, Bernard A. 1958. *They Gathered at the River—The Story of the Great Revivalists and Their Impact on Religion in America.* Chaicago: Little Brown & Co.

Weisman, Leslie Kanes. 1992. *Discrimination by Design: A Feminist Critique of the Man-Made Environment.* Urbana: University of Illinois Press.

Welter, Barbara. 1978. "The Cult of True Womanhood: 1820–1860." In *The American Family in Social-Historical Perspective* (2nd ed.), ed. Michael Gordon, 313–33. New York: St. Martin's Press.

Westermarck, Edward. 1922. *The History of Human Marriage.* New York: Allerton.

Wicklund, Susan. 2007. *This Common Secret: My Journey as an Abortion Doctor.* New York: Public Affairs/Perseus.

Wills, Garry. 2007. *Head and Heart: American Christianities.* New York: Penguin.

Winner, Lauren F. 2005. *Real Sex—The Naked Truth about Chastity.* Grand Rapids, Mich.: Brazos Press.

Wolfe, Alan. 2009. *The Future of Liberalism.* New York: Knopf.

Wolfe, Tom. 2000. *Hooking Up.* New York: Farrar, Straus, and Giroux.

Wolfe, Tom. 2004. *I Am Charlotte Simmons.* New York: Farrar, Straus, and Giroux.

Wollstonecraft, Mary. 1792/2001. *A Vindication of the Rights of Women: With Strictures on Moral and Political Subjects.* New York: Modern Library.

Wood, Gordon S. 1992. *The Radicalism of the American Revolution.* New York: Knopf.

Wood, Gordon S. 2006. *Revolutionary Characters—What Made the Founders Different.* New York: Penguin.

Wuthnow, Robert. 2006. *Saving America: Faith-Based Services and the Future of Civil Society.* Princeton, N.J.: Princeton University Press.

Zeitzen, Miriam Koktvedgaard, 2008. *Polygamy—A Cross-Cultural Analysis.* New York: Berg/Oxford.

Zernike, Kate. 2006. "Use of Contraception Drops, Slowing Decline of Abortion Rate." *New York Times* (5 May).

Zezima, Katie. 2008. "More Women than Ever Are Childless, Census Finds." *New York Times* (19 August).

Index

women taking charge and taking care,
109–12; religious right's worldwide
war on sex among less-advantaged
persons, 106–9; responsibility and,
91–94, 100–101; sexual sins, 90–91;
sexual smarts, autonomy, and economic advantage, 104–6; single persons and sex, 28–34; social evolution
of views on abortion, 117–21; spawning
of religious right, 42–48
Sexually transmitted diseases (STD), 98,
101, 102–3, 106–11
Sexual smarts: autonomy and, 101,
104–6, 190–91; contraception and,
102–4, 106–9; cultivating, 100–104
Single blessedness, 150–51, 196–97
Single persons and sex, 28–34
Sizer, Ted, 169–70
Skilled workers, 69
Slaves and slavery, 15–17, 175–76
South Africa, 111
Southern Baptist Convention (SBC), 60
Stanton, Elizabeth Cady, 20–21
Surnames of women after marriage,
73–74

Teen sexuality, 97–100
Temporary marriage, 141–42
Terry, Randall, 117
Thomas, Sherry, 58–59
Tolstoy, Leo, 4

Uganda, 106–7, 110
Upper middle class, 65–66, 69

Veevers, Jean, 149
Vera Drake (film), 114
Violence against partner,
82, 102
Virginity, technical, 32–33

Wage gap, gender, 54, 63–64
War and Peace (Tolstoy), 4
Warner, Judith, 76–77, 84
Wilberforce, William, 119, 175–76
Wimp factor, 84
Wolfe, Tom, 81, 84
Wollstonecraft, Mary, 13
Womanhood cult, 17–20, 62–63
Woman of the Year (film), 185
Work: autonomy and, 56, 72–74, 191;
gender identities and economic
disadvantage, 82–85; independence
and, 55, 71–72; inventing "radical"
family values for middle class
women, 59–61; liberation from, 53;
material aspects, 54, 61–63; men
and women as problem-solvers
together, 75–82; mothers' wage gap,
63–64; new world of, 67–70;
problem solving in, 54–57, 69, 71;
respect and, 56; serving others via,
56–57, 74–75; spiritual aspects,
54–57, 67; stay-at-home moms,
64–66; traditional roles of women
and men, 57–59; woman's obligations
to herself in, 70–75
World War II, women workers
during, 75–76

About the Author

JOHN H. SCANZONI, author of more than a dozen books, is an internationally recognized expert on family change. He has taught sociology at several universities, and is currently a professor at the University of Florida. Educated at Wheaton College and the University of Oregon, Scanzoni's career-long fascination with the evolution of families is reflected in his books *Designing Families: The Search for Self and Community in the Information Age; Contemporary Families and Relationships: Reinventing Responsibility;* and *Shaping Tomorrow's Family: Theory and Policy for the Twenty-First Century.*